CONTESTING NATIVE TITLE

CONTESTING NATIVE TITLE

FROM CONTROVERSY TO CONSENSUS IN THE STRUGGLE OVER INDIGENOUS LAND RIGHTS

DAVID RITTER

Routledge
Taylor & Francis Group
LONDON AND NEW YORK

First published 2009 by Allen & Unwin

Published 2020 by Routledge
2 Park Square, Milton Park, Abingdon, Oxon OX14 4RN
605 Third Avenue, New York, NY 10017

Routledge is an imprint of the Taylor & Francis Group, an informa business

Cataloguing-in-Publication details are available
from the National Library of Australia
www.librariesaustralia.nla.gov.au

Index by Tess Burton
Set in 11.5/15 pt Minion Pro by Bookhouse, Sydney

ISBN-13: 9781742370200 (pbk)

CONTENTS

FOREWORD

The history, politics, law and process associated with the recognition and protection of native title in Australia has produced a very large array of articles, collections of essays and monographs since the High Court delivered its decision in the *Mabo* case in 1992. The common law as declared in that case was channelled into the framework established by the *Native Title Act 1993* (Cth) which was subject to contentious amendments in 1998, inspired in part by the decision of the High Court in *Wik Peoples v State of Queensland* in 1996. Further amendments to the Act since that time reflect concerns that the statutory process for the recognition and protection of native title has not met expectations and, in particular, has cost far too much and taken far too long. The large range of publications on the topic of native title demonstrates its difficult history, its complex multidimensional character and the need for inter-disciplinary approaches to its understanding.

This book puts the law and history of native title in Australia into its multidisciplinary context. Through the interlacing strands of the histories and political science of the institutions centrally involved in native title, David Ritter has woven a rich, fascinating and instructive tapestry. The text is at times unashamedly argumentative and not all of its readers will agree with all of its observations and conclusions. But this is quality polemic and worth reading to stimulate reflection and response, even if only by way of disagreement or quiet fury.

I was directly involved in two of the institutions of which the author writes. One was the National Native Title Tribunal. The other was the Federal Court of Australia. As President of the Tribunal from 1994 to 1998, I also had dealings with the other institutions discussed in his book—the vehicles of national Aboriginal leadership including ATSIC and the Native Title Working Groups, the native title representative bodies which were regionally organised, the various levels of government, Commonwealth, State, Territory and local, and the mining and pastoral industries and other industry groups affected by native title.

David Ritter was my Associate in 1995 during the time I was President of the National Native Title Tribunal. He also subsequently served as the Principal Legal Officer of a native title representative body, the Yamatji Barna Baba Maaja Land and Sea Council.

The institutional experiences to which David Ritter was exposed have obviously informed his writing, but they have not narrowed his focus. For myself, and for others who have been closely involved in the institutions and organisations he describes, it is a refreshing and salutary experience to review the sweep of events over the last fifteen years through his eyes. Sometimes the stimulation is the slightly shocking one of a cold shower of realistic appraisal.

There is a melancholy theme in the book that much of what was promised has not been achieved. But it is not in any sense depressing nor does it sink to despair. As the author remarks towards the end of his text:

> Fifteen years of native title is a story of winners, losers and pragmatic settlers, not a castle in the air in which everyone is happy with their lot.

He accepts that there has arisen an overwhelming view that native title issues are best resolved through reaching agreements but observes, correctly in my opinion, that 'the transformation is a product of hard-fought contests having been played out'. In that connection the role of the courts in settling the 'terrain' has made its own contribution to allowing what David Ritter calls 'the edifice of negotiated relationships' to take place.

The book will not please everybody, but that is not its purpose. It is an unsentimental, richly informed account of a fascinating period in the history of Australia's relationships with its indigenous people. It is unsparing in its references to the false starts and wrong directions that have been part of the history. I commend the book to its readers.

Chief Justice Robert French
May 2009

PROLOGUE

One day in the north

Sometime in the late nineties I found myself in the refuse-strewn front yard of a house, one in a row, in a coastal town in Australia's north-west, having an awkward conversation with the Aboriginal woman who lived there. I knew the lady of the house and her husband reasonably well as I'd been one of their native title lawyers for some years. Both were formidable people of considerable cultural and political stature in their community who exercised great tactical dexterity. On the day in question the woman and I were both ill at ease as the reason for my visit was intrinsically uncomfortable. I had been told that her husband had decided not to come to a crucial meeting later in the day and was hoping to find him in time to invite a change of mind, as he was expected to be an important participant in enabling a decision to be taken by the community. I held out little prospect of success, but felt some obligation to at least make the inquiry. I asked a few questions about the husband's whereabouts as politely as I knew how, but was gently rebuffed, albeit with a slight unease to the woman's tone. It was just another hot, humid day and I could feel myself burning and perspiring as I stood in the yard making no progress in the heavy air. Frustrated and slightly embarrassed, but understanding the futility and impropriety of exhibiting any disquiet or pushing the point further, I found myself gazing absently at a heap of rubbish to one side of the porch and realised that I was staring into the face of a recently decapitated kangaroo's head. At more or less precisely that moment a stereo somewhere nearby suddenly opened into the insufferable Billy Ray Cyrus song, 'Achy Breaky Heart'. It was just one particularly surreal moment of lived experience in what is antiseptically called 'the native title system'.

This book is about the native title system: that peculiar set of institutions and processes that was established after the *Mabo* decision to manage the disputation over traditional Indigenous land rights in Australia under the Commonwealth's *Native Title Act 1993*. The subtitle of the book includes the phrase 'from controversy to consensus' to express the flavour of the overall trend. On and off between 1992 and 1998, native title was staggeringly divisive and controversial; the subject of immense political storm and legal battles giving rise to numerous banner headlines, blockbuster parliamentary debates and marathon litigation in front of the High Court. At times, wilder opinion forecast the break-up of Australia, the collapse of the economy and outbreaks of violence. To the extent that the statute was intended to bring to an end the hullabaloo over the recognition of traditional Indigenous rights in land in Australia, eventual success within those terms seems palpable. Students born in the last twenty years often look up from their desks in some puzzlement when one tries to evoke the hysteria and volume of debate that once existed over the recognition of native title. For these younger Australians, *Mabo* has simply always been there, a part of the national 'vibe', to borrow from *The Castle*, perhaps the most popular cultural artefact associated with the case.[1] Native title is now just part of the furniture; or maybe, so dim is the collective awareness of the legal doctrine once dubbed a 'revolution', that it can be thought of as no more than a design on the national wallpaper. This book explains how and why native title became so comparatively invisible.

The Australian constitutional system allocates power and sets out restraints, within which governments pass laws that in the case of disputes are interpreted by independent courts. In the world of native title, actors are bound by the Native Title Act and have engaged in fierce contest within the arena of that legislation. Often, though, efforts were made to shift the boundaries through lobbying of governments to make new laws, or by prosecuting litigation before the courts.

Thus, organisations and individual actors have had a decisive effect on the distribution of rights and power within the native title process through their contest both within and over the rules of the game. The development of native title is sometimes described in rather passive tones as—after an admittedly fiery beginning—the 'evolution' of laws and procedures that have incrementally come to be accepted by the parties concerned, almost all of whom are now reconciled to resolving matters by agreement.[2] This book takes a somewhat different view, arguing for an understanding of the native title system that is steeped in ideological and economic contest. The aim here is to understand the history and politics of native title, by approaching the subject through a number of the principal organisations which have administered or engaged with the system. The intention is to understand these bodies and to see how imperatives have been manifested in actions and rhetoric, changing over time in response to shifting circumstances.

The focus in this book is more heavily weighted towards the formative years of the native title system in Australia. Indeed, one of the implicit themes is path dependency, suggesting that what happens in the future in native title in Australia is heavily constrained by that which has already occurred. Evolution is not preordained or the triumph of the ideal, but the strengthening of tendencies that were the most sufficiently adequate at the time.[3] The comparative openness of vista that existed after *Mabo* was handed down in 1992 was to a very considerable extent indelibly framed by Paul Keating's legislative response. When John Howard won the prime ministership in 1996, the terms of the native title debate that ensued were largely defined by Keating's existing framework. The changes eventually made by the Howard Government were of course significant, but much of the foundation of the original system remained intact. In a triumph of path dependence, the political brawling in 1996–98 and the more timid exchanges in 2005–07 resulted in reforms to the existing system, rather than any *de novo* reordering consistent with new conceptions of the ideal. Among the judiciary, the whole purpose of the doctrine of precedent ensures that principle is accrued over time. At an operational level within the native title system, the interaction and behaviour of the largest actors are constitutive. Institutions are self-reinforcing and historical events lock in particular legal, economic and administrative formations.[4]

The institutional approach taken in this book is intended to explain how the native title system has come to be as it is, through political and legal struggle within Australia's liberal democratic system. It is a repudiation of the myth of passive evolution. The broad consensus over native title that has now been reached is not a product of the slow fruition of benevolent attitudes through a kind of awakening acceptance. Negotiation has not become the dominant paradigm because the principal players have foresworn interest in power. Rather, agreement-making is an expression of power relations that were the subject of vigorous contest and have now settled into a configuration that the principal parties either broadly accept or lack the facility to meaningfully seek to overturn. This book charts the course of the disputation, setting out the way in which various organisations discharged the competition over rights and influence in the native title arena, making and remaking their public and political positioning depending on the outcome of key engagements and the resolution of critical issues.

The history of the native title system in Australia is not a simple (post)colonial morality tale. The 'contest' of this book's title refers, in truth, to a multitude of engagements. The politics of native title may sometimes look like a convenient binary, echoing the 'applicant versus respondent' bifurcation of civil proceedings, but the reality has been far more complex and equivocal. The contests over native title have not simply been between claimants and respondents or between Indigenous and non-Indigenous people, but amount to a compound of struggles, transactions and relationships undertaken within and between a wide range of organisations and interests as strategic opportunities have shifted with events and over time.

The main entities that are dealt with in this book are:

- the Federal Court of Australia
- the National Native Title Tribunal
- the Aboriginal and Torres Strait Islander Commission (and various peak-level Indigenous working groups)
- native title representative bodies

- peak bodies representing primary industry
- executive government of the states and territories.

What each of the organisations covered by this book has (or had) in common is a peak role within the native title system. Not included are the Commonwealth legislature and the High Court of Australia, which are in a different category because they have the ultimate power to determine the law. The organisations featured here have quite different roles and degrees of power that necessarily require differential analytical treatment. The National Native Title Tribunal and the Federal Court both umpire and facilitate the system, with the latter also subjecting the former to judicial oversight. The Aboriginal and Torres Strait Islander Commission, the native title representative bodies and the executives of the states and territories all represented a certain collectivity of interests, while having responsibility for administering parts of the process under the Native Title Act. The industry peak bodies and the various Indigenous working groups played a purely representative role, with no formal statutory function. Organised collectivities of parties united by a common interest are quite different in nature to the governmental institutions invested by the Native Title Act with the function of administering or adjudicating process: the difference between players and referees. Nevertheless, this work proceeds on the assumption that all organisations have interests: even the most impartial operate on the basis of a certain view of how the world should work.

The expressions 'NNTT' and 'Tribunal' are used interchangeably for the National Native Title Tribunal and the same is done with 'NTRBs' and 'rep bodies' for the native title representative bodies, in both instances simply to give variety of expression to the reader. Although 'Aboriginal' and 'Indigenous' are not generally treated as interchangeable (because the latter is usually taken as not including Torres Strait Islanders), I have similarly attempted to mix my use of the expressions where not inappropriate. In Chapter 2 I explain in more detail that the basis upon which I use the vexed expression 'the Indigenous leadership' in this book, is as a catch-all to describe the organised Indigenous leadership in the context of native title, including the Aboriginal and Torres Strait Islander Commission, the National Indigenous Working Group, the

Queensland Indigenous Working Group, the Western Australian Aboriginal Native Title Working Group, the National Native Title Council and the National Indigenous Council.

Existing accounts and explanations

This is the first full-length history of the native title system, but there is a voluminous literature dealing with other dimensions of the phenomenon. Existing legal analysis has, quite reasonably, been centred on the state of the law, offering either compendious summary[5] or critical analysis.[6] Anthropologists[7] and historians[8] have also written important accounts of native title through their respective disciplinary lenses, while the multi-disciplinarity of the area has itself provided a focus of interest.[9] Native title has also attracted authors writing within cultural studies and influenced by the literature of post-colonialism.[10] There is also a developed body of work about the place of Indigenous peoples within the liberal democratic state.[11] Various commentators have written about the policy detail associated with the native title process, with 'agreement-making' in particular attracting considerable attention.[12] There is also a plethora of material promoting reform of the native title system one way or another, often comprising advocacy as much as analysis.

This book draws on the disciplines of political science, history and jurisprudence in aiming to offer an account of the attitudes and actions of organisations within the native title system. The existing scholarship to which this book is closest includes the political and historical analysis of Tim Rowse and Murray Goot[13] and the specialist work produced by current and past members of the Centre for Aboriginal Economic Policy Research dealing with the institutions and economics of native title, including particularly various reports by Jon Altman, Julie Finlayson, Diane Smith and David Martin.[14] The account of native title provided here has also been assisted by the critical scholarship of Ciaran O'Faircheallaigh and Tony Corbett, who have sought to test many of the rhetorical claims made about the future act system and by the National Native Title Tribunal in particular.[15] This book can also be seen as drawing on the insights of a range of historians, including Bain

Attwood, Michael Belgrave and Giselle Byrnes, who have shown how the expression of Indigenous land aspirations is historically contingent.[16]

Although this book is in the critical tradition in that it accepts that law is indeed a discourse of power, the emancipative claims and achievements of the liberal-democratic legal system are not simply dismissed as an exercise in the maintenance of the status quo. Although not strictly a 'law book', if considered within jurisprudence, this study is more closely associated with legal realism than with critical legal theory seeking to understand the life of the law as experience rather than logic, but still taking the claims of the system seriously at face value.[17] Law, then, is conceptualised not in positivist terms as a system of logic that exists independent of reality, but as both produced by and constitutive of economy and society. This study traces not only the way the law of native title has been made by organisations contesting the boundaries of the doctrine in the courts and agitating for reform by parliament, but how legal rules have conditioned the way in which actors have pursued their goals. In native title, the contestants argued everything from the toss onwards—and sometimes convinced the umpire—but simultaneously were required to play by whatever rules were in force at the time.

Sources and experience

This study is based largely on the abundance of source material that exists in the public domain. Most of the organisations that are featured produced annual reports and many also produced newsletters, circulars, position papers and the like. Great numbers of conference papers and speeches were given by key figures within the institutions in question, many of whom also made contributions featuring in scholarly and professional journals. Parliamentary inquiries, some of which dealt specifically with the functioning of the various native title organisations, were an important source of information. Promotional material has also provided some rich insights, including not only brochures but video and audio products and even memorabilia. (When government institutions start giving out glossy bookmarks and calendars promoting their work, it may tell you something about priorities within the system.) Given that the native title era in Australia roughly coincided with the emergence of the internet, there are also very significant web-based sources to be taken into account. Finally, there are the media releases that were issued in relation to many of the major native title events during the period. This is not a work of oral history and no interviews have been conducted as part of the research, though the author has benefited from many conversations that are acknowledged below. Neither is this study in the nature of a memoir. Inevitably, though, given that the author worked within the native title system in various capacities for more than a decade, there are no doubt times when analysis is influenced the writer by simply having been there at the time.

ACKNOWLEDGEMENTS

This is necessarily a critical book, but it is not an attack or a denunciation. I hope that I have managed to write with empathy and respect. Native title has often been described in terms akin to 'a national journey', but the process—which established new organisations, social roles and previously unknown jobs—also provided paths for individuals. My own work within the native title system—from judge's associate, to commercial lawyer, to Principal Legal Officer of the Yamatji Marlpa Land Council, to then teaching and researching about the subject in both law and humanities at university—was a personal and professional trajectory as much as a voyage through the system that is described in this book. My views on native title have changed substantially over the years, in light of evidence, further thought, shifting historical context, new experiences and countless conversations. My appreciation to those who have generously contributed to the development of my thinking along the way is both deep and broad.

This book would not have been completed without a grant provided by the Australian Institute of Aboriginal and Torres Strait Islander Studies that enabled me to work on the project in the course of 2006–07, for which I offer grateful thanks. I also thank and acknowledge my initial referees for the grant application. Within AIATSIS, I owe particular appreciation to Patrick Sullivan and Lisa Strelein. I am also grateful to the Faculty of Law at the University of Western Australia for auspicing the grant and in particular to Bill Ford and Barbara Williamson. I was affiliated with both the Faculty of Law and the History Discipline Group in the School of Arts, Humanities and Social Sciences during this project and would like to thank my colleagues within both departments, including Tony Buti, Mark Edele, Andrea Gaynor, Sharon Mascher, Neil Morgan and Simon Young. I especially thank Richard Bartlett, Michal and Richard Bosworth and Rob Stuart.

In late 2006 I was hosted as a visiting scholar by the Castan Centre at Monash University and would like to thank my institutional host and Melissa Castan in particular, as well as Melissa and Rob Lehrer for their kindness and hospitality. In February 2007 Informa conferences gave me a useful opportunity to test out some of the ideas contained in this book in Melbourne. The Australian Mining and Petroleum Law Association also gave me the chance to make some comments influenced by this project at their national conference in 2006 and I thank especially Carol Bartlett. The Institute of Progressive Policy in Perth was kind enough to hold a forum to discuss some of the ideas then being developed for this book and I thank them for holding the event and disseminating the notes of the conversation. My gratitude goes also to the library at the National Native Title Tribunal, particularly Kathy Wright. At the Federal Court I thank Louise Anderson and June Eaton. I thank the libraries and staff at the University of Western Australia. Much of the final writing and editing was carried out in the British Library in London and I thank the staff of that institution.

I would also specifically like to acknowledge conversations with many people who have increased my understanding of native title as reflected in this book including thanks to Parry Agius, Jon Altman, Melinda Ashley, his Hon. Justice John Basten, Paul Burke, John Catlin, Fred Chaney, Jennifer Clarke, Rachel Connell, Tony Corbett, Gillian Cowlishaw, Mick Dodson, Martin Dougherty, Julie Finlayson, Merrilee Garnett, Gary Hamley, Paul Hayes, George Irving, Patricia Lane, Tony Lee, Ron Levy, Greg Marks, David Martin, Bardy McFarlane, Greg McIntyre, Marshall McKenna, Michael Megaw, Simone Muller, Graeme Neate, his Hon. Justice Anthony North, Ciaran O'Faircheallaigh, Noel Pearson, Frances Peters-Little, Susan Phillips, Richard Potok, Eric Ripper, Mark Ritter, Tim Rowse, Doug Sanders, Diane Smith, Andrew Solomon, Marcus Solomon, Chris Sumner, David Trigger, Geoff Walker, Eric

Walsh, Lisa Wright and many others. I owe very special thanks to Hal Wootten. I have benefited too from the numerous insights of the students of Indigenous Peoples and the Law and Legal History, which I was fortunate enough to be able to teach over a number of years in the UWA Law Faculty. I owe a specific debt of gratitude to Chief Justice Robert French. I am particularly grateful to his Honour for generously agreeing to provide a foreword to this book. I would also like to thank Judy Sulcs for her assistance.

I acknowledge the various governing committees and executive directors Clinton Wolf, Roger Cook and Simon Hawkins of what is now known as the Yamatji Marlpa Land Council where I worked between 1999 and 2005. Very special thanks and acknowledgement to all of my former colleagues at Yamatji, including particularly Malcolm Allbrook, Christina Araujo, Tess Burton, Nathan Cammerman, Mark Chambers, Simon Choo, Justin Cvitan, Cedric Davies, Zen Davison, Veronica de France, Justin Edwards, Tony Farnham, Frances Flanagan, Kim Fleet, Donna Friedl, Nicholas Green, Justin Hannah, Pam Kaye, Helen Lawrence, Pam McGrath, Adrian Murphy, Jodie Neale, Marnie Parkinson, Marcus Priest, Michael Robinson, Jeremy Ryan, Michael Ryan, Raina Savage, Emma Smith, Nick Smith, John Southalan, Louise Southalan, Robin Stevens, Carolyn Tan and Tony Wright. Thanks too, to the numerous student clerks who donated their time to Yamatji.

I also give special thanks and acknowledgement to my colleagues at Chalk & Fitzgerald Lawyers & Consultants, including Jason Behrendt and Andrew Chalk and especially James Fitzgerald.

In the production process, I was well supported by Tess Burton, Jessica Panegyres, Zoey Irvin and Andrew Thackrah as able and interested research assistants and am especially thankful for their efforts. I am also grateful for access to unpublished research work by Andrew and Jessica, as well as by Daniel Vujcich and Sarah Knuckey. Jon Altman, Sarah Burnside, Michael Dillon, Frances Flanagan, Julie Finlayson, James Fitzgerald, David Martin, Tim Rowse, Carolyn Tan and Diane Smith were all generous enough to have important communications with me about elements of this book. Thanks, too, to the readers retained by Allen & Unwin for their invaluable comments.

The writings of philosopher Raimond Gaita on animals provide reassurance that I am being more than just sentimental in acknowledging that three cats, Graeme, Nino and Fruitcake, were companions through much of the writing process. Outside of the native title system, I have been lucky enough to share helpful conversations on matters related to this book with Bain Attwood, Giselle Byrne, Shirli Kirschner, Carmen Lawrence, Robert Manne, Gavin Mooney, David Moore and Henry Reynolds. I also thank Matt Anstey, Frank Bongiorno, Kirsty Mackenzie, Willie Mackenzie, Tamson Pietsch, Andy Tait, Terri-ann White and Kevin Young. I thank my parents and family for their love and support.

I am most grateful to Allen & Unwin for publishing this book and in particular to Elizabeth Weiss for her suggestions, support and encouragement and to Ann Lennox for her editorial support and assistance.

Traditional owners should be warned that some of the individuals whose names are mentioned in the following paragraph are now deceased.

I have learned much, too, from the many native title claimants for whom I acted in one capacity or another (some of whom were also my fellow staff members at Yamatji and so earn my double thanks) including Teddy Allen, Don Bell, Benny Bellotti, Jeff Brown, Alum Cheedy, Peter and Charlie Coppin, Glen Councillor, David and Tootsie Daniel, Violet Drury, Doris Eaton, Gavin Egan, Neil Finlay, Neata Fishhook, Gloria Fogarty, Percy and Ollie George, Colin Hamlett, Roderick Hedlam, Pansy Hicks, Bobby Holt, Kenny and Maudie Jerrold, Oldie Kelly, Albert, Hazel, Victor and Terrence Little, Bill and William Mallard, Alec Ned, Taffy Papertalk, Slim and Guy Parker, Yvonne Radcliffe, June Ruffin, Lucy Ryder, Charlie Smith, Fred Taylor, Roy and Julie Tommy, Bridget and Yilbie Warrie and Donny Wilson and many others that space precludes me from mentioning.

Finally, I would like to profoundly thank my dearest friend, my wife Frances. This book is dedicated to her with my love.

The views and conclusions represented in this study are mine alone and do not represent the position or views of any of the organisations with which I am currently, or have been, associated. All mistakes are of course solely my responsibility.

1

READING THE PORRIDGE

Introducing the native title system

From the Dreaming to the day

The Australian native title system has an often turbulent short history, but origins in the deep past. This chapter is an overview, first of the long genesis of native title, followed by an account of the *Mabo* case and then a précis of the legislative system in operation. The processes of native title are infamously labyrinthine and so a digest of their design is inevitably something of a catalogue of winding passages. The detail can be dreary but all the more devilish for the dullness, because the extent to which law and procedure constrain social and political choices can become obscured in the dry. The rules of the native title system restrict the options of the actors and condition the ways in which underlying interests can be expressed. On the other hand, merely understanding how the statute works provides only a partial and imperfect guide to explaining what happened. The functioning of the native title system then is more than the sum of the various instrumental parts and this chapter finishes with some specific 'complications' associated with the process. Some readers may prefer to start not with the evolution of the law but with the discussion of complexities at the end of this chapter, or indeed to skip to Chapter 2 and read this chapter only when the rest of the book has been completed.

The southern continent

Tens of thousands of years ago, human beings first arrived in Australia from the north and established societies that were largely isolated from the rest of humanity until well into the second half of the second millennia AD. In civilisational seclusion, the first inhabitants of Australia developed a distinctive culture, marked by the existence of hundreds of small entities with separate territories, languages and customs yet linked by systems of trade, cultural exchange and religious worship in networks that spanned the continent. Although these Aboriginal groups were nomadic to varying degrees, movement occurred inside broad boundaries and according to certain rules. It is thought that, in 1788, as many as 500 distinct indigenous societies covered the Australian mainland in a geopolitical patchwork. Other indigenous communities existed on the various islands off Australia's coast. There was of course fluidity, change and conflict and while customary boundaries and entitlements can be presumed to have shifted over time, it is clear that indigenous civilisation in Australia involved a clear sense of ownership of land and waters. Under the various systems of law and custom the numerous societies present in pre-contact Australia each owned their respective countries.

No recognition of native title in Australia between 1788 and 1992

The formal acquisition of sovereignty over Australia by the British Crown occurred incrementally, between 1788 (New South Wales) and 1829 (Western Australia). In the course of colonisation the pre-existing indigenous societies were not acknowledged as having any particular rights under the new sovereign and were regarded as subjects of crown authority. Australia has no history of treaty-making.[1] The elaborate system of customary land title that existed prior to the arrival of Europeans received no acknowledgement. Indigenous societies were effectively treated as itinerant and stripped of their property at the convenience and to the advantage of the colonials.[2] The idea of 'native title', meaning a form of real property arising out of traditional law and custom that is acknowledged under the common law of the colonisers, was not recognised in any of the six British colonies in Australia. When the colonies federated to form the Commonwealth of Australia on 1 January 1901, the remnant indigenous peoples played no part in the process and native title was not considered a live question to be addressed. Nevertheless, the Commonwealth Constitution was not silent on the more general 'native question', among other things expressly prohibiting the new federal government from making laws in relation to Aboriginal people, a situation not remedied until the passage of the referendum in 1967.[3]

Although it had long gone without saying, the question of whether Indigenous customary land titles were capable of recognition under the common law of Australia was not tested in court until the late 1960s, in an action eventually decided by a single judge of the Northern Territory in *Milirrpum v Nabalco* in 1971.[4] His Honour Justice Sir Richard Blackburn was faced with the difficulty that elsewhere in the common law world, including New Zealand, Canada and the United States, native title had indeed been recognised and there seemed to be no judicial precedent which explicitly explained why Australia was the exception. It was a legal and historical puzzle with no obvious solution. The judge attempted rather courageously (and as it turns out, wholly wrongly) to explain the anomaly by reference to different modes of acquisition of sovereignty and reached the conclusion that there was no doctrine of native title known to Australian law.[5] *Milirrpum* was not appealed. Instead, the political momentum for some form of recognition of traditional rights over land was answered with a legislative land rights scheme in the Northern Territory.[6] Statutory land rights, though, do not represent 'native title' in a technical sense: the former is created by parliament while the latter refers to an inherent common law right, the recognition of something already there, with origins not in the authority of the settler state but in pre-existing systems of law and custom. It is the difference between a right and a favour.

The native title question was not agitated again before the courts until 1982, when a group of Meriam people led by Eddie Koiki Mabo initiated proceedings in the original jurisdiction of the High Court of

Australia seeking a declaration of exclusive use, possession and ownership of the island of Mer, in the Torres Strait off the coast of far northern Queensland. Critical to the success of the case was the enactment of the Commonwealth's *Racial Discrimination Act 1975* (RDA). The Commonwealth Constitution contains no bill of rights or constitutional entrenchment of equality and the passage of the RDA marked the first time that discrimination on the basis of race had been proscribed in Australia. Under the Constitution, valid federal laws prevail over state laws to the extent of any inconsistency and so once the RDA had been enacted, it became impossible for a state government to act in a racially discriminatory fashion.[7] The presence of the RDA meant that the State of Queensland could not, as it tried to do, simply pass a law to wipe out any native title that might exist before the *Mabo* case even reached trial.[8] Instead, the litigation was able to proceed and in June 1992, by a majority of six judges to one, the High Court held that *Milirrpum* was wrong, that Australian law recognised the doctrine of native title and that the Meriam people were entitled to 'possess, use, occupy and enjoy' Mer as against the whole world.[9] The logic of the High Court was, at its essence, that Australia could not sensibly be distinguished from the rest of the common law world and the continent was not to be treated as if it had belonged to nobody before the arrival of the colonisers.[10] Although *Mabo* caused political convulsions in Australia, the High Court's decision was conservative to the extent that it simply applied the common law as already well known elsewhere in the world.[11] Where it could be proven on the facts, as it had been in the *Mabo* case, native title survived in Australia.

The post-*Mabo* dilemma, 1992–93

In deciding the *Mabo* case, the High Court was only required to determine the specific legal dispute at issue, but in so doing necessarily had to elaborate a broader doctrinal position on which to base the decision. The crucial implication of *Mabo* was the prospect that much of the Australian land mass could be the subject of future native title claims. After *Mabo*, the way was open for the various native title claims of other

Indigenous peoples in Australia to be lodged in state and territory supreme courts and, indeed, in 1992 and 1993 a variety of such actions were initiated or reached an advanced stage of preparation.[12] However, what was not clear from *Mabo* was how native title interacted with other forms of tenure that had been granted both by the colonies and after federation. What happened when native title clashed with a pastoral lease, mining tenement, pipeline easement, national park or countless other forms of title? The general principle that the High Court set out was that native title was extinguished where there was a clear and plain intention to do so and to the extent of the inconsistency.[13] *Mabo* made it clear that native title was extinguished by freehold title and exclusive leasehold (the 'suburban backyard' was always 'safe' from claim), but how the rule might be applied to other tenure types remained a subject for furious debate. *Mabo* also left open the possibility of claims for compensation for any native title that had been extinguished since the passage of the *Racial Discrimination Act 1975*.

The uncertainties created by *Mabo* were a dilemma for the Labor Commonwealth Government of Prime Minister Paul Keating (1992–96), which could either attempt a national response to *Mabo* or take no action, leaving the law of native title to be developed on a case by case basis through further litigation. Debate over what the Commonwealth should do was intense and prolonged, culminating in dramatic parliamentary sessions where the final shape of the Act was hammered out.[14] The states and territories, the peak bodies representing primary industry and so-called 'A' and 'B' teams of Aboriginal negotiators, were all involved in an arduous process of lobbying the government and the Opposition, as well as the minor parties (the Greens and the Australian Democrats), which then controlled the balance of power in the Senate.[15] The final shape of the *Native Title Act 1993* (NTA) was a product of petitioning, alliance-building, negotiation and compromise that in the end and for diverse reasons was supported by Labor, the minor parties in the Senate, most of the Aboriginal leadership, the Labor-held state governments and the National Farmers' Federation, but opposed by the Liberal and National parties, the Minerals Council of Australia, the states held by the parties of the centre-right and the government of the Northern Territory. The Western Australian Government attempted to circumvent the Commonwealth Act by enacting its own legislation, just prior to the passage of the NTA, which purported to extinguish all native title within the jurisdiction and to substitute a form of statutory title. Unsurprisingly, the Western Australian law was struck down in emphatic fashion by the High Court as unconstitutional because it was inconsistent with federal legislation.[16] The creation of the NTA was an intensely political and politicising event, making it inevitable that the operation of the new statute would be controversial and vigorously contested.

1 January 1994: Australia's new native title system in outline

The NTA created a system under which Indigenous people could lodge claims for the recognition of native title over land or waters in Australia with a newly established body, the National Native Title Tribunal (NNTT).[17] A claimant application for a determination of native title needed to specify some named applicants, the group on behalf of whom the claim was being brought and the land and waters over which title was being sought. Although any Aboriginal group could make a claim supported by whatever advisers or representatives they might choose, the NTA also established a process for the Commonwealth Minister to recognise Aboriginal corporations as 'native title representative bodies' (NTRBs) with specific functions to facilitate and assist claims. Once a claim had been lodged, the Tribunal notified all interest holders within the area of the claim (pastoralists, miners, resource explorers and so on) who might be affected. The Commonwealth, the relevant state or territory and all local government municipalities were automatic parties to each claim. When the list of responding parties ('respondents') to a claim was finalised the Tribunal then initiated a process of mediation for the purposes of trying to resolve the claim through a 'consent determination' of whether native title existed or not, who held it and how it interrelated with other legal interests.[18] Consent determinations would be given final legal effect by order of the Federal Court.

The NTA did not assume that all mediations would be successful and provided the Tribunal with the power to refer any claim that could not be settled to the Federal Court for determination by trial. If a claim went to litigation, the claimants would need to present the same proof of native title that had been set out in the jurisprudence of the *Mabo* case: the existence of a social group with a continuing traditional connection to the land claimed unbroken since sovereignty. If a trial occurred, the claimants would need to demonstrate their case by adducing sufficient evidence to satisfy each of the factual elements giving rise to the existence of the title. The NTA also made it possible for non-Indigenous interests to bring their own actions, known as 'non-claimant applications', to establish whether there might be any native title over a particular area not yet under claim. If a non-claimant application was met with a claim, then the latter simply proceeded and the former fell away, but in any other case there could be a determination that no native title existed.

The legislation explicitly guaranteed the validity of all existing property rights so, from the commencement of the NTA's operation, non-Indigenous interests did not have to be concerned about actually being dispossessed of any valid existing interest. However, the NTA did not for the most part confirm or impose extinguishment of native title by any particular class of tenure. Rather, all holders of non-extinguishing legal interests in an area covered by a native title claim were separately given the automatic right to respond to the application by becoming a party and so joining in the process of resolving the matter through mediation and litigation if necessary. As a consent determination could only be achieved with the acquiescence of all parties, in theory every respondent possessed something near to a right of veto over the settlement.[19]

Where a claim had been made but not yet decided, the NTA set out an elaborate set of procedures governing how new interests could be obtained in the meanwhile. The critical policy question at stake was one of balance: how much of a say should native title claimants get over dealings on land subject to claim? Under the Australian federal system, the power over land titles generally resides with the states so the effect of the NTA was to impose overarching national rules and conditions over the normal processes for how interests in land are granted. Once a claim had been lodged with the Tribunal it was made subject to a secondary acceptance procedure which, if passed, resulted in formal 'registration' giving the claimant group a 'right to negotiate' over 'future acts' on the land in question, including the creation of new mining rights and compulsory acquisitions. The 'future act system' operated quite independently from the claims process proper and required the state or territory government making the grant to negotiate 'in good faith' with registered native title claimants. Grants and land acquisitions that occurred without compliance with the future act system were at risk of invalidity. If no claim had been made over an area, the state or territory government in question was still required to advertise a proposed grant or acquisition, giving potential native title claimants a window of opportunity in which to have a claim lodged and registered. The NTA also created a short cut, known as the 'expedited procedure', which could potentially remove the right to negotiate in relation to certain less invasive types of exploration tenement. An act attracting the expedited procedure could be converted to one accruing the right to negotiate via a process of objection and inquiry. Where the right to negotiate did apply, if negotiations did not result in an agreement about the act being done (that is, the tenure being granted or the land being acquired) then the NNTT would arbitrate on the matter, subject even then to ministerial override on public interest grounds. Apart from the future act system, the NTA also allowed claimants to surrender native title, but it was otherwise inalienable and so not susceptible to being commercially sold on the open market.

The native title system in operation

It is possible to discern three phases of the operation of the native title process since 1994, differentiated by marked shifts in the rules and politics governing the system.

1994–98: Flux

The NTA was difficult legislation to understand (once described as like attempting to 'read porridge'[20]); not only intrinsically complex, but open-ended. Although the Act established a system for dealing with claims, there were many fundamental matters that were still left to the elaboration of the courts. After following some complicated process in the NTA through various sub-sections to a logical conclusion, the reader might come up with a reference to common law principles which were as yet undetermined. The statute offered a string through a maze that might lead nowhere except to an indefinite wait in some judicial ante-room. Precedents in Canada in particular suggested that native title was a robust form of legal entitlement that could include or give rise to commercial rights of resource exploitation and even limited self-government, but whether Australia would follow suit was completely unknown. In relation to extinguishment, the NTA gave little direction as to the effect of pastoral or mining tenure on any underlying native title. The parties to native title claims and the claimants themselves were in a state of some considerable confusion and uncertainty as to what exactly was even in issue. The system's functionaries were often forced to address the rage or perplexity of the parties by iterating the honest but inherently unsatisfying position that nobody yet knew the answer at law.

The internal logic of the NTA also became considerably distorted by a number of early judicial decisions which enforced statutory interpretations rather different from those that Parliament had intended.[21] Most significantly, a decision of the High Court in early 1996 effectively gave immediate access to the right to negotiate to every claimant application, regardless of merit and no matter how rudimentary and imprecise the document setting out the basis of the case.[22] The result was a snowballing of native title claims:

> The growth curve from 1994 to 1998 was exponential. In the first six months to 30 June 1994, 14 claimant applications had been lodged. By 30 June 1995 this had grown to 82. And by 30 June 1996 . . . to 367. By 30 June 1997, the numbers had reached 552, and on 30 June 1998, there had been 804 applications lodged . . .[23]

The machinery of the NTA also failed to prevent or deter overlapping native title claims, which proliferated. The most infamous congestion occurred in the Western Australian Goldfields where, by mid-1998, in some places there were more than 30 overlapping native title claims. Under the NTA there could only be a single determination of native title for any given area, so all overlaps would need to be resolved as a precondition to obtaining a consent determination. Meetings called by the Tribunal to resolve the miasma at first drew large attendances that were often angry and unsettled, but which later gave way to dwindling participation as parties grew to perceive the futility of the exercise. The geographical spread of claims was also perhaps greater than had been expected, with multiple applications made over capital cities, as well as ambit assertions for vast swathes of ocean extending out into the high seas. The spread of native title claims seemed unrestrained and the overall picture was not promising. Later recording his personal reflections, the first President of the NNTT commented that the NTA's processes had turned out 'to be convoluted, impractical, conceptually confused and, at their end point, unconstitutional'.[24]

The broader political situation also contributed to the uncertainty. Those who did not consider the native title question to be settled to their satisfaction acted strategically to try to undermine the functioning of the system in order to strengthen the political case for amending the NTA. The opportunity for change arrived in 1996 when Prime Minister Keating was swept from office and replaced by the Liberal–National Coalition government of John Howard (1996–2007). For a long time in Australian political history, Indigenous affairs had been largely bipartisan, but that tradition was fractured by disputes over native title and other issues in the early 1990s. By the middle of the decade Indigenous affairs had become understood in partisan terms, with Labor clearly identified as the party that was expected to support Aboriginal causes. The new Howard regime was, rightly, presumed to be hostile to native title rights as they then stood. In the first year of the new government the High Court handed down the much-anticipated decision of *Wik v Queensland*, which decided that pastoral leases did not extinguish native title in that state. When in opposition, Howard had advocated changes to the NTA, and the *Wik* decision provided a political opportunity for embarking on a process of ambitious legislative reform. The government, though, did not command a majority in the Senate and so any amending legislation required the support of at least one non-government vote in the upper house, necessitating a process of negotiation and bargaining. The protracted set of public and parliamentary debates continued until the Commonwealth's *Native Title Amendment Act 1998* was finally passed in mid-1998 (the 1998 Amendments).[25] The functioning of the NTA was altered in important respects, including moving the processing of claims from the NNTT to the Federal Court, adulterating the strength of the future act processes and reinstalling a threshold test for access to the right to negotiate.

1998–2002: Definition

The passage of the 1998 Amendments comprised the legislative component of a second phase in the operation of the NTA, characterised by increasing certainty and definition about the distribution of rights and power within the native title system. The other source of growing sureness was the various cases that answered key uncertainties about how the system established by the NTA worked in operation. The laws of the game were becoming progressively more fixed and the players more accustomed (or resigned) to the rules. *Yorta Yorta*, *Yarmirr* and *Ward* were the three crucial test cases, each decided episodically before the Federal Court, then the Full Court of the Federal Court and then the High Court, between 1998 and 2002.[26] *Yorta Yorta* set out the minimum requirements for proving traditional continuity, *Yarmirr* explained the relevant principles as they applied offshore and *Ward* went to the content and nature of native title. Though the claimants succeeded in some respects in *Yarmirr* and *Ward*, all three cases were disappointing in the context of the broader Indigenous agenda. *Yorta Yorta*, *Yarmirr*, *Ward* and other significant precedents also showed conclusively that many of the more expansive predictions about the potential reach of native title were unfounded under Australian law. It became clear, for example, that there was no unitary title[27] and that the 'bundle' of rights were amenable to piecemeal extinction,[28] there could be no exclusive possession of offshore waters,[29] no claims to mineral resources[30] or intellectual property[31] and that native title was inherently 'weak' and 'fragile'.[32] It was possible, by the end of 2002, to say with considerable confidence as a matter of law where native title could exist, what it was and how you proved it. Litigation still occurred thereafter, but the nature of the issues being tested would perforce be finer points of law or disputed questions of fact.

2002 and beyond: Agreement-making and consensus

Though the basic intention of the NTA was to encourage the resolution of native title matters through alternative dispute resolution, the trend was slow in developing. One of the key impediments to reaching deals was legal uncertainty, meaning that many parties lacked the confidence to know whether it was wise or advisable to enter into an agreement in any given circumstances. However, following the period of definition, the practice of agreement-making burgeoned and was matched by a convergence in public rhetoric. Broad consensus on agreement-making being the best way of dealing with native title issues continues to reign. The most recent tranches of amendments to the legislation, enacted by the Commonwealth in 2007, encountered negligible political controversy and did not displace the widespread policy accord.

Complexities I: Wider meanings of 'native title'

Native title, it might be said, is a set of relationships and not a thing.[33] One of the complexities in understanding native title is the tendency for the term to be used to describe a number of quite different phenomena. Among lawyers, 'native title' refers to the relevant body of legal doctrine, but is also the noun for the common law proprietary right that arises from recognising traditional customary rights in land. The full content of the expression has fluctuated over time as the law has changed: the substantive and technical meaning of 'native title' has its own historicity. Yet confusingly, there has also been a tendency for the term 'native title' to be used to describe an Indigenous sense of traditional ownership, regardless of the common law position. The distinction is between what the common law recognises and what Indigenous people believe, feel and avow. So, for instance, an Aboriginal person may assert the survival of their 'native title', irrespective of the formal position under the non-Indigenous legal system.[34] Similarly, 'native title' might be envisioned as a matter of cultural relations, rather than official relationships; that is, 'about people, not legal technicalities'.[35] As a matter of social fact or political positioning, Aboriginal people may continue to assert their 'native title' regardless of the actual state of the law.

Significantly, the recognition of native title was seen as being merely one of a number of phenomena that catalysed the relationship between the Indigenous people and the state in Australia in the mid-1990s, including growing popular awareness of the widespread historical forced removal of children (the so-called 'Stolen Generations'), the national 'reconciliation' process initiated by the Hawke and Keating governments, the Commonwealth's professed commitment to a policy of 'self-determination' and populist events like champion sprinter Cathy Freeman's display of the Aboriginal flag at successive international athletics meets. Yet however much the confluence of political and cultural events suggested a coherent agenda of Indigenous empowerment and emancipation, there were sharp conceptual disjunctions. The removal of children, for example, was widely argued to merit reparation, yet in the context of native title was more likely to be productive of evidence of the loss of traditional connection rather than the awarding of title.[36] Making the point with brutal simplicity: if cultural succession within an Aboriginal group was decimated by forced child removals, then how could there be the continuing traditional connection demanded by the doctrine of native title? Whatever the universal justice of the situation, there is nothing logically inconsistent about forced child separation leading to the destruction of social norms (indeed, that was to some extent and at times the whole point of the policy) but the consequence seemed deeply hurtful and ironic to those who understood native title as remedial in character.

The conceptual relationships between native title and both reconciliation and self-determination were also fraught. In order for native title to be iterated as either part of the reconciliation process or an exercise in self-determination, certain features of the process would have to be highlighted while others overlooked or suppressed. There might be an element of 'self-determination' in the making of a claim for native title, for example, but it was hard to see how the same appellation could be applied to a process that mandated the manner and form of the assertion to country and where the ultimate decision on the legitimacy of the application was decided by state authorities. The conceptual wooliness of reconciliation meant that it was simpler to characterise native title as one dimension of the project, but there were still problems.[37] For instance, where the native title process engendered a legal result that sharply antagonised an Indigenous group because of a perception of injustice, how could the outcome be said to be conducive to 'reconciliation'? The agreement-making emphasis of the NTA did perhaps appear as concomitant with reconciliation, given the latter's etymology, but even that supposition relied on the arguable assumption that reaching a deal implied a level of 'coming together' with a sociocultural meaning broader than mere contracting.

There are many things that native title, as a matter of law, was not but was widely thought of as entailing. From the outset, the doctrine was saddled with broad cultural and political connotations. *Mabo* was 'no ordinary judgment' with the implication that native title was 'more' than merely a form of property.[38] 'Native title' has, for example, been rendered as a harbinger of the *zeitgeist*,[39] the inspiration for an artistic movement,[40] a lens through which to understand Australian film,[41] a critical determinant of trends in historiography,[42] giving rise to a discursive sense of 'unsettlement-in-the-midst-of-modernity'[43] and a matter worthy of broad and lasting political mobilisation.[44] Among some Aboriginal people, 'native title' stood as shorthand for wider programs of political and economic emancipation. The gulf between doctrine and sociocultural understandings is not addressed by merely noting the extent to which the latter may be wrong as a matter of law, because ideas can be politically and legally affective. The actors within the native title system have attitudes shaped by what is going on in society around them. Each of the organisations discussed in this book engaged with broader readings of the meaning of 'native title', not infrequently drawing on the wider discourse for politically instrumental uses.

In historical terms, the recognition of native title was seen by some commentators as the latest in a line of events that together constituted a recent teleology of Indigenous emancipation in Australia: the Constitutional referendum of 1967, the enactment of the RDA in 1975, the creation of Aboriginal land rights legislation in the Northern Territory in 1976, the first *Mabo* decision in 1988, the establishment of reconciliation and self-determination as paradigms of public policy and discourse, the formation of the Aboriginal and Torres Strait Islander Commission (ATSIC) in 1990 and then *Mabo (2)* in 1992 and the NTA a year later. The problem with this Whiggish view of Aboriginal history is that it came to a sharp impasse with the election of John Howard (and Pauline Hanson) in 1996. A certain assumed path of history no longer seemed to make sense. For a time it might have been believed that Howard was an anomaly, soon to be corrected by the electorate, but the Coalition government's narrow survival in 1998 suggested that an ideational and political fog of greater density and persistence had descended on the land. In legal terms, the 1998 Amendments marked a range of crucial changes to the NTA, but it is useful to conceive of a 'long 1998' with more emblematic meaning. The 'long 1998' encompassed Howard's political victory in getting his Amendments to the NTA through the Senate, as well as his multiple re-elections, empowering a government that changed the course of Indigenous affairs radically, rendering many of the fond myths of the Keating era problematic or hollow. In a broader political context the 'long 1998' implies a politics of intolerance and fear-mongering that would later also encompass harsh treatment of asylum-seekers and the shrill insistence on a certain discourse of 'Australian values'. For believers in the redemptive qualities of *Mabo (2)*, the 'long 1998' was when everything went wrong.

Complexities II: Native title and the puzzle of historical time

Within the native title system the movement of time was uneven and multidirectional and must have left many participants in the system feeling vexed and bewildered. The logical paradox at the heart of *Mabo* was that the case recognised native title, not only as a matter of future law, but as having always been there. Native title was not, in other words, only prospective, but backward looking: a matter of recognition, rather than the creation of a grant. The concept of a 'legal fiction', a fact or situation assumed or created by a court that is later used to resolve a matter before it, is well known to the common law, but what marked native title aside was the historical scale and political implications of the device in application. The High Court had acted to go back in time, in order to include Indigenous property rights in Australian legal history. Native title had not been recognised until 1992, so the deeds of the various historical actors (including Indigenous people themselves) had never, as a matter of reality, been predicated on the assumption that customary property rights were enforceable as a matter of law. However, the Court imagined that native title had been there all along, even if it were 'invisible'.[45] Thus the NTA provided a method for developing an imagined history in which native title had existed in 1788 and—having been in existence—could have been impacted upon by adverse historical events or extinguishing acts.

The consequence of the legal fiction necessitated by the logic of the recognition of the doctrine of native title was that, in the last year of the twentieth century, the courts were given the task of deciding upon meanings that could not possibly have been intended by the actors in their historical context. It was not logically feasible, of course, to give native title holders any capacity to enforce their retrospectively (and often posthumously) recognised rights. The native title that was projected backwards was mute and defenceless: a constructed thing that could be acted upon, but was not amenable to imaginative protection. The courts could indeed engage in the doctrinal equation of pre-existing native title minus colonial land grant equalling either complete or partial extinguishment, but there was no way of inserting agency into the process, giving long-gone traditional owners access to remedies of law and equity that might have arisen had they been recognised as property owners at the time.

Making matters even more complicated, developments in the law of extinguishment worked like a kind of doctrinal parallax, in that the presumed effect of tenure granted in the past apparently changed not because the past acts in question themselves altered, but because of shifts in the point of judicial observation. The question of the effect of pastoral leases on native title illustrates the analogy: in 1992, 1995,

1996, 1998, 2000 and 2002, the legally presumed impact of an identical grant of tenure made many decades previously oscillated not because new historical information had come to light, but because of instability in the state of the most authoritative judicial opinion on the subject. The legal fiction that native title had 'always been there' meant that litigation in relation to extinguishment was a contest to determine the legal and social implications of historical events. The consequence could produce political puzzles, as parties went to court to argue for a particular interpretation of law and history then, once the matter had been judicially determined, would be required to act as if it had always been thus. In *Wik*, for example, the dispute was in relation to what the effect had been of pastoral leases granted in the first decades of the twentieth century on native title which (as a matter of historical reality) had not then been recognised as existing. After making submissions as to what history should have been, once the High Court had decided the matter the past became fixed: pastoral leases did not wipe out traditional ownership in Queensland. The political contest over native title was in a very real sense a dispute over the past, the effects of which would be jurally determinative in the present. The juridical construction of native title thus requires an intellectual exercise that is both counter-factual and historically constitutive. The consensus on native title that has now been reached is predicated in considerable part on a retrospective construction of the past, decided by the courts after extensive litigation. Legal history has been constructed in hindsight through court processes, contributing to the allocation of rights and power in the present.

The division of sovereignty in Australia also meant that 'time' did not move evenly in the native title system. It is possible to think of the episodes in the development of the law of extinguishment as analogous to Australia's division into time zones. The law associated with the impact of pastoral tenure, for example, was definitively known in Queensland following the *Wik* decision in 1996, but not finally established in Western Australia until *Ward* or in New South Wales, in *Wilson v Anderson*, until 2002.[46] To some extent at least, 2002 in Western Australia was the equivalent of 1996 in Queensland, while in New South Wales, where the High Court decided that grazing tenure extinguished native title, 2002 might be seen as marking a return to 1992, when the prevailing assumption had been that pastoral tenure did indeed wipe out any pre-existing customary entitlements. The incremental and diverse development of the law in the various Australian jurisdictions was in a simple sense merely an expression of the historical and legal reality of federalism, but the analytical consequence is that care must be taken in assuming the political conditions of the day in any particular state or territory based simply on a bird's-eye view of the development of the national jurisprudence of native title.

Complexities III: Cross-cultural communication

Native title processes required intensive and extensive communication between Indigenous people and non-Indigenous systems of authority and bureaucracy, including the organisations dealt with in this book. The NTA was legislated by the Commonwealth Government to provide the primary interface between traditional rights over country and the state system of property law, necessitating extensive communication across cultural boundaries. Indigenous people observing traditional law and custom were placed in the exquisitely difficult position of having to try to apply customary precepts to making decisions under the NTA. Should a claim group object or simply let the exploration occur? If there was not one exploration licence application to consider but twenty, how would a group decide what to do? What did traditional law and custom say about prioritisation of responses? Choices could be stark. If an agreement was offered, how might a community decide when to accept the complete spoliation of an area of country in exchange for payments, jobs and other benefits particularly given that veto was not an option? On the other hand, native title also placed considerable obligations on the organisations administering the system to communicate clearly. The discharge of these requirements was conditioned by a certain awareness that had developed, no doubt spurred on by the Royal Commission into Aboriginal Deaths in Custody 1987–91, that the legal system was often not understood by Indigenous people who were in turn dealt with by lawyers, administrators and judges who knew little about the challenges of communicating across culture.

Unsurprisingly, given the broader meanings attached to *Mabo* and native title described earlier, there was common commitment that this time it would be different.

The challenges of cross-cultural communication under the NTA quickly proved to be substantial. The communal, consensus-based, decentralised and non-delegable nature of much Indigenous decision-making is hardly well suited to the sharp choices required of native title claim groups. Although the Act required the naming of applicants with the power to make decisions about the claim, social realities often rendered the statutory scheme unfeasible in practice, necessitating the development of broader and more amorphous decision-making structures.[47] Within meetings, any number of cultural norms could have an impact, including language taboos, avoidance relationships and restrictions on sharing information. Some claimants simply did not speak English or could not read or write, while others talked in 'Aboriginal English', with great attendant potential for misunderstanding.[48] Advisers to native title claim groups often found themselves in the invidious position of having to elicit instructions from a community feeling stressed and uncertain. The stark demographic reality of Indigenous Australians suffering higher rates of youth morbidity, chronic physical and mental illness and substance abuse directly impaired the functionality of many native title meetings. Sometimes, and regardless of any imperative derived from external procedural urgency, it was impossible to progress matters at all because of traditional funereal practices or ceremonial law business.

'Claimant group meetings' are so central to the functioning of the NTA as it has evolved, indeed are in many ways the system's most basic unit of operation, that it is worth condescending to some specifics in describing the complexities involved.[49] Although it was typical for a whole day (or days) to be set aside, it was not unusual for meetings not to begin until mid-morning or later because of cultural attitudes to time, enormous distances to be travelled, unreliable vehicles or perhaps actual unwillingness to start for reasons that might never become clear to outsiders. These gatherings might be held in fairly rudimentary facilities or in more plush locations (like mining company offices, municipal chambers or NNTT premises) that although nicely appointed, were hopelessly ill-fit for the purpose. Then again, holding meetings 'on country' might mean anything from an urban nature reserve to a dry riverbed in the true outback, a long way from any bitumen. Meetings could well be marred by interjections from a person off their medication or embroiled in some argument completely unassociated with native title. On some occasions, disputation between claimants might result in everyone walking out, or in an actual physical fight. 'Pushing on' to try to finish with agenda items could be totally counter-productive, particularly given the prevalence of diabetes in many Aboriginal communities. Lunch might well take hours and leave the company reduced in number, sleepy from heat and food and with perhaps little time left in the day once travel home had been factored in. Dogs and vigorous children also made regular appearances, creating a racket that was often more absorbing than the formal business at hand. Claimant meetings often faced long agendas, including presentations from multiple government agencies and resource companies, each with their own maps, documents and positive intentions. It is not surprising that many meetings ended in a decision to have another meeting. After a gathering, specific matters might have to be followed up with individual claimants, sometimes to almost absurd lengths.[50]

When the native title system was first established, there was an inevitable 'shock of the new' associated with the novelty of the process. For many non-Indigenous people who had not previously worked with Aboriginal communities, the challenges were no doubt striking and daunting. Quickly, though, a discourse developed about how to manage the complexities associated with communicating across cultures that became increasingly institutionalised in a set of practices and conventions as to how the work should be done. Expressions like 'cultural sensitivity' and 'cross-cultural awareness' became commonplace by the mid-1990s, used to describe the goals of 'cross-cultural education' or 'communication training'. With differing degrees of intensity and formality, every one of the organisations profiled in this book had some form of corporate engagement with learning about 'cross-cultural communication'. At the NNTT, for example, cross-cultural communication was seen as 'fundamental' and the goal was set that all staff 'be able to display sensitivity to Indigenous issues'.[51] On the back of the emergence of the native title system, learning about 'doing business with Aboriginal communities' became a growth enterprise in itself, giving rise to a mushrooming range of conferences, seminars and training courses.[52]

It seems unarguable that the cross-cultural communication project 'worked', insofar that many problems of miscommunication and offence were no doubt avoided through the effort.[53] Yet hazards lay in exaggerating what was achievable. According to one senior staff member from the Tribunal speaking optimistically in 1996, it was 'possible, if the mediators in the process are culturally sensitive to indigenous decision-making', for mediation to be 'conducted in a manner which is understandable to all of the parties', enabling outcomes to be reached that were 'just and fair'.[54] The evidence that exists is less sanguine, suggesting that concrete instances of the cultural divide, including those relating to seating arrangements, time frames, speaking protocols or feelings of power disparity, remained enduringly problematic.[55] At times the whole enterprise descended into little more than 'neo-colonial farce'.[56] In June 2005, the Tribunal publication *Talking Native Title* recorded how, after a role-swapping relationship-building exercise involving both claimants and industry executives in South Australia, the Chief Executive Officer of the SA Chamber of Mines and Energy, Stephanie Walker, said that after the process the parties 'could start talking as friends and build up good relations'. *Talking Native Title* reported that Walker

> was surprised by the depth of feeling generated when the negotiating parties from the State and the Chamber took on the role of traditional owners and 'experienced' having their land invaded by others.[57]

Even the most obvious of communication complexities, the language barrier, was not necessarily dealt with adequately.[58] A little knowledge being a dangerous thing, there was always the risk that well-meaning non-Indigenous people might unsuspectingly completely misunderstand the nature of an exchange of which they had just been part. More subtantively, far from being a way of dissolving difference, effective cross-cultural communication may actually function to demonstrate the gulfs that exist by making plain the values that are not shared and through isolating the incommunicable.[59] Despite good faith and best endeavours, there is simply a limit to how cultures can be bridged without engendering some internal transformation.[60] It seems more than possible that 'successful cross-cultural communication' was as much a consequence of Indigenous people increasing their participation and fluency in the norms and conventions of modernity as of non-Indigenous people learning how to 'talk to the natives'.

The concept of 'cross-cultural communication' also posed the danger of being over-determined, unhelpfully setting up a notion that world views are bifurcated between 'Indigenous' and 'non-Indigenous' spheres. Effective cross-cultural communication in the best sense is highly nuanced and attenuated to specific circumstances. However, more rigid adherence to learned tenets of cross-cultural communication could actually have a flattening effect, to the extent that a particular stereotype of an Indigenous person became the imagined other. In reality, varying life experiences and social realities give rise to divergent ways of engaging, regardless of genealogy. As Hal Wootten observed, '[i]t may be of little relevance that an experienced businessman happens to be of Aboriginal descent'. Indeed, the demographic reality was that by 1992, only a fraction of Indigenous people in Australia experienced lived realities governed by the kind of non-modern traditions that continue to characterise some communities. Again, as Wootten noted:

> in the non-Aboriginal community in Australia, one can usually assume an understanding, and in most cases an acceptance, of the capitalist view of the world. You can of course find plenty of Aboriginal people who share this view, and still more who, even if they do not share it, understand that it is the view of the world held by white people with whom they have to deal. If businesses are dealing only with such people, they may not need to vary their approaches and practices to any significant degree.[61]

Like the rest of the human race, Indigenous people in Australia are also divided by class, religion, geography, ideology, education, gender, sexuality, occupation, ability, life experience, taste and so on, and it would seem an exercise in reductionist identity politics at its most vulgar to demand that indigeneity necessarily comes first.

Indeed, as it became institutionalised, the peril emerged that cross-cultural communication would become a matter of ritual more important for what it signified than for any functional purpose. At the same time, as the native title system matured, it can be assumed that the Indigenous participants became savvier in how the machinery worked, or at least more settled in accepted understandings. The risk was that 'being culturally aware' ceased to be a matter of ethical obligation, professional competence and commercial due diligence, to instead become a kind of imagined elevation amenable to being enacted as a sort of moral fashion statement. The 'formal' acknowledgements of 'traditional ownership of country' that became so ubiquitous at meetings and events in the native title era, for example, offered a classic opportunity for demonstrations of ersatz cultural sensitivity, often displaying an ironic disjunction between the literal implications of formal words used and the nature of the gathering and venue in question.

One way of interrogating the meaning of the widespread embrace of cross-cultural communication is to understand its implications for the wider distribution and exercise of power within the native title system. The intention behind cross-cultural communication was to 'empower' Indigenous people which, as an alternative to business as usual, can be considered to have been successful. However, the institutionalisation of cross-cultural communication also acted to legitimise the native title system because of the assumption that the substantive allocation of power was made more just because of the way in which it was talked about. There is some force in the point, to the extent that what is incomprehensible inevitably seems arbitrary and capricious. Yet the hard facts of power are not dispelled simply because they are understood. Cross-cultural communication may give Indigenous people more informed agency, but does not shift the material allotment of rights. Nevertheless, it would be wrong to assume that the discourse of cross-cultural communication was just another conning of the hapless indigenes. Indeed, in a local sense, native title claimants with an awareness of rhetorical commitments to cultural sensitivity were able to act tactically in holding others to certain standards of behaviour. The particular vogue for certain actions as demonstrating 'cross-cultural sensitivity' may even have fostered patterns of behaviour among Indigenous people themselves. Cross-cultural communication was constitutive as well as enabling; serving to both produce and validate certain manners of acting in ways that were complex and unpredictable.

Complexities IV: The making of the claimant

The NTA provided an opportunity for Indigenous people who considered that they had rights to land arising from traditional law and custom to assert that ownership, potentially leading to some degree of recognition under the Australian legal system. In order to gain access to what the NTA offered, Indigenous people were required to become institutionalised as 'claimants', constructed in the way required by the statute and accompanying regulations. The NTA provided certain rules and parameters, requiring the people concerned, once transformed into 'claimants', to behave in prescribed ways and to make particular kinds of decisions within specified time periods. Indigenous people might be flesh and blood, but the status of 'claimant' was a function of the operation of the Act. Prior to the 1998 Amendments the laxity of criteria for the lodgment and registration of a native title claim meant that there was little control over who was eligible to become a 'claimant'. Indigenous people themselves often engaged in bitter disputation over the 'claimant' status of others, asserting that particular claims were bogus or that individuals had no right to membership of a group.[62]

Aboriginal people claiming customary rights over lands and waters, including all those with the formal status of native title claimants, have often been dubbed with the umbrella term 'traditional owners'. However, the operative element common to all Indigenous people who make claimant applications is not 'tradition' or 'ownership', but statutory eligibility giving rise to certain rights.[63] 'Claimants' are a statutory 'entitlement group' who may not in fact turn out to be traditional owners. It is arguable that nobody has protested the point as much as some Indigenous people themselves, in instances when one group has been seeking to deny the assertions of another. Officials often found the term 'traditional owners' to be a convenient catch-all that could be used, without making any qualitative judgment, to include a number of overlapping claim groups as well as Indigenous people who had not even lodged claims but might do so in the future. However, more than one native title claim group found themselves deeply angered and frustrated by the NTA according rights to others whose declaration of customary connection they hotly disputed.

Yet despite formal equality, within the discourse of native title not all claimants were regarded equally. In the minds of administrators, 'good claims' were compromised by groups that met regularly and without incident, were free of overlaps, inclusive of every Aboriginal person who asserted interest in the area in question and where the claimants engaged with future act processes willingly and in a timely way. Being a 'successful' and 'effective' native title claimant who understood how to respond and deal with the conventions of the system was a socio-legal role that was learned. Proficiency in dealing with process, though, was not necessarily coincident with authority under traditional law and custom. It could well be the case that a group or individual learned with great dexterity how to maximise their statutory entitlements and please officials, perhaps even complete with eloquent displays of great charm and cultural charisma, yet held little or no traditional authority. No moral judgment should be attached to those who made the most out of what the law offered, but equally, while the NTA required claims to be treated with formal neutrality, it would be wrong to imagine that the status of all native title claimants was the same under traditional law and custom.

Those native title claim groups that are successful in achieving determinations are then required by the NTA to engage in a further process of construction. In what is sometimes referred to as the 'post-determination' environment, now prescribed bodies corporate (PBCs) take the place of claim groups exercising procedural rights on behalf of the recognised native title holders. The legislation requires the nomination of a prescribed body corporate as either an agent or trustee on behalf of the successful claimants. It is to some extent one of the ironies of the native title system that Indigenous societies which have proved their claims are then directed on the form of the corporate structure through which their title must be held. PBCs are burdened with a considerable array of administrative and legal tasks. In the longer term, the performance of PBCs will be of critical importance to the functioning of the native title system.[64]

2

THE DILEMMAS OF THE BLACK LEADERSHIP

ATSIC, the native title working groups and their successors

Representing constituents and speaking for country

The promising and bold expression, 'the Indigenous leadership' hides a multitude of ambiguities and is often used to describe individuals who differ greatly in terms of the nature and source of their power and influence.[1] In this chapter the expression is confined to mean the official 'Indigenous leadership' in the context of native title. For most of the history of the NTA, the formalised Indigenous leadership was constituted by the Aboriginal and Torres Strait Islander Commission supplemented by a number of peak-level 'native title working groups'. However, in 2005 the abolition of ATSIC was followed by the establishment of two new bodies, the National Indigenous Council and the National Native Title Council. Among the Indigenous leadership, lines of authority and mandate always remained contested and ambiguous, a phenomenon of varying voices and shifting spaces. In the politics of native title, the locus of Indigenous power proved elusive and contextual, and the omnipresent question of 'who speaks for the blacks' was incapable of an unconditional answer. Tensions between different kinds of Aboriginal representation are an enduring theme in Indigenous affairs in Australia.

> Few things have given rise to more strife in Aboriginal affairs in the last 25 years than the attempts of governments to insist on Indigenous Australians working through representative, accountable organizations. People of European background treat such bodies as a universal norm, for they are heirs to a long struggle to develop representative institutions to wrest power to make binding community decisions from monarchies and oligarchies.[2]

Disjunctions existed between the elected authority of ATSIC politicians, the executive power of Indigenous government appointees and public servants, NTRB leaders and Aboriginal men and women of high degree exercising culturally based clout. Whatever else can be observed about ATSIC, it was a top-down creation with ultimate facility and funding depending on the imprimatur of government. The democratic structure of ATSIC was mandated in statute and was always at odds with traditional law and custom, which necessarily privileged those with cultural authority to speak for kin and country.[3] According to anthropologist Gillian Cowlishaw, seeking a position with ATSIC offered

> access to a new social identity . . . Well paid jobs, social esteem and public respect entirely reshaped many individuals' lives at the same time as they created divisions within communities. An ATSIC representative, a board and committee member . . . would find themselves in an invidious position. Kin networks are not only affective and symbolic but entail responsibilities which readily take priority over responsibility to the state . . . Local organizations thus became a fraught domain of complex and tense social action.[4]

Although the ATSIC zones and regions were to some extent designed around traditional cultural boundaries, the organisation was not 'organic' and exercised no customary legitimacy within Indigenous society, making local rivalries endemic. The uneasy power relationships which existed were complicated further by the extent to which individuals could exercise multiple roles, creating dynamic tensions that spilled promiscuously across organisations and circumstances.

Despite the complex undercurrents and with various exceptions, the Indigenous leadership was largely able to maintain public unity. Representations were generally made, either implicitly or explicitly, on behalf of 'Indigenous (or Aboriginal) People (or Peoples)' (or sometimes 'traditional owners') and comparatively rarely received challenge from any nonconforming voice. Such dissentients as became heard were mainly confined to the level of the local newspaper. Indeed, on the face of it, the position of the Indigenous leadership in relation to native title might be thought to be quite clear and readily amenable to political solidarity. On closer inspection, though, the confused patterns of mandate and authority are expressive of other complexities. The Indigenous leadership routinely supported and promoted native title, but that advocacy was expressed in varying ways over time, and meant diverse things to different people, all on shifting grounds. The breadth of significance attached to the expression 'native title' as described in Chapter 1 meant that the focus of Indigenous advocacy was not always plain or self-evident. Further, even if 'native title' was being defended in the narrow doctrinal sense of the term, there were still multiple (and sometimes inconsistent) reasons why the law might be thought to be, or endorsed as, a good thing. Despite the universalising tendency of the verbiage, there was never an unqualified and singular 'Indigenous position' in support of native title, but rather a variety of rationales determined by a range of factors, including external political and strategic considerations, as well as differences in ideological proclivity. Although the contradictions were seldom exposed, the Indigenous leadership advocated for native title on a range of bases that could oscillate radically.

ATSIC, NIWG, QIWG and WAANTWG

ATSIC was established by Bob Hawke's Labor government in 1990 as a statutory body designed to enable a form of limited 'Aboriginal and Islander self-management' in a manner that was to be both 'effective and accountable'.[5] ATSIC divided Australia into a number of Regional Council areas to decide on local priorities and larger zones that returned Commissioners to a national board, presided over by a chair. The first two Chairpersons of ATSIC, Lowitja O'Donoghue (1990–96) and Gatjil Djerrkura (1996–2000), were appointed by the Commonwealth, while the third and last, Geoff Clark (2000–04), was elected from among the Board of Commissioners. At regional, state and national levels, the elected arm of ATSIC was assisted by a substantial bureaucracy of Commonwealth public servants initially drawn from existing government agencies.[6] Only Indigenous people registered on the Commonwealth electoral role were permitted to vote and participation was voluntary, with actual turn-out estimated to average around 20–25 per cent of the total eligible population.[7] ATSIC could only ever exercise a highly contingent form of independence from the federal government. As Minister for Aboriginal Affairs, Gerry Hand, told the House of Representatives at ATSIC's birth, the body's power was entirely 'derived from legislation' and was entirely 'accountable to the Minister' and Parliament.[8] ATSIC was sometimes held out as an exercise in 'self-determination', but in truth the organisation's fate and funding remained always at the caprice of the Commonwealth.[9]

Native title was seen to herald a new 'operating environment' for ATSIC, but the only statutory function specifically provided to the national body under the NTA was a discretionary power to provide financial assistance to native title representative bodies.[10] Although native title program funding was quarantined from other areas of expenditure, in years when ATSIC had a surplus, the Board of Commissioners could exercise discretion to allocate extra money to NTRB programs and often did.[11] More amorphously, the Commission also exercised responsibility for broad-based advocacy in relation to native title pursuant to a general statutory mandate to represent the interests of Indigenous people.[12] A third function undertaken by ATSIC was to provide advice to the Commonwealth Minister in relation to the operation of the NTA. ATSIC's *Annual Report 2000–2001*, for example, noted that the organisation had 'played a major role in advocating an Indigenous position', which 'involved . . . provision of advice to governments; participation in interdepartmental committees; [and] maintaining constructive working relationships with relevant government and non-government bodies'.[13] The Commission was cast in the role of interlocutor between Aboriginal and Torres Strait Islander people and NTRBs on the one hand and the federal administration on the other. It was the fate of ATSIC to be perpetually caught in the middle, sometimes accused of being 'just another government agency' yet simultaneously trying to pursue the particular interests of its constituents, often against the tide of a broader Commonwealth agenda.[14]

More informal than ATSIC were the various peak bodies brought into existence to lobby on native title issues: the National Indigenous Working Group (NIWG), the Queensland Indigenous Working Group (QIWG) and the Western Australian Aboriginal Native Title Working Group (WAANTWG). All of the working groups included representatives from both NTRBs and ATSIC, while NIWG also incorporated representatives from certain other agencies.[15] In each case the impetus for the establishment of the working group was three-fold. First, the ambiguous nature of ATSIC in relation to native title meant that, without augmentation, it was regarded as an unsuitable representative by the leadership of some NTRBs who craved a more direct and independent collective line to government. Second, the absence of an overall peak body for NTRBs and the diffusion of jurisdiction among a number of rep bodies in Western Australia and Queensland in particular meant that it was strategically advantageous, both nationally and in those two states, to establish some level of coordination. Third, the specific imperatives for cooperative action were various clear and present dangers that emerged at both state and national level insofar that the advances achieved in *Mabo* and the original NTA were at risk of being legislatively undone: the WA government's attempt to extinguish all native title by legislation in 1993 precipitated the formation of WAANTWG,[16] the election of the Howard government in March 1996 prompted the establishment of NIWG[17] and QIWG was hastily set up when the Labor administration led by Premier Peter Beattie proposed to implement certain state-based reforms.[18] All three working groups received ATSIC funding to operate.[19]

The vexed question of coordination

It was always conventional wisdom that 'coordination and funding of claims on a state, and preferably on a national basis' would feature as part of any sensible strategic approach by the organisations representing native title claimants.[20] A country-wide effort would presumably have involved the selection and pursuit of the most promising test cases run by top counsel, as well as careful benchmarking of negotiated outcomes, complemented by horizontal integration between NTRBs sharing accumulated experience and the systematisation of precedents. Ultimately, though, the system was not conducive to a synchronised approach and hopes of national coordination were never fully realised. Centrifugal concerns and the realities of the distribution of decision-making power largely overcame centripetal aspirations. The result was a system driven by local needs and pressures, subject to a limited degree of broader dialogue generally in response to government. Decisions on priorities and funding at a national level invariably trailed events, rather than dictated them. In practice, the cases that set precedents were rarely, if ever, chosen after some preliminary process of state or national evaluation, but rather 'followed the fact' of individual actions having been initiated by particular claimants or rep bodies.

It is not clear that the Commission ever understood the extent of its own operational frailty, often making rhetorical claims well beyond the organisation's actual capacity. In its *Annual Report 1995–1996*, for example, ATSIC indicated that it would seek 'better prepared and researched claims being lodged and processed' and 'a significant advance in the progress' of applications, both of which, though laudable objectives, were well beyond the Commission's volition.[21] Again, in 1997–98, ATSIC included as a performance indicator the 'number of native title agreements and determinations reached'—both matters which were very clearly outside of its control.[22] In one of its last gasps in 2003–04, ATSIC increased 'the input' of its Regional Councils 'into the setting of native title policy' but apparently with little idea of what the initiative could possibly mean in practice.[23] Matters were made worse by what seemed at times to be a fairly superficial understanding of the native title system among parts of the Commission. In 1996–97, for example, amidst the wild proliferation of overlapping applications in some areas, ATSIC nevertheless indicated that one of its key performance indicators for NTRBs was the blunt quantitative measure of 'number of claims lodged'.[24]

ATSIC and the working groups were weak organisations in the sense that they had little capacity to bind individual NTRBs and, still less, particular claim groups to a particular position or course of action. Any potential for voluntary harmonisation of approach was undercut by the fact that the bodies that needed to cooperate to make any hope of coordination meaningful were actually engaged in competition over an insufficient and finite pool of resources. A national perspective, which contemplated allocating resources on the basis of a more global appraisal of strategic needs, was clearly not the same as the organisation-specific imperatives driving each NTRB to maximise their share of the available funding by concentrating on local priorities. NIWG, QIWG and WAANTWG competed for allocations from the same funds with the NTRBs, which also vied with each other, creating inevitable contention over the relative merits of priorities and without any clear and transparent basis for resolving the contest. Whatever the external displays of Indigenous unity and blustering about the need for intra-organisational cooperation, behind the façade was internecine competition for scarce resources.

The 'Indigenous position'

ATSIC described its primary role in relation to native title as 'advocating an Indigenous position' to government and in the community at large.[25] By the time ATSIC was established, the idea of forging a common Indigenous position already had a substantial heritage. At least since the formation of the Federal Council for the Advancement of Aborigines and Torres Strait Islanders (FCAATSI) back in 1958, campaigns over constitutional reform, land rights and other issues had often been characterised by expressions of pan-Aboriginal solidarity. All who could show some ancestry and identified as 'Aboriginal' were welcomed within the broad tent, despite huge variations in geography and experience.[26] The social reality, particularly after a long history of colonisation, was that experientially, what it meant to be an Indigenous person differed dramatically depending on individual life trajectories. If, as historian Bain Attwood observed twenty years ago, colonisation made 'the Aborigines', the process also manufactured a new patchwork of Indigenous diversity because the 'making' did not occur evenly throughout the continent.[27] In 1958 when FCAATSI was formed, for instance, some traditional owners of the Gibson Desert had not yet encountered a non-Aboriginal person. The necessary political consequence was that any campaign on behalf of all Indigenous people in Australia would need to encompass the full breadth of experience but simultaneously assert the community and solidarity of the whole.

In the context of native title, acknowledging diversity yet proclaiming unity was accompanied by an elision of the historical reality of numerous distinct societies before colonisation ('Aboriginal peoples' rather than 'Aboriginal people') with contemporary variety in Indigenous social experience. The neatness of the positioning meant that current differences among Aboriginal people and communities could be bracketed with tribal and regional differentiations that had existed before 1788, with the implication that less traditional Indigenous groups in the present should be accounted for as merely an extension of the original diversity. The conflation solved the discursive problem that all native title claims had to be made on the basis of 'traditional connection', no matter how the group was constituted or actually experienced life. In terms of arguments about where native title existed, the measure of greater or lesser traditionality was necessarily discarded in favour of a reframing that insisted instead upon varieties of tradition that could admittedly look either more or less like pre-colonisation culture. Indigenous society, it was asserted, took countless and varied forms as it always had done; any argument to the contrary was ignorant and essentialising at best and straightforwardly racist at worst. Importantly, though, sociocultural variety was not to be confused with significant political divergences or any fracturing of pan-Indigenous solidarity. Cultural multiplicity was paired with political singularity. As leading Indigenous academic Larissa Behrendt put it in 2003: '[a]lthough from 500 different groups, Indigenous people from diverse cultural groups remain politically united against the dominant culture'.[28] Legally, every community asserting native title had to claim to be 'traditional' and, politically, all were seen to be preoccupied with the same agenda. The foundation of native title in 'tradition' associated with the paradigm of pan-Aboriginal unity of purpose bolstered the notion that Indigenous people's rationale for supporting the doctrine was organic and self-evident.

The political reality, though, was that native title did not impact upon all Aboriginal people the same way. Further, the rationales for native title that were provided by the Indigenous leadership were both changeable and inconsistent. It is a well-observed irony of post-colonial 'struggle' that 'the colonized's success in overcoming their subjugation depends on them becoming adept in the use of the colonizer's political instruments'.[29] Throughout the native title era, the Indigenous leadership showed willingness to adopt the political argot of the moment to articulate justifications for supporting native title which, it was believed, might prove more likely to achieve success. However, when setbacks occurred a willingness was evinced to adopt more radical positions, though generally out of frustration rather than any kind of operable threat. At no stage in the context of native title has the Indigenous leadership seriously veered towards a strategy of peaceful direct action or, thankfully, violent confrontation.

During the period between the enactment of the NTA and the downfall of the Keating government, the default Indigenous position was to side with the Commonwealth Labor regime against attacks on the new legislation.[30] Nevertheless, the Indigenous leadership's support for the NTA was always provisional on certain other promised initiatives, namely a land-purchasing fund and a broad social justice program.[31] What had already been achieved had to be shielded, but very much more was still hoped for. According to Noel Pearson, then Executive Director of the Cape York Land Council, speaking in March 1994, *Mabo* had been a 'pragmatic' decision and the NTA was 'a fair result', but the next question arising from the decision was how to go from the 'remnant title' that had been recognised to achieving full 'social justice'.[32] Support for the NTA should also not be conflated with passive acceptance of the administration of the new processes. Pat Dodson, one-time director of the Kimberley Land Council, remarked as early as September 1994 that it was 'a matter of continuing hurt' for Indigenous people to be meeting other parties as 'supplicants pleading for our interests in the face of those who have in the past, and who continue to, deny the existence of our rights'.[33] Lowitja O'Donoghue commented in mid-1995 that, in contrast to the 'exhilarating achievements' of *Mabo* and the enactment of the NTA, the procedures of the new statute seemed rudely constipated, making 'indigenous Australians frustrated at an apparent lack of progress'.[34]

Once the Howard government had been elected, articulating the Indigenous position at a federal level became a tougher business, requiring arguments more in keeping with the values of the new administration. Howard had been elected by promising to govern 'for all of us', and in a climate increasingly ill-disposed towards the kinds of sectional interests that were perceived to have been favoured by the previous Labor government, it was politically attractive to attempt to iterate native title as a phenomenon consistent with mainstream values.[35] *Wik*, for example, was universalised as 'all about mutual respect for different interests in land'[36] and 'a victory for commonsense and fairness',[37] while the doctrine of native title itself was said to 'benefit the whole community' or even given as a reason for feeling a wider patriotism.[38] It was also increasingly emphasised that native title could promote development, while any adulteration of the right to negotiate would 'destroy an opportunity for economic independence just as it [was] beginning'.[39] At their most ambitious, economically progressive rationales for native title became inflated to include claims that agreements over new resource developments not only benefited Indigenous people, but were even 'good for business' too. NIWG asserted in 1996 that companies 'negotiating agreements with indigenous people' were 'gaining a competitive edge in the market place'.[40] Given the extent to which the Australian economy is predicated on primary industry, it is ironic but not surprising that the 'Indigenous position' so quickly evolved to include the argument that native title should be supported on the basis that it was good for the resources business.

The consequence of rhetorical malleability was internal consistency, though admittedly there is no particular reason for thinking that a more coherent position would have been more politically effective, at least in the short term. Nonetheless, with hindsight the disjunctions can be striking. There was, for example, a genuine tension between the conservative argument that native title was based on and preserved tradition and the economically progressive case that the right to negotiate would stimulate development and modernisation.[41] The complex question of the ongoing engagement between tradition and modernity is one of the foundational paradoxes of Indigenous affairs, and each person's answer will necessarily be predicated on perceptions of what constitutes a good society. However, in the crucible of the native title debates in the mid-1990s, contradictions were staunched with sentiment and blandishment, in the typical manner of stump-politics. So, for example, Gatjil Djerrkura told a Senate Committee on one occasion that it was 'attachment to our country' which gave Indigenous people 'a strong basis to participate in and contribute to contemporary Australian life, whether it be economic or cultural'.[42] Needless to say, suggesting that traditional societies' socio-religious attachment to land provides an obvious foundation for participation in a modern industrial economy seems arguable at best. However, the politics of the time dictated that the Chair of ATSIC should attempt to equate vibrant participation in a pre-modern cultural system with market readiness.

The period of just over two years, from the formation of NIWG in April 1996, to the passage of the amended NTA in September 1998, probably marked the pinnacle of national Indigenous coordination since the native title legislation had been enacted. NIWG met six times in the course of 1996–97 and was allocated scarce program funds by ATSIC to obtain legal advice and maintain a small secretariat.[43] The struggle that took place involved both lobbying the Howard administration to try and ameliorate the proposed amendments but also, as the fail-safe, persuading the Australian Labor Party, minor parties and independents in the Senate to vote down unacceptable changes. In the post-NTA environment, the Indigenous leadership's efforts to combat the Howard government's proposed changes to the Act constituted an extraordinary and sustained effort of political campaigning. However, the debates proved gruelling and the way in which the amending bill was finally passed by the Senate was deeply embittering, as well as bringing a result that was considerably worse than the leadership had hoped might be salvaged. The government's changes to the NTA had only been possible through an accommodation being reached with the independent Senator from Tasmania, Brian Harradine. The dynamics of the ultimate settlement—'based on a political compromise, to which Indigenous interests were not a party'—was supremely galling.[44] Mick Dodson described the passage of the Amendments as 'the spectacle of two white men, John Howard and Brian Harradine, discussing our native title when we're not even in the room'.[45]

After the Amendments had been passed, positions hardened. In the period from March 2000, when a majority of the Full Court of the Federal Court overturned the first-instance ruling in *Ward* in critical respects,[46] through to the High Court's decision in *Yorta Yorta* in December 2002, the jurisprudence turned sharply against the interests of native title claimants. The result was that the Indigenous leadership lost considerable faith in the redemptive power of the domestic jural system, perceiving, in the words of one ATSIC commissioner, 'an ever increasing gap in Australia between native title law and justice'.[47] Clark argued that 'Indigenous people should not have to fight tooth and nail to win recognition of every right we have as the first peoples of this nation'.[48] In response to *Yorta Yorta* in particular, Clark and others also began to advocate a radical view of native title as premised on 'original ownership' derived from 'birthright' rather than current social practices.[49] Native title rights, Clark now believed, should be respected 'without having to prove them to a Federal Court', and in a sweeping move promptly launched a renewed push for a national treaty under the auspices of ATSIC, a process in which the Howard government did not evince the least bit of real political interest.[50] Internationally, things were even more hopeless. ATSIC embarked on a successful campaign to have the Amendments condemned by the Convention for the Elimination of Racial Discrimination Committee of the United Nations.[51] However, resorting to the international arena was politically impotent: the Coalition government did not appear to care less and may even have electorally benefited from being seen to stand up to overseas meddling.[52]

Frustration at the trend of the development of the law, resignation at the re-election of Howard in late 2001 and no doubt general weariness at the slow speed with which native title determinations were being achieved, eventually led Clark and others to take the extreme position of attacking native title, ostensibly in order to save it. The ATSIC Chairperson repeatedly railed against the native title process as 'costing too much money', 'taking too much time' and creating 'too much uncertainty'.[53] He was not alone. Pat Dodson complained that the Amendments to the NTA had not only been unjust to Aboriginal people, but 'created nightmares for all the serious stakeholders'.[54] Speaking, perhaps, to the concerns of 'all of us' in 2002, Clark claimed that 'everyone' would 'agree that the system is not working':

> At the rate we are going, land claims will still be running in the next century. It will have cost the Aboriginal people, governments, industry—taxpayers—billions of dollars for Aboriginal people to get their title recognised. We need a better system.[55]

In corroboration of his radical conclusions, Clark was not averse to quoting from among the most intractable opponents of native title.[56] Adopting the arguments of your adversaries to further your own end is one of the oldest political debating tricks in the book. However, appropriating the preoccupations of your antagonist does not mean that peace or compromise will follow on the terms you are hoping, for the simple reason that agreeing on a problem does not necessarily equate to sharing a view on the ideal solution. There may indeed have been a common view, in Clark's words, that the native title system was 'not sustainable', 'unfair', 'expensive' and 'delivering uncertainty instead of just outcomes',[57] but that did not mean that either industry or conservative politicians would come to share an 'Indigenous position' which favoured stronger and more entrenched rights: it was a logical *non sequitur*. Espousing the concerns of business overlooked the basic reality that the interests of resource companies and native title claimants are not the same. Clark's own solution was a new 'national land settlement acceptable to all parties' and he called 'on the Prime Minister to take a lead'; a plea that was ignored.[58] The Coalition government was never going to be won over to the cause of strengthening Aboriginal rights, no matter how many Indigenous leaders professed to have got with the program.

The decline of the old order and the makings of the new

Once the 1998 Amendments had gone through, the immediate purpose of NIWG in particular seemed no longer apparent. The last NIWG event—a national conference of Indigenous leaders and their advisers in relation to the implementation of the Amendments to the NTA—took place in May 1999, after which, deprived of further ATSIC funding in June of that year, the organisation collapsed. In any event, the priorities had become the need to contest the possible introduction of alternative state regimes, as well as dealing with the complexities posed by the implementation of the Amendments at a regional and local level.[59] An attempt to resuscitate a national action group in September 2002 in Cairns came to nothing.[60] On another occasion Clark, as chair of ATSIC, proclaimed the formulation of a range of portfolio positions and working groups, including one for native title, involving most of the unelected peak Indigenous leadership, an extraordinary announcement which also quickly fizzled out.[61] The Commission's funding of WAANTWG and QIWG continued until the end of the 2002–03 financial year, after which the Western Australian body closed down, while the Queensland equivalent continued to function on the basis of contributions in kind from its member organisations.

ATSIC itself was in steep decline by 2004. The corporate memory of the Commission in relation to native title had already been weakened through staff losses incurred by repeated restructuring and multiple office relocations across state borders.[62] The last years of ATSIC's existence were tortured and controversial. Both Clark and his deputy 'Sugar' Ray Robinson were implicated in a number of unsavoury personal scandals, but refused to step aside, and there were broader questions raised about organisational propriety.[63] The truth, as demonstrated by a Commonwealth auditor's report, was that ATSIC could demonstrate accountability well above acceptable public service levels, but that was not the impression that was generated in the media.[64] ATSIC was also unfairly held responsible for the absence of any improvement in Indigenous health and education, despite the reality that it possessed no funding or statutory obligations in relation to either.[65] Perceptions, though, were everything and in the hard, volatile, unrepentant and allegedly violent Clark, the Coalition government had a target that could not be much larger or more inviting.

There is little doubt that the Howard government pursued the path of destruction, regardless of the evidence and notwithstanding any of the actual failings in ATSIC's leadership. A wide-ranging review was initiated by the Commonwealth Minister into the future of ATSIC in 2002, but before the report had even been brought down legislation was introduced denying the elected arm of the organisation supremacy over the administrative side.[66] The executive component, renamed the Aboriginal and Torres Strait Islander Service (ATSIS), was no longer answerable directly to the popular representatives. The new arrangements, with power divided between ATSIS and ATSIC, lasted a single dysfunctional year before the federal government moved to full abolition mode. The final decision to eliminate both ATSIC and ATSIS was made in April 2004 amid a new commitment to 'mainstreaming' of Indigenous service delivery.[67] Any potential serious partisan political opposition was ruled out when the then leader of the federal Labor Party, Mark Latham, said in March 2004 that he would close down ATSIC if elected.[68] In May 2004 the Howard government introduced legislation to abolish ATSIC, which was passed by the Federal Parliament in the following year.[69]

After the demise of ATSIC, the last remaining Indigenous national configuration of any ongoing relevance was the annual Australian Institute of Aboriginal and Torres Strait Islander Studies (AIATSIS) native title conference which, although well-attended by Indigenous leaders, was an event rather than a political structure. Many of the *Mabo* generation of Indigenous leadership had already departed the scene, no longer holding official positions within any native title organisation. Pat and Mick Dodson, Peter Yu, Lowitja O'Donoghue, Noel Pearson, Marcia Langton and Aden Ridgeway, among others, had hardly abandoned politics but were exercising their 'Indigenous leadership' roles in new ways. Nevertheless, the departure of many of the stars from formal native title structures undoubtedly contributed to the overall sense of systematic decline. The Howard government, though, had no intention of just leaving a void and in 2005 announced the creation of an advisory National Indigenous Council (NIC), with an appointed membership. In an effort to avoid accusations that the NIC was merely a stooge organisation, among those appointed were retired magistrate Sue Gordon from Western Australia, who enjoyed the trust of the local Labor government, as Chairperson, and senior Labor figure and Executive Director of the New South Wales native title representative body, Warren Mundine.[70] The old guard, though, was conspicuously absent. True to its name, the NIC had a purely advisory role and commanded no staff to speak of, or any operational budget. When the federal government again moved to amend the NTA, though the political context was admittedly vastly different, the contrast with the efforts of 1996–98 could not have been greater: the NIC did not even make a submission in relation to the Commonwealth Native Title Bill (2006).

Perhaps the most significant idea fostered through the NIC, though never actually endorsed, was the notion that communally held Indigenous land should be privatised. Although always directed more at various land rights regimes and particularly the Northern Territory system which gives rise to a form of communal statutory title, the privatisation proposal nevertheless had potential application to native title. The notion that customary ownership giving way to fully fungible private property rights was essential to economic development and prosperity had obtained a broad currency.[71] Howard was enthusiastic about the prospect that became euphemistically dubbed 'Indigenous home ownership'. Significantly, though, it was Warren Mundine who emerged as one of the principal advocates, potentially placing him at odds not only with his own NTRB and with the Australian Labor Party, but also precipitating open conflict among the Indigenous leadership. The audacity of Mundine's effort was not only in the content of the idea, but the basis of his thinking. Here was a senior Aboriginal leader who was saying out loud that not all Indigenous people were 'traditional' and that land was more culturally important for some than others:

> Well, it was almost like a myth . . . we believed that once we had land rights all these wonderful things were going to flow from it, that we were going to have a land of milk and honey; there was going to be economic development, our communities would be safe, we'd reverse

> the ills and problems that colonisation put upon us, and we'd have this great lifestyle. When we go back now over 20 years that isn't the case . . . You can't get away from the fact we're coming from a society that was very much spiritually, economically, land-based, and it meant that it's very much a great part of our lives, and of course that was the process; if we did get separated from our land then it could cause death in the past. But we're living in the 21st century now. Many Aboriginals are living off their lands . . . we're not going to die.[72]

The result was a rare fracturing of the public unity among the national Indigenous leadership. Among the broader NTRB community, there was great disquiet at the privatisation proposals and Mundine was subject to excoriating criticism from peers at a conference in Coffs Harbour in mid-2005 and on other occasions.[73] Yet the sense was that the politics was moving fast in the direction of the privatisation of Indigenous land.

In response to concerns that the NIC in general and certain individuals in particular had seized the national agenda and in alarm at what the Commonwealth Government might be about to do next, a new body was established in 2005 and incorporated in 2006, known as the National Native Title Council of Native Title Representative Bodies and Service Providers in Australia (NNTC). The unwieldy name was a product of the shift that had occurred in the provision of Commonwealth funded representation to native title claimants, from the land council model to that of corporate service provision, which is described in Chapter 3. The result, though, was that the basis of the NNTC's platform was ambiguous from the outset.[74] In particular, an accelerating trend towards non-Indigenous chief executives running native title service providers created new complications associated with the meaning of 'Indigenous leadership'. Brian Wyatt, the long-standing Executive Director of the Goldfields Land and Sea Council, well known for his economically progressive pronouncements on native title, was made the inaugural Chairperson of the NNTC.[75] Without funding or staff, the NNTC had little capacity and grasped at a wide variety of rationales for native title, sometimes evincing little coherence.[76] Like its predecessors, the NNTC attempted to catch the prevailing political wind and, although opposing the mantra of privatisation, certainly foregrounded economic development arguments in favour of native title.[77]

Coming home

In assessing the Indigenous leadership in the history of the NTA, three overriding points seem obvious. The first is that if the original legislation is taken as the benchmark, the rights of native title groups have since gone backwards (particularly when seen in relative terms to those of primary industry as discussed further in Chapter 5), which rather bluntly suggests that the Indigenous leadership suffered a long political defeat. The reversal seems closer to a rout when it is added that the Indigenous leadership as it had been constituted at the beginnings of the native title era was entirely destroyed, with much of the accompanying ideology widely unfashionable or discredited in mainstream political discourse. In the end, black feet of clay had proved sublimely vulnerable to sustained outside attack: before leaving office Howard's regime had smashed the organised Indigenous leadership as it had previously existed. In ATSIC's case, that few mourned at the organisation's passing (which is distinct from outrage at the unfairness of government dealings) showed that public discourse had changed along with the facts of power. A third observation, though, perhaps suggests that a rather more nuanced appraisal may be appropriate. Native title may have been diminished but had not been the subject of wholesale national extinguishment. Despite the demise of ATSIC, the rise of new political directions on Indigenous affairs and the push towards a privatisation of communal Aboriginal land, native title had survived; albeit in more attenuated form.

In any event it is open to debate as to how much any of these results can be ascribed to the doings of the Indigenous leadership given their lack of power and limitations on action. Whatever dexterity of stratagem or sheer tenacity might have been exhibited, inherent structural weaknesses imposed deep-seated restrictions on what was possible. The Indigenous leadership ultimately relied on the grace and favour of the Commonwealth for standing, status and resources. Indeed, one way of understanding the fate of ATSIC and NIWG was being doomed to bite the feeding hand with all their vigour, a course of action that was never likely to cultivate organisational longevity. Perhaps it might even be suggested that for all its substantial imperfections, it is some small testimony to ATSIC's positional integrity that the Howard government bothered with the organisation's obliteration. The diffusion of Indigenous authority created particular limits to what might be done, manifested in the functional inability to direct and maintain operational priorities in any kind of coordinated national approach. Associated with the basic vulnerability of native title to the Commonwealth legislature was an instrumental willingness on the part of the Indigenous leadership to continually refashion their position on native title in the political language of the day; a form of tactical agility in response to strategic weakness, but which came at the price of some logical and ideological incoherence.[78] If a plurality of arguments could have been made, openly recognising the existence of a spectrum of 'Indigenous positions' on native title, then the tortured nature of some of the reasoning might have been avoided; but Aboriginal politics just has not worked like that, instead being actively predicated on the solidarity of a unitary position. In any event, it is at best arguable that greater attention to consistency and coherence would have led to any stronger outcomes.

Even had ATSIC and NIWG not been swept away, it is perhaps inevitable that, as the law and politics of native title settled and consensus deepened, the Indigenous leadership would have become diminished in weight and profile. In the absence of great issues and stirring controversies, there is less of a call for big personalities or intensive policy attention. Maybe some new configuration of Indigenous leadership will attempt to reopen the fundamental framework of native title, but at present it is hard to see how momentum for a reformation that would increase Aboriginal rights might be generated. The job from now on might be no more than to stand watch on the system, seeking incremental and instrumental improvements in funding and administration, but without disturbing the basic distribution of rights and power that has been established. Meanwhile, on a regional and local level, there is still a great deal of work to be done, conducting negotiations and settling claims, even if the horizons of what is possible are now far more circumscribed than was dreamed in the early 1990s. The current generation of the Indigenous leadership in native title is necessarily more preoccupied with the proximate than the continental, one sense at least in which the operation of the NTA has indeed brought Aboriginal people home.

3

LIKE UNACKNOWLEDGED BASTARDS

The native title representative bodies

How shall the work be done?

Whatever the statutory settlement that followed *Mabo* was to look like, one thing was clear: there would be an awful lot of work to be done. Exactly who would do the job of representing Indigenous people wanting to pursue native title claims and how it would be paid for were two of the critical policy questions that had to be decided. There was an existing model on show, namely the large statutory Indigenous land councils of the Northern Territory, which since their inception in the 1970s had held monopoly powers and independent income streams through mining royalties. However, for the states, much of industry and even some Aboriginal groups who were defensive of local autonomy, the consolidation of control represented by the Northern Territory example was precisely what had to be avoided.[1] Those fearful of too much centralised control prevailed in the debates and, in accordance with current ideals of service provision, it was intended 'that indigenous native title parties should have maximum flexibility in the representation of their interests'.[2] In contrast to the monopolistic Northern Territory model, there would be a system in which Aboriginal organisations applied to the Commonwealth for official native title representative body status and funding and multiple bodies could have NTRB status over a single geographical area, creating a competitive environment in which claimants could choose their preferred representative. The result was a mess from the very beginning.[3]

The NTA simply required an interested organisation to be able to satisfy the criterion of being 'broadly representative' of the Indigenous people of the relevant area before the Commonwealth Minister was able to bestow NTRB status, but it was not particularly clear how such a standard should be demonstrated.[4] The functions of NTRBs were rather loosely defined in the statute and there was no 'rigorous assessment undertaken of their roles, responsibilities and of the workloads that they might face and the sorts of funds they might require'.[5] Among the entities that achieved rep body status were some pre-existing statutory land councils and Aboriginal legal services,[6] various corporations of long-standing non-statutory operation[7] and some new bodies that had been established since *Mabo* for the specific purpose of dealing with native title issues.[8] The result was a deep unevenness in purpose and capacity among NTRBs, plus rife instability in some of the weaker organisations and across the scheme as a whole.[9]

While the particularities of their constitutions differed, all rep bodies were Aboriginal corporations with an elected governing committee that appointed a chief executive officer. Mostly the CEOs of NTRBs were Indigenous, but there was no legal compulsion to that effect and a number of non-Indigenous people held executive positions at rep bodies from time to time. Typically, the CEO was supported by a complement of professional and administrative employees, including corporate services, lawyers, anthropologists, community liaison officers and others. Work that could not be performed by staff would have to be contracted out, invariably at greater expense. The size of the staff group depended on the organisation in question, but ranged from between around ten to more than 70. NTRBs almost always operated offices within the jurisdiction they were representing, although it became common for regional bodies to also maintain capacity in their state capital. Rep body work was heavily dependent on long drives and air travel, servicing an often far-flung client base and constituency. NTRBs fulfilled a broad range of functions, including intra-Indigenous dispute resolution, preparing applications, providing representation and advice on mediation, litigation and negotiation of claim and future act matters, convening and supporting claimant meetings, participating in state and national processes (including some of the Indigenous leadership bodies described in Chapter 2) and responding to broader government requests for consultation on a wide array of policy matters.[10] While the workload was formidable enough on the face of it, the actuality was even more intricate and convoluted given the cross-cultural and geographic dimensions of what was involved.

The rep bodies were a cornerstone of the native title system, yet the NTRB system always suffered from a kind of structural illegitimacy in which the nature and role of the organisations were overburdened, contested and beset with contradictions.[11] Long-standing native title lawyer James Fitzgerald has commented that all too often the NTRBs have been treated 'like unacknowledged bastard children, paid minimal maintenance by a begrudging, estranged government that took no interest in their progress as long as they didn't cause trouble'.[12] As children of uncertain lineage, rep bodies struggled with their place in the world: were they 'Aboriginal organisations' furiously contesting the legacy of colonisation at every step, or docile servants of government policy faithfully achieving key performance indicators? The gnawing contradictions of the NTRBs, twisted creatures from the outset, were never resolved.

NTRBs 1994–98

After less than one year of the NTA's operation, the ATSIC Board initiated a review into the effectiveness of NTRBs, under the titular chairmanship of Guy Parker, an ATSIC Commissioner from the Pilbara in Western Australia who had portfolio responsibilities for native title and was assisted by a highly skilled and experienced review panel. The 'Parker Report' was handed down in August 1995 and recommended a significant re-envisioning of the NTRB system, involving both legislative change and administrative re-tooling. The Parker Report argued that the native title system would be best served by a patchwork of between 20 and 30 native title representative bodies, each exercising exclusive jurisdiction and with sole control over government funding for progressing native title claims within each region. NTRBs should be adequately resourced, but with increased reporting obligations and a greater interface with ATSIC as the principal funding agency. Specific recommendations were made for the recognition of particular rep bodies where none currently existed. The overall approach was to sort out the chaos in favour of cleaner lines of responsibility and greater overall systematisation.[13] As two of the Parker review team related to a workshop in September 1995, their findings went against the prevailing tenets of governmental thinking which was 'very much anti-monopoly, anti-trust, pro-competition' and instead argued that what would be most effective was the establishment of 'representative bodies with monopoly powers to represent native title parties in relation to native title issues': a rejection of the neo-liberal orthodoxy of competition and transition, in effect, to something much closer to the Northern Territory land rights model of representation.[14]

The election of the Howard government in 1996 meant that the whole matter of NTRB functioning was again up for review. However, the fate of the rep bodies was not a first order issue in the tortuous debates that preceded the amendment of the NTA in 1998 and did not, for example, feature under any of the items contained in Prime Minister Howard's 'Ten Point Plan' for reform released in May 1997. In the event, although the Amendments substantially altered the functioning of NTRBs, in important respects the content of the changes reflected many of the concerns of the Parker Report, as the federal government was quick to point out.[15] Nevertheless, the scale of the transformation of the NTRB system as a consequence of the 1998 Amendments exceeded anything previously proposed. In sheer numerical terms, the rep bodies' part of the NTA swelled from less than a page and a half of text to nearly 40 pages in length. The coming into effect of the relevant provisions was stepped, with the first wave commencing on 30 September 1998 and the second and more onerous set beginning 30 June 2000. The Amendments converted the NTRBs from loosely scrutinised organisations with broad discretionary functions to heavily regulated entities obliged to perform specific tasks in a pre-determined order of priority, the content of each of which was spelled out in detail. Statutory grant conditions were imposed, accompanied by new obligations to strategically plan, hold appropriate accounting records and submit annual reports to Parliament. Powers were created allowing government to inspect NTRB records and the executive office holders of each rep body were made subject to specific liabilities, including those arising under the *Commonwealth Authorities and Companies Act 1997*. The overall effect was to enforce the creation of a set of new bureaucratic standards among NTRBs.[16]

Accompanying the changes to how the rep bodies were regulated were broader alterations to the native title system, which had the effect of greatly increasing the workload. The initial 'avalanche' facing the NTRBs under the amended NTA was the imposition of a new registration test on existing native title applications, which required extensive work to ensure that claims remained registered so as not to lose the right to negotiate.[17] A range of novel and more complicated future act processes were also introduced by the Amendments that had the general consequence of making it harder and more labour intensive for claimants to assert procedural rights, thereby creating further work obligations for their representatives. The removal of the basic carriage of native title claims from the National Native Title Tribunal to the Federal Court brought an associated stiffening of procedure and the imposition of judicial powers of direction, which also acted to enlarge the burden on NTRBs.[18] Multiple processes with converging obligations amplified the overall pressure, a general condition that came into specific focus when Federal Court and National Native Title Tribunal limitation periods and return dates created competing obligations. One counsel described the cumulative effect as 'Kafkaesque'.[19]

The 1998 Amendments also required all existing rep bodies to reapply for recognition. The Commonwealth Minister divided Australia into various 'invitation areas' and then asked all NTRBs that had previously enjoyed jurisdiction over part of the region in question to make application to be re-recognised now as having sole jurisdiction for the entire district.[20] The effect of the re-recognition process was to set up what was effectively a competitive tendering environment pitting existing

NTRBs against one another for exclusive status. The jurisdictions of some smaller former NTRBs were completely subsumed within larger areas; others were merged, while in several instances as many as five NTRBs were eligible to seek re-recognition for the same region. Many organisations would be required to greatly increase their compass if they wished to survive, while others seemed bound to lose representative status. The process of re-recognition was quite intense, requiring both the lodgment of an extensive submission addressing comprehensive statutory criteria and the conducting of on-site investigations by multi-person review teams.[21] Re-recognition was intended for final completion by 30 June 2000, but in some regions no NTRB was recognised until considerably later. When re-recognition was complete, the jurisdictional map had been significantly redrawn: eight NTRBs had disappeared or lost their status, another five new ones had come into being and all the original rep bodies which had survived engaged in varying levels of restructuring to secure their continued existence.[22]

In general, between the passage of the 1998 Amendments and the stabilisation of the new NTRB system in 2000–01, the rep bodies (and often claimant groups themselves) were preoccupied with responding to the changes in the NTA at the expense of much substantive work to actually progress native title claims. It would be wrong, though, to characterise the Amendments as only having made things more difficult for NTRBs. As the Cape York Land Council noted optimistically in its *Annual Report 1998–1999*, as distracting as the implementation of the new provisions had been, the organisation had as a consequence obtained a 'greater degree of consistency and direction in its operations' as well as an improved commitment to general statutory compliance.[23] The 1998 Amendments created a framework that demanded greater professionalism and invited a higher standard of performance from the NTRBs. The kind of shoddiness that had accompanied a considerable proportion of rep body work in the past would in theory no longer be tolerated. One analyst described the Amendments as giving rep bodies the 'chance to excel'.[24] However, the possibility of success always depended on the availability of realistic levels of funding; no operational improvements resulting from finer statutory prescription or the imposition of higher benchmarks unless adequate resources were provided for improvements to be made.[25]

Spiralling down

In the first years of the NTA's operation there was an under-appreciation of the costliness of the work that was to be performed. However, the findings of the Parker Report, accompanied by successful lobbying, saw levels of funding rise significantly. Money provided by ATSIC to the NTRBs increased from just under $10 million nationally in 1993–94 to over $37 million in 1996–97. It was generally recognised within ATSIC that the federal Coalition government elected in 1996 was not likely to be predisposed to increasing the level of resources provided to rep bodies. Accordingly, in 1998, in a bid to substantiate the case for enlarged financial support, ATSIC commissioned a report by an accountancy firm, Senatore Brennan Rashid, and the partner of a large law firm who had made a name for himself in native title by representing pastoral interests in native title claims, Mark Love of Corrs Chambers Westgarth.[26] What became known as the 'Love Rashid Report' was handed down in 1999 and the stark finding was that the NTRBs would simply 'not be capable of professionally discharging their functions under the new regime within the current funding framework' given an overall national level of under-funding in the vicinity of $30 million per annum.[27] However, despite the findings of the Love Rashid Report, only a minimal increase in Commonwealth support followed when, in 2001, ATSIC received an additional $17.4 million to be spent over four years, mainly on so-called 'capacity building' initiatives.[28] The theory behind 'capacity building' was that increased base capability would reduce the need for higher recurrent funding, though there was probably always a wishful exaggeration of the potential in what was possible.

Many sectors of society consider, no doubt with strong justification, that they are not adequately assisted by government. However, the NTRBs were in the position of having been given compulsory duties by the government that they were then denied the resources to perform. It was not the case that rep bodies were able to adjust their obligations to the level of resources that were available, because the NTA did not allow that discretion. Forced to undertake more work than funds allowed, the NTRBs' functioning and development were predictably impaired. In contrast, both the Federal Court and the National Native Title Tribunal received significant funding increases in 2001. The methodical underfunding of native title representative bodies became the system's perpetual problem, hampering and hovering over every discussion of how matters might be more quickly or efficiently progressed.[29]

The Love Rashid Report had warned that without the necessary augmentation of NTRB resources, the organisations would become beleaguered and suffer a 'spiral down into a cycle of immediacy'.[30] Certainly the evidence suggests great problems in the rep body sector following the turn of the new millennium. Applications to adjourn litigation on the basis of funding simply having run out became a not uncommon feature of Federal Court directions hearings,[31] while studies pointed to dysfunctional turnover rates among professional staff.[32] The Kimberley Land Council delivered an impressive string of victories in the Federal Court in the first years of the 2000s, but had to engage in redundancies, the sale of assets and the abandonment of much future act work to sustain the effort.[33] Staff salary levels and conditions were typically lower than the private, government and mainstream legal aid sectors and were accompanied by the stresses of incessant travel, remote locations and constant exposure to all the tensions of cross-cultural communication. Resource companies, government departments and private firms of lawyers and consultants were perpetually recruiting from the NTRB training ground, offering better wages and easier working conditions. Reflecting on the Parker Report which, with others, they had co-written, Altman and Smith wrote in 1995 that they had

> tried to present two pictures in the vision statement. One was a very positive picture which proposed a situation of harmony and workability that would result from the existence of a nation-wide system of efficient and effective representative bodies. But we also tried to present the other side of the coin and say that, without these sorts of bodies, there would be a very negative situation where costs and chaos would result from an absence of representative bodies.[34]

A decade later, the Commonwealth's failure to finance the NTRBs at an appropriate level had ensured that the 'very negative situation' predicted by the Parker Report had come into being. The starving of resources from NTRBs was deliberate Commonwealth policy. The rep bodies were regarded as anathema by a Howard government that was deeply ideologically opposed to both collectivism and Indigenous particularism.[35] Yet despite the antipathy, it was not really clear how else the work might be done and so the Howard administration did not do away with the NTRBs altogether. Contracting the work to law firms, though perhaps more consistent with the Coalition's preference for outsourcing and privatisation, would have been vastly more expensive and there was no clamouring for the work from the big end of town. Gross under-funding was a political outcome that satisfied the Coalition government's paradigmatic dislike of NTRBs, tempered with the pragmatic acknowledgement of the need for their ongoing existence. The government simply continued to reject all recommendations that funding be increased.[36] As described further in Chapters 4 and 5, sometimes, out of sheer frustration and motivated by their own needs, either state governments or resource companies provided additional funding to NTRBs. However, process funding supplied to rep bodies by respondents was always in order to progress particular matters and was never able to remedy deficiencies in structural capacity. Treated miserably and never taken into the fold, the bastard children of the native title system were to be kept in the poor house. Funded to fail, it is unsurprising that the rep bodies often did.[37]

Measuring rep body performance

Not all NTRBs operated sub-optimally all the time; indeed, some rep bodies achieved reasonable steadiness in patches even while the system faltered as a whole. Organisational stability, though critical, is of course a rather modest measure of success. Yet trying to establish clear criteria by which to measure whether an NTRB was doing well proved elusive.[38] For example, how does one evaluate the performance of the WA Aboriginal Legal Service, which won a number of important victories in court between 1994 and 1998, but never acted for more than a handful of claimant groups for which it received disproportionate funding at the expense of other NTRBs?[39] Further, in a system that valorised alternative dispute resolution, wasn't winning in court rather problematic as a gauge of achievement? Indeed, for other NTRBs avoiding litigation was held up as the hallmark of commitment to the process.[40] Some NTRBs spent years principally engaged in the exercise of attempting to remove overlapping native title claims, while for others a multitude of future act agreements were achieved but few or no native title claim determinations. Future act agreements were invariably represented as successful in public but, given that confidentiality conditions applied in almost every case, effective benchmarking was not possible, and it was a matter of common notoriety that there was a wide range in performance.

ATSIC tried and failed to establish a meaningful range of performance indicators for NTRBs. An initial quantitative approach, concentrating on numbers of claims and objections lodged, failed for the obvious reason that merely lodging applications was hardly a guide to good practice. Later approaches attempted to instil more qualitative elements but were stymied by the impossibility of comparing apples with pears: for instance, if an NTRB did not have a jurisdiction rich in minerals prospectivity, then there was no way of 'doing well' in terms of number of future act agreements because the miners simply were not there with whom to agree. Attempts at having NTRBs engage in realistic budget submissions setting out operational targets were also a failure, as ATSIC never had the funding necessary to support the work that was reasonably predicted. It was, as one senior ATSIC staff member privately conceded, all merely an exercise in 'make-believe'.[41] Budgetary submissions were made for funds that didn't exist but for work that would have to be completed anyway, with the shortfall presumably being taken up in practice by unpaid overwork, process funding from companies, shoddiness in the job being done or not being completed at all. In 2002–04, as ATSIC entered its terminal phase and responsibility for the NTRB system was briefly handed over to the Aboriginal and Torres Strait Islander Service, the process-achievement requirements imposed on the rep bodies changed multiple times again, engendering further confusion.

As a general rule, when NTRBs managed a measure of observable stand-out success it was not because the system was succeeding, but because one of five anomalous factors was present. First, the Northern and Central Land Councils, which were Northern Territory land rights legislation bodies that had successfully applied for NTRB status, were more stable and successful because of their origins and structure. Second, bigger NTRBs generally had a better chance of achieving a portion of reasonable performance because of economies of scale and the increased resilience that went with larger size. Third, in instances where a particular rep body could get access to additional discretionary funding, it might be possible to build capacity and alleviate pressure. The Yamatji Marlpa Land Council, for example, was able, by leveraging off economic development on a world historical scale with the Chinese demand for iron ore from within its jurisdiction in the north-west of Western Australia, to increase its funding and capacity. Fourth, the ease of the task at hand made a big difference. The Ngaanyatjarrah Council, for instance, was responsible for desert regions with clients that boasted perhaps the strongest evidence of native title in Australia and, facing few third party respondents, enjoyed natural advantages. Finally, the presence of charismatic and competent leadership could make all the difference to NTRB performance. Indigenous leaders who could 'cut through', by being equally capable of picking up the phone to the Prime Minister's office, getting access to top-shelf journalists or facing down local community politics, provided an incalculable asset. The successes of the Kimberley Land Council, when led by Pat Dodson and Peter Yu, and the Cape York Land Council under Noel Pearson, are prime examples of the phenomenon, though inspirational leadership also had its pitfalls, including the inevitable difficulties associated with succession.

Tensions and contradictions

One of the consequences of systemic under-funding preventing any serious chance of the proper functioning of the NTRB system was that conceptually more intractable issues were often obscured. The scarcity of resources came to dominate the problem of representation. Yet even if the NTRBs had been properly resourced, their muddled nature would have made effective functioning still very difficult. Within the native title system, rep bodies were stuck in a range of middles, occupying what Diane Smith called 'an interstitial political position' beset by conflicts and tensions.[42] These various difficulties are now dealt with in turn.

Intra-Indigenous conflict

The unamended NTA required NTRBs to be 'broadly representative of the Aboriginal peoples or Torres Strait Islanders in the area'[43] and referred to the provision of assistance to such 'individuals or groups'.[44] The 1998 Amendments tightened the definition of the constituents of representative bodies to that class of 'persons who hold or may hold native title' but also imposed an obligation to 'consult effectively with Aboriginal and Torres Strait Islanders living in the area'.[45] The social reality behind these general statutory formulations was a seething complex of intra-Indigenous cultural politics that made the representative role of NTRBs inordinately difficult to discharge. Quarrelling and competition existed among applicants, between 'traditional' and 'historic' peoples,[46] within claimant groups and between overlapping claims.[47] 'Historic people' in particular—the term referring to those who had moved, including often having been forcibly relocated, some time earlier but whose traditional country was elsewhere—could not hold native title over the area in which they were now living, unless some form of customary process of succession or absorbtion could be demonstrated. In Kalgoorlie the Chairman of the Goldfields Land and Sea Council reported sadly in 2002 that native title had 'pitted family against family as connection to country is claimed and counter claimed'.[48] Some disagreements arose out of the native title process, while others simply reflected a new manifestation of feuds going back decades.[49] Unresolved latent tensions over who spoke for a given area, for example, might be brought into the open and exacerbated, or native title could be an arena for continuing local politics that had originally emerged in another sphere altogether. Bad blood might date back to some infidelity or violence, real or imagined, in the distant past that had neither been forgiven nor forgotten. In the midst of intra-Indigenous turmoil, the role of NTRBs was generally to encourage actors to submerge their differences within inclusive claims: success was mixed at best.

Rep body appeals for unity and inclusiveness were necessary in order for claims to be progressed. Not only would respondents largely refuse to deal with overlapping groups in mediation, but in the end there would have to be some reckoning because the NTA provided that there could only be one determination of native title for each area. The worst possible scenario was for overlaps to be maintained into litigation, with Indigenous witnesses outdoing each other in bitterly denouncing one another's evidence. The problem for rep bodies was that having a claim lodged—and registered—gave a splinter group or an individual considerable power that would have to be surrendered in order to create a more inclusive vehicle. In prospective areas, having one's 'own' claim meant exclusive rights to potentially lucrative negotiations with resource interests, but even in geologically barren areas there was some degree of status attached to driving a native title application.

Thus, rep bodies were required to try to prevail upon individuals to surrender positions of influence and power in the name of the common good. The fundamental contradiction, then, was that it was in the short-term interests of smaller groups and individuals to lodge and pursue their own claims and to string out the process; but NTRBs had to advise that consolidated applications were ultimately more likely to succeed. The system drove putative claimants, acting rationally in their own interest, in one direction while driving their representatives to give advice to the contrary. NTRBs told their clients and constituents that 'together you are stronger'; but the perverse reality was that in many situations individuals and smaller groups might well be better off on their own for some time. Indigenous systems of collective decision-making provided their own source of restraint and it is no doubt due to the stickiness of customary power and forms of association that in many parts of Australia—including some of the most minerals-rich areas—there were not more overlapping claims, effectively a highly valuable service that traditional law and custom provided to the broader economy that has seldom been acknowledged. Sometimes, though, cultural strictures proved to be insufficiently compelling or more honoured in the breach.

Terry O'Shane, then Chair of the North Queensland Land Council, wrote in 2001 that his organisation had

> seen the ugly face of greed. We have seen the destructive nature of the promotion of individual rights over the collective rights of all native title holders and we have heard individuals say that if they don't get what they want then no one will get anything.[50]

More than one claim group that fully grasped the NTA's procedural opportunities was quite prepared to keep dancing until the music stopped.

Simultaneously opposing and serving the state

The rep bodies were 'institutional servants of a state system' to the extent that it was their responsibility to carry out the functions ascribed to them under Commonwealth legislation, regulations and grant conditions.[51] NTRBs were expected to act as intermediaries between their clients and government in relation to native title by litigating, negotiating and lobbying, as and when instructed. The relationship was vexed and multifaceted, because it was the Commonwealth Government that gave NTRBs their status, provided them with their funding, held ultimate legislative power over the future of the NTA, and it was also the Crown (in right of the territories, states and Commonwealth respectively) that responded to individual native title claims. NTRBs were thus in the uneasy position of deriving their status and money from the government in order to litigate (if necessary) against it, knowing all the while that the rules could be changed or the supply of funds reduced or suspended if the displeasure of the Commonwealth had been too greatly incurred.[52]

The provision of representation and service was an apparatus of power by which the Indigenous response to the *Mabo* decision was shaped and conditioned. Though NTRBs were instructed by their clients, in instrumental terms rep bodies acted to fashion Aboriginal political and cultural formations under the NTA. As the Kimberley Land Council frankly revealed in its *Annual Report 2000–2001*, there was at times a clear divergence between what claimants expected and the statute required:

> KLC is a Native Title Representative Body and consequently has particular statutory responsibilities to fulfil under the Native Title Act, 1993. Additionally, native title holders in the Kimberley have an expectation that KLC will continue to assist them to both gain 'country' and to 'look after country' as has been KLC's established role for more than 20 years.[53]

Much NTRB staff time was spent explaining to Aboriginal people what was not possible under the NTA and further, how if traditional owners did want to access such rights and protections as the statute did offer, they would need to organise themselves in a given way and submit to the authority of the system. Indeed, the internal structure and geographical scope of many native title claims were determined at least in part by NTRB advice as to best practice, as much as by any underlying 'organic' response from Aboriginal societies.[54] Similarly, dealing with future act notices commonly occurred not because of 'grass roots' community reaction, but in line with standing instructions sought from a claimant group by rep body staff in accordance with the position generally understood to be procedurally optimal. The notion that native title claim groups themselves responded to future act notices was largely a procedural fiction, and in prospective areas would scarcely have been possible given the swift flow of tenement applications. Even the very way in which native title business was transacted—through a limited range of meetings usually organised by the NTRB—was, if not imposed on claimant groups, certainly instilled as 'the way business was to be done' through rep body practice.

However, it would be wrong to imagine that the relationship between NTRBs and their clients all went in a single direction, one in which the rep bodies acted as 'agents of the state' who disciplined unwilling indigenes. In reality, the pressures on rep bodies to produce results in conformity with the statutory ambitions of the NTA, and to demonstrate productivity, created a situation in which native title claimant groups could exert influence on NTRBs in exchange for the former's constructive involvement in the process. NTRBs decided on priorities within their own regions but were themselves captive to the decision-making processes of native title claimant groups while, even within the claims, individuals named as applicants exercised near autonomy as statutory actors.[55] The NTRBs' need for 'outcomes' and to consolidate their own regional legitimacy created a dynamic political opportunity for and among traditional owners. NTRBs represented only one of a number of available external sources of potential power and influence for claim groups. The fact that rep bodies did not have a monopoly meant that claimants acting strategically often played off NTRBs by seeking direct relationships with resource companies and government and by retaining private advisers. Rep bodies needed quantifiable results in order to defend their performance and to preserve and expand their meagre budgetary allocations. While determinations, agreements and wins in court were being pursued on behalf of traditional owners, each of these results was iterated as a bureaucratic 'outcome' and benefited the NTRB. A native title claimant group may have reached agreement and gained some tangible benefits, but it was the rep body that chalked up another key performance indicator. NTRBs needed the constructive acquiescence of their clients and the latter could obtain considerable political capital as the reward for their participation. The boundaries between claim groups and NTRBs were also neither rigid nor impermeable, with claimants often serving as governing committee members, staff or in irregular liaison roles and capable of exercising agency to pursue multiple agendas.

Bureaucracy and tradition

NTRBs were explicitly expected to act cross-culturally, informing and advising traditional owners about the whitefeller law of the NTA and receiving evidence, decisions and aspirations from the blackfeller domain. In relation to specific transactions and relationships, NTRBs were intended to play a translating role, making possible dialogue between claimants, governments and third parties. The ambition of cross-cultural communication required NTRBs to attempt to straddle vastly different milieux. As political theorist Duncan Ivison observed in 2002, 'tensions' were inevitable for NTRBs 'between the requirements of modern liberal democratic governance on the one hand, and those of the particular indigenous communities they are meant to serve'.[56] The rep bodies were required to perform their functions in a culturally appropriate manner, but also in accordance with liberal notions of transparency and accountability and in compliance with the laws and regulations of the Commonwealth.[57] It was common for NTRBs to implicitly assert that they were bridging the divide, by insistence on simultaneous fidelity to the dictates of both modern accountability and pre-modern tradition. The Central Queensland Land Council, for example, asserted that it valued

> above all else, local Aboriginal morals, local Aboriginal heritage, local Aboriginal lore/law, local Aboriginal culture/s, local Aboriginal relationships, local Aboriginal views on ancestors, life, and death, local Aboriginal prior ownership of all land and waters

but, rather quixotically, announced it was striving to 'honour these values' by 'carrying out statutory functions and powers; in an open, transparent and publicly accountable manner; in a fair, just, economic way; with professionalism, integrity and honesty'.[58] Just up the road, the North Queensland Land Council recorded its 'values' as those that:

> demonstrate respect for Elders and traditional laws and customs they hold; service the native title community in a professional and accountable manner; maintain our commitment to securing the traditional land, waters and sea country of native title holders in an efficient, transparent and diligent manner; provide a suitable workplace to progress native title claims that is safe, harmonious and productive.[59]

Adherence to liberal conceptions of good governance and respect for traditional law and custom are no doubt both laudable ideals but they are hardly the same thing and one is not the expression of the other. Rather, the notion that customary tradition could be honoured and observed simultaneously with compliance with bureaucratic accountability simply acted to obscure the internal contradictions between the two imperatives through the device of cross-culturalist sanctimony.[60]

Representation and representativeness

Writing in 2000, academic Tracy Summerfield wondered whether, when the NTA said 'represent' in the context of native title representative bodies, the statute was 'referring to the need for NTRBs to advocate for constituents, or to represent their viewpoints': was it 'concerned with representation or representativeness?'[61] There is a fundamental difference between an entity being 'representative of' a constituency in the sense of being 'derived from' some process of group decision-making and the alternative interpretation of providing 'representation to' a specified class of person. The distinction might be expressed as being between an 'Aboriginal organisation' and one that merely represents Aboriginal people.[62] Rep bodies were expected to provide 'representation to' native title claimants and holders, but to an uncertain degree were also regarded as being 'representative of' (some) Aboriginal people within their jurisdiction, such as when making submissions to government on matters of general concern. In particular, the geopolitical nature of the origins of native title created an impression of a representative role closer to a form of pseudo-governance. The fact that native title involves the recognition of collective identity bonded to territory through a system of laws meant that NTRBs had just the hint of being emerging regional polities. It seems likely that ATSIC officer-bearers watched any NTRB dalliance with broader political ambitions with some ambivalence.[63]

The distinction between 'representation' and 'representativeness' was sometimes muddied even further by the assumption that there was an *a priori* link between the two, implying that if the latter was more entrenched, the former would be better provided. The presumption was that superior representativeness would lead to enhanced representation. The argument often found expression in assertions that it would be preferable if Indigenous people had more power to direct affairs, at the expense of non-Indigenous lawyers, anthropologists and bureaucrats: a political argument that went directly to the intrinsic rep body crisis of legitimacy by decrying the prominence of the professional staff that had usually come in from outside the community.[64] As Noel Pearson, for example, remarked in 2003, 'allowing native title to continue as a delegated industry involving lawyers and anthropologists . . . will get many of our clients nowhere'.[65] There were often calls for NTRBs to employ more Aboriginal staff in order to make the organisations more 'representative'. However, while demands about Indigenous 'control' seem reasonable enough in the context of representativeness, they are far more contestable when it comes to representation.[66]

NTRBs were always an unhappy hybrid of community organisation and professional service provider with the tendency inexorably shifting towards the latter over time. The presence of elected or appointed Indigenous governing committees always created the strong impression that rep bodies were grass roots social organisations. Some of the first NTRBs, including the Kimberley Land Council, the South Australian Aboriginal Legal Rights Movement and the Foundation for Aboriginal and Islander Research Action (FAIRA), certainly had long histories of activism. However, achieving rep body status implied a shift of organisational emphasis to a more professional and bureaucratically accountable footing, associated with statutory obligations and funding conditions. As the native title system evolved, there was a steady transition on the part of NTRBs away from community orientation towards service provision. The public idiom of rep bodies may have remained of the people, but the imperatives were increasingly dictated by Canberra with an ever decreasing margin of discretion available to governing committees and chief executives. Carpentaria Land Council, for instance, claimed in 2002 to be 'very strongly committed in developing a strong grass roots organisation' but the organisation's objective was no more than 'carrying out the functions, powers, duties, responsibilities and rights' of a service-providing NTRB.[67]

Central Queensland too, despite the organisation's emphasis on local culture noted earlier in the chapter, had the objective of performing 'the functions of a native title representative body in a timely manner' and explicitly acknowledged that 'the limits of the resources available' would define what was possible.[68] Freedom of action declined as more and greater constraints on funding and functions were imposed by the Commonwealth. As NTRB executives had fewer options and more obligations, so their clients and constituents may have experienced more professional representation but a tangible sense of decreasing representativeness.

In any event, even in the early days of the NTA, it was never entirely clear what 'greater Indigenous control' might actually have meant in practice, as attempts to actually flesh the matter out tended to demonstrate. In 1995, for example, Jackie Morris from FAIRA stressed the critical importance of 'ensuring that the process of claiming native title is controlled by the claimants and not by the lawyers, anthropologists or even the representative body itself', a process she said might be achieved by setting up a 'steering committee for the claim which is acceptable to the community and which will carry out appropriate consultation of the community in relation to major decisions about the claim'.[69] Whatever else a committee might be, it would hardly seem to be a peculiarly 'Indigenous' way of conducting business. Ultimately any attempts to explain what a more 'Indigenised' process might look like were doomed to be unconvincing because seeking to obtain a determination of a form of tenure which is amenable to recognition pursuant to statute is simply not an 'Indigenous' process. Once the decision had been made to participate within the native title system, Indigenous discretion in that arena was limited to the array of available statutory options, implying severe constraints on any demand for greater volition over the process.[70]

What did they think they were doing?

Given the wider cultural meanings that attached to native title, the broad assortment of rationales that were offered in support of the doctrine and the general ambiguity surrounding the role and function of the rep bodies, it is unsurprising that considerable uncertainty existed among the NTRBs themselves as to their nature and purpose. It seems likely that individual staff and committee members enjoyed some quite different conceptions of what constituted the 'good rep body'. Considerable variety is demonstrated in the various ways that the rep body mission is stated in annual reports. The Goldfields Land and Sea Council, for example, saw itself among other things as 'encouraging the creation of economic independence . . . through commercial and other activities'.[71] The South West Land and Sea Council explained its task in particularly expansive terms as being to 'rebuild a strong and proud nation' leading to the 'unification' of its constituents, 'protecting the spiritual . . . connection to land of members and their extended families in accordance with their traditions, laws and customs', the promotion of 'Aboriginal reconciliation as a basic tenet of Australian society' and 'tackling social and economic disadvantage'.[72] Carpentaria Land Council also expressed an economic welfare role, describing its role as including the provision of 'basic community services to members of the Association to alleviate Aboriginal poverty', while also '[p]romoting and preserving Aboriginal culture and language' and being 'specifically concerned with the support of Traditional Owners in the security, control, protection, conservation and management of their lands, waters, and natural resources'.[73] Queensland South was especially strident in its iteration of the work at hand:

> If the future of the indigenous culture is becoming part of the so called 'lucky country' the Traditional Owners will have to share all the country has to offer—quality of life, services, by also participating fully in some of the more commercial and perhaps uncommon aspects of capitalism of modern day Australia. That will mean involving indigenous people in direct negotiations for all aspects of future development, creation of wealth, legal power and areas of the delivery of medical, housing, education and unemployment.[74]

A number of observations can be made about the way that rep bodies described themselves. There was obviously considerable enthusiasm for stating organisational purpose in language that was much broader than envisaged under the NTA. However, while there was nothing to prevent rep bodies having wider functions and ambitions than native title, the funding and capacity would need to come from elsewhere and if it didn't then there was liable to be disappointment that certain stated aims had been rendered hollow. In particular, despite sometimes expressing the ambition, NTRBs were not established to facilitate economic development on the part of their clients beyond assistance in negotiations and generally lacked the kind of resources and expertise that would logically be demanded for such work.[75] It can also be noted that the way in which NTRBs self-described their missions was prone to contradiction and ideological leaps of faith. It was unclear, for example, how commercialisation could be encouraged at the same time as tradition could be preserved, or why it might be necessary to unify those who purportedly already lived under a common set of traditions, laws and customs. Given that there were differing (and not always clear) representations of what NTRBs were meant to be doing, it seems likely that particular employees, committee members, clients and constituents were perpetually feeling aggrieved because the organisation was not living up to their own vision of what the 'good rep body' should be like. The staff of rep bodies might well find themselves at cross-purposes not only with clients but each other, grasping at different rationales and priorities.

Service mentality

In 2001 the New South Wales Aboriginal Land Council—the native title representative body for the whole of New South Wales—was de-recognised by the Commonwealth Minister and later replaced by an incorporated body with a non-Indigenous person as director. In 2003, New South Wales Native Title Services was joined by Native Title Services Victoria after Mirimbiak Aboriginal Nations Corporation, which had been re-recognised as the NTRB for Victoria, lost rep body status. Each of the native title services was funded by ATSIC like an NTRB and was able to exercise most if not all relevant powers under the Act. However, unlike representative bodies, which had to be Aboriginal corporations with elected boards, native title services were ordinary corporations with unelected directors and so were spared the governance issues of NTRBs. Where native title 'services' were created, any notion that the work at hand was to represent communities, rather than to provide professional representation, was finally dispelled. Ambivalences were associated with the change; for good or ill, something of the legitimacy and organisational culture of rep bodies was undoubtedly lost, but the gains were greater liberal accountability and stability. The unloved and unacknowledged bastards had been replaced with hired help. The potential for rep bodies to be substituted by native title services also sent out a clear warning to remaining NTRBs that might be suffering from a surfeit of 'community' to change their ways or expect de-recognition.

In 2007 the last remaining NTRBs faced a new round of reforms, the most significant of which was to require all rep bodies to again apply for re-recognition, which would this time only be granted in finite time extensions of up to six years. In announcing the new changes, the Minister accepted no responsibility for the disarray of the rep body system, preferring instead to blame the victims:

> In the past a number of NTRBs have been plagued by serious administrative and financial difficulties significantly affecting their capacity to resolve native title claims . . . There is a large backlog of native title claims across Australia and this has created uncertainty not only for Indigenous people but business and government.[76]

Under-funded, under perpetual pressure and scrutiny and—unsurprisingly—often under-performing, NTRBs were now also under permanent notice that their future was not assured. The justifications for time-limiting rep body status were always spurious and are best understood as part of the Howard government's disciplinarian approach to social services provision and civil society. The new regime of fixed-term recognition of NTRBs converted organisations that were already inherently wobbly into being innately transient, always a prescription for ever more unquestioning compliance rather than improved stability. Uncertainty of future was not likely to promote professionalism, staff retention or community confidence. More NTRBs lost status under the new system and by the end of 2008 only ten remained, confined to parts of Queensland, Western Australia and the Northern Territory, elsewhere replaced by native title services.

Neither one thing nor the other

Perhaps a certain limited romantic mythology was attached to NTRBs. In Australian domestic society the work was as exotic as any to be found and, if not exactly 'letting the slave go free', appeared to involve giving the legal and political system a gentle nudge in an emancipative direction.[77] Nudging, though, can be pretty mundane in practice. In reading the annual reports of the rep bodies, the disjunction between the breadth of ambition and the humdrum reporting of service provision amply discloses the hollowness of any simplistic imagining of NTRBs as brave crusaders for social justice. In 2001 the Cape York Land Council—in many ways always one of the more bravura of rep bodies—in its annual reporting specifically sought to link the organisation's 'key objectives' to particular statutory functions with the result that, for example, '[g]et our land back' became 'facilitation and assistance; certification function; dispute resolution; notification [and] agreement-making', while '[s]peak up for our people' was transmuted into 'agreement-making' and 'other'.[78] Bold slogans were translated through the language and categories of the NTA into statements of compliance, as was inevitable for organisations that received recognition and funding for that very purpose.

The function of NTRBs was, in a real sense, to implement governmental policy by providing representation to native title claimants of the kind that was deemed appropriate by the state. The potential for divergences of purpose to become apparent was largely addressed through common adherence to alternative dispute resolution and mediation as best practice in native title. If rep bodies agreed with the Commonwealth and with respondent parties that the aim was to resolve claims through agreement, then to a considerable extent any tendency towards arguing about the fairness of the rules was discouraged. Instead, the role of NTRBs became one of facilitating and enabling the participation of their clients and constituents within the system. As anthropologist for the Kimberley Land Council, Patrick Sullivan observed with irony in 1995:

> Mediation is nowadays a very fashionable principle and it is very difficult to speak against it. Opposed, by definition, to conflict, it is so obviously a good thing.[79]

The hegemonic attachment to the ideal of resolving native title matters by agreement obscured the structural and unavoidable conflict of interest inherent in a state simultaneously funding and opposing native title claims. It was the rep bodies that bore the brunt of the contradiction, by being expected to provide frank and fearless representation to native title claimants, but to do so in a conciliatory manner and with an insufficient resource base, guiding their clients to an embrace of the precepts of alternative dispute resolution.

It simply was not an option for an NTRB to reject the terms of the NTA and to retain representative status under the Act. In order to become and to remain a rep body an organisation had, above all, to demonstrate acquiescence to the rules, and NTRBs could implement their clients' wishes only to the extent sanctioned by the government. At times, the tensions became explicit: in 2004, for example, Wayne Bergmann recorded with exasperation

> a growing level of conflict between the operation of the KLC as an independent representative body setting and determining our own priorities and Commonwealth agencies dictating what those priorities should be.[80]

If conflict became absolute, it was clear that the wishes of the state would prevail.

However, recognising the ambiguities associated with the role of NTRBs does not mean that the organisations should be summarily dismissed as having been agents of 'deep colonisation'.[81] Although NTRBs were forced to adopt strict policy adherence and to share the managerial priorities then in vogue in order to retain funding and recognition, capacity still remained for the pursuit of rebellious agendas. There was always some wriggle room. Indeed, each vision of native title that went beyond what the NTA allowed and that was disclosed on the face of an annual report might be seen to some extent as representing a subversion of the system as much as an exercise in wishful thinking. NTRBs were able to complicate and sometimes frustrate state imperatives, even as they were the instruments of implementation. Ultimately, rep bodies were neither one thing nor the other; doing their best in the circumstances but tormented by the uncertainty of their composition and deprived of resources, they ended up hopelessly stranded amidst a complex of competing forces and imperatives and never achieved any sure foundation.

4

STATE EXPECTATIONS

Executive government of the states and territories

New reasons for old arguments

Federal–state relations are the ants at the picnic of Australian public life, getting into things and spoiling perfect plans; but then the whole point of federalism is to place limits on power.[1] At best, federalism provides healthy democratic checks; at worst it promotes blame-shifting and is a cause of governmental incapability in solving problems. The constitutional history of Australia has seen the steady shift of control from the states to Canberra.[2] In Aboriginal affairs the transformation was particularly abrupt, with the 1967 referendum removing the prohibition on the Commonwealth making laws with respect to 'the Aboriginal race in any State'. Thereafter, Indigenous issues became just another area for playing out the long federal quarrel. Following *Mabo*, a number of state governments were among the most outspoken critics of the doctrine that they perceived as having been foisted upon them by the Commonwealth's High Court. Once Canberra had decided to establish a national legislative framework for native title, any prospect of one or more of the states going it alone became impossible, as the High Court confirmed when it shut down Western Australia's attempt to act unilaterally as unconstitutional.[3] It was clear that the states could not evade the operation of the NTA and possessed only so much freedom of choice as the Commonwealth's native title legislation let them have.[4] The Premier of Western Australia denounced the statute as a 'classic case of a federal government introducing legislation which has effectively neutered the states' ability to control land and resource management'.[5]

However, although the Commonwealth had demonstrated constitutional supremacy in relation to native title, the states still possessed considerable autonomy within the system. The NTA gave all the states and territories the automatic right to be respondent parties to native title claims, with liberty to decide how they would respond. Additionally, because the states exercise exclusive control over the issuing and registration of property entitlements, they would necessarily play a pivotal role in the operation of the future act processes. It was as if two sets of games were being played simultaneously, with one set of rules about native title and the other about the ordinary system of property law, with the former dominating over the latter but never to the point of total eclipse. The executive governments of the states and territories, then, were among the principal actors within the native title system as the 'first respondent' to each native title claim and the 'government party' that granted tenure within the future act system.

State governments were required to participate under the NTA's processes but could simultaneously be engaged with the Commonwealth, trying to achieve changes in the rules through legislative amendment, regulatory adjustment or shifts in policy. How the dynamics worked, in terms of relationships with both Indigenous parties and Canberra, would often depend on which party was in power where. In general terms, native title might be considered to span four political periods in federal relations: 1992–96, when the Keating government dealt with state regimes of mixed political stripe; 1996–2001, during which Howard did the same; 2001–07, in which the conservatives held power in Canberra but nowhere else; then followed by the return of Labor to Commonwealth office under Kevin Rudd. However, while party allegiances were important, they were not always determinative; differences of political culture and economy could also be decisive. On the other hand, some patterns, like state governments wanting to avoid any attempts at federal cost-shifting, persisted regardless of who occupied whichever treasury benches. Some administrations simply produced ministers with greater talent or interest in native title than others, or allocated the portfolio to a more or less influential figure within cabinet. Timing in the electoral cycle could also be crucial in deciding how brave a particular government was prepared to be in relation to Aboriginal rights.

The nature of native title, involving complex and novel questions of governance and law associated with Indigenous affairs, planning, infrastructure, land, water, mining, agriculture, fishing, heritage, judicial administration and so on, meant that there were also a large number of state agencies that became involved. The proliferation of bureaucratic interests, each with their own procedures and imperatives, presented a genuine stumbling block to progressing native title matters. In 1996, for example, the President and Registrar of the NNTT highlighted an occasion when 30 distinct sections of state government had become involved in dealing with a particular matter.[6] Native title claimant groups could find that 'dealing with government' or 'talking to the state' did not involve a single relationship so much as a multiplicity of overlapping dealings that varied widely in their nature. Eventually, all states and territories allocated responsibility for native title matters to a dedicated unit which, in addition to dealing with claimants, was encumbered with the considerable obligation of herding other departmental cats to ensure compliance with law and policy. An exceptional role was also played by the various state law divisions that often appeared to be particularly influential in shaping government policy through the legal advice that was given.[7] Ultimately, it is the courts that decide whether or not native title exists over any given area in Australia, making the performance of state law offices singularly prominent in the recognition process.

Within the overall ambit of executive government, there is competition for power, influence and budgetary share. Sometimes divisions between agencies or ministers are caused by no more than the silo-ing of responsibility or the exercise of individual ambition, while others can be as a consequence of departments serving diverse or opposing visions of 'the public', creating loyalties defined by sector. State agencies may be prone to championing their own principal stakeholders, with ministries of mining favouring miners, fisheries favouring fishermen and so on. Public service schizophrenia can no doubt frustrate ministerial intentions, but it may also oblige political agendas, as shades of policy preference represented under different departmental hats can allow a government to appear to simultaneously pursue multiple priorities, that are in tension with one another to serve diverse segments of the community. At their worst, departmental cleavages can be deeply corrosive in the successful implementation of complex aims. It has been accepted at the highest levels of the Australian public service that a failure of bureaucratic coordination has seriously impinged the effectiveness of government in Indigenous affairs: native title has not been immune from the problem.[8]

The state as 'government party' in the future act system

The future act processes set up by the NTA are a tripartite affair composed of the native title group, the resource interest that wants the tenement and the state or territory government that is to grant the tenure in question. As the 'government party' in dealing with future acts, states have the role of issuing notices about what is proposed, responding to the objections of native title parties and participating in the various consultation, negotiation and arbitration procedures that follow. The NTA separates all future acts into an assortment of categories, each with their own procedural requirements for native title groups, resource interests and state governments. However, by applying the broad criteria of considering the state's actual level of interest and participation, it is possible to isolate four general categories of future acts that are clearer to understand and give a more accurate impression of political economy than the plethora of legal processes described in their statutory form. These categories are more important in those jurisdictions with a greater area of land subject to native title claim and higher minerals prospectivity: Queensland, the Northern Territory and particularly Western Australia.

Exploration tenements[9]

The minerals industry is constantly in search of new resource bodies to exploit, a process that generally occurs on large numbers of prospecting and exploration tenements that are granted by state governments for that purpose. Although the hunt for minerals can be invasive and involve considerable disturbance to land, the absence of commercial production means that there are few occasions when any monies will be paid over to native title groups holding the right to negotiate. Exploration without a find is not profitable in and of itself. Instead, for the most part, the convention has become that the explorer will pay for an Aboriginal heritage survey to be conducted, creating a short-term casual economic opportunity for the participants to assist in preventing any damage to sites or areas of particular significance.[10] In the formative years of the NTA, state governments had little direct involvement in the process of resolving objections to exploration tenements. The exception was where matters could not be solved by private agreement and ended up in litigation when government would appear and invariably take the part of the explorer in arguing that objections should be dismissed in order that tenements could be granted. More recently, some state Labor governments have sought to resolve the question of exploration tenements more systematically, through the negotiation of regional arrangements. The purpose of regionalisation is to achieve a more standardised approach with fewer transaction costs associated with the processing of each tenement.

Production tenements[11]

Where there is a known resource body and tenements are being applied for to support or allow for extraction, the imminent need for the tenure provides any native title group holding procedural rights with sufficient bargaining power to secure an agreement that contains significant valuable consideration. Deals may include monetary payments, protocols to protect and rehabilitate land, business and employment opportunities, equity allocations and other benefits. Under the letter of the NTA, whenever the right to negotiate applies, the state is meant to be involved in good faith negotiations with the resource interest and the native title group to see if a deal can be reached to get the tenement granted. However, notwithstanding the formal position under the statute, government almost never becomes involved in the substance of talks, which are left to the resource interest and the native title group to conduct between themselves and then record in a private arrangement. Again, though, the exception is where negotiations break down and litigation ensues, when governments will usually carry the burden of arguing that the tenements should be granted.[12]

Flagship projects

Although this category is not situated in any procedural distinctions under the NTA, it is useful to distinguish those projects which involve a private third party proponent but that are of such scale and importance that their progress becomes a matter of more general notice. Where a project has achieved notoriety, a government may take the unusual step of becoming directly involved in the substance of agreement-making. In the Century Zinc case, for example, both the Queensland and Commonwealth governments made substantive contributions to the quantum of consideration offered to the native title claimants for their agreement to the project proceeding.[13] Flagship projects are anomalous in that they draw resources from well outside what is usual in the native title process.

Compulsory acquisitions

In each of the three cases outlined above, there is a private interest that is seeking the grant of tenure from the government. However, in some instances, where the state requires land for its own purposes, there is no third party involved. Here, the state will need to compulsorily acquire the tenure in question and will have to conduct the negotiations and offer the consideration for agreement itself. The distinction is significant, because private proponents have greater flexibility in what they are able to offer native title groups. In some instances the difference may be somewhat clouded where a third party interest is identified to whom the state is proposing to on-sell the tenure, and so which becomes involved in the negotiations. Unlike private contracts, the content of an agreement facilitating a compulsory acquisition is likely to be in the public domain because it involves the expenditure of state revenue.[14]

In summary, then, state and territory governments have preferred to play a non-participatory and non-interventionist role in the future act system, letting the grantee and native title parties negotiate their own agreements. Exceptions to the laissez-faire approach to future act negotiations have largely occurred only when a party has directly required the formal participation of the government pursuant to the NTA or when some anomalous imperative has demanded state involvement. The single overriding exception to the rule that governments try and stay out of future act proceedings when possible is that if a matter ends up in litigation, then generally the state will take a leading role advocating for an interpretation of the law that will favour the grant of the tenement in question as expeditiously as possible. One of the general rules of understanding how the native title system works is that, when matters end up in court, ordinarily even the most politically progressive of state regimes will try to defeat the claims of the Aborigines.[15]

The states as 'first respondent' in the claims system

All layers of government have automatic party status under the NTA but it is the states and territories, as the administrators of the property system, that are the primary respondents to native title claims, take first position on court documentation and will lead on process. Frequently, meetings will occur between representatives of the state and the claimants with no other party or intermediary being present. Overlaying basic options about when to negotiate and litigate are innumerable smaller decisions in regard to how relations with claimants and third parties are conducted. In both the court and the conference room, state officials can be more or less cooperative and facilitative, making apparently minor choices that can sometimes have great impact.[16]

In the period of flux described in Chapter 1, the ambiguity of the law made it highly unlikely that state governments would be prepared to settle claims. Despite the optimism and urgings of the NNTT, Indigenous representatives and others, there was never 'any real prospect' that state and territory governments as 'land managers' would agree to determinations of native title before key legal principles were clarified.[17] The uncertainty of the law, particularly in relation to where native title had been extinguished, fostered an environment in which prudent administration meant not agreeing to anything. In the event that a state was prepared to tolerate the uncertainty of the law, the abundance of overlapping claims was enough in some regions to ensure that proceedings were bogged down in intra-Indigenous disharmony, effectively shutting out the possibilities of advancing matters with the government.

Even if circumstances were somehow locally conducive, state governments were still faced with the overall policy dilemma of how to decide whether or not to actively engage in mediation and then whether native title actually existed. It was commonly assumed that in order to achieve a consent determination, claim groups would still need to demonstrate some evidentiary foundation to support their assertion of customary title. Even among Indigenous people, indignation at having to present factual information about what seemed culturally self-evident was tempered with an awareness that it was necessary to prevent tradition-deaf officials being duped by plausible cultural interlopers claiming country to which they had no right. At the NNTT's first public stakeholder conference in 1994, Michael Dillon, a senior public servant with the Office of Indigenous Affairs in the Department of Prime Minister and Cabinet, stressed that '[g]ood research by claimants [would] increase the likelihood of mediated outcomes'.[18] Dillon also noted the importance of the 'pre-acceptance filters' in the NTA, but within a short period of time the statute's filtration mechanisms had broken down entirely under judicial scrutiny, leaving the onus of deciding which claims had prima facie merit making them worthy of mediation to fall squarely on state governments. As the President of the NNTT put it, the executive would need to be satisfied that there was 'a basis for the assertion of an appropriate traditional connection between the applicants for recognition of their native title and the land which is the subject of the application'. Hopefully in more obvious cases 'the evidentiary threshold set by government for accepting traditional ownership need not be particularly high'.[19]

Initial state government responses to the question of how to evaluate claims tended to be fairly imprecise and generic. In June 1996, the President and Registrar of the Tribunal advised the Commonwealth that:

> One State Government has indicated that it requires 'credible evidence' of the elements of native title before it will agree to its existence. This is a standard of indefinite content, 'credibility' being in the eye of the beholder. No principle underlying the application of that criterion has been set out. Another State Government has begun enunciating in ongoing mediations a new requirement of a 'high standard of proof' of connection before it will agree to recognize native title. Attempts in mediation to elicit a more precise formulation of this criterion have not been successful. The question must be asked whether the proof on the standard of probabilities would be sufficient to meet this standard. If not, then the particular government may be setting a higher standard than would be applied by a court. The lack of a clear policy foundation for, and enunciation of, the government's position generated some resistance from Indigenous parties who questioned the utility of further negotiations in the face of an apparently open ended requirement for proof of connection.[20]

The question of how state governments assessed claims became more urgent as the incremental clarification of the law and the resolution of many of the overlaps, removed other impediments to matters being resolved by agreement. As is discussed further below, the policy positions of state governments throughout Australia became unambiguously accepting of native title and in favour of resolving claims by agreement, but the transformation in attitude did not answer the mechanical question of just when a state should begin mediation and, even more importantly, what criteria should be applied in deciding that a consent determination was appropriate. The key institutional development was the formalisation of the practice of governments requiring each claim group to submit an evidentiary summary known as a 'connection report', usually written by one or more senior anthropologists briefed by the claimants' lawyers and prepared in accordance with state criteria, as a pre-condition to the mediation of native title claims.[21] As senior anthropologist Julie Finlayson explained:

> Objectively speaking, government's insistence on production of a Connection Report provides a degree of certainty for establishing the identity of the applicant group, the area of land with which connection is asserted, and the legitimacy and nature of that connection.[22]

Although it was not the objective, the formalisation of the method of receipt and evaluation of connection reports to some extent marked an informal recovery of power by the states: a de facto assertion of control over the claims process, even within the Commonwealth-controlled native title jurisdiction.

The ostensible advantage of the connection report process was to provide states with a way of receiving and evaluating evidence in a way that was faster, cheaper and more informal than the forensic adversarialism of litigation. However, the comparative lack of formality did not imply anything about the content of what was being submitted to the state. It soon became apparent that even if the modus operandi was more casual, there was to be little relaxation of the standard of proof required for a positive determination. In each set of connection guidelines it was clear, as the Court Liberal government's guidelines put it, that the 'detail provided' in a connection report was to be 'no less than is required to prepare a case for the Federal Court'.[23] Claimants would still have to prove their case; they just did not have to do it in a courtroom. Although the wording was sometimes more relaxed, procedures produced by state Labor administrations were not any softer in substance. So, for example, under principles adopted by Geoff Gallop's Labor government, which succeeded the Court government in Western Australia, native title claimants had to 'show that the claims made in the application can be established at law'.[24] In each case, the connection guidelines also contained an explicit statement that it was not possible for any government to agree to a determination of the existence of native title where the necessary factual foundation could not be shown.

The assessment of connection reports by state administrations created a new set of complexities, calling for the involvement and retention of lawyers, historians and anthropologists and the development of additional procedures and protocols. Although it had not started out that way, the connection report process ultimately proved to be time-consuming and arduous.[25] One judge of the Federal Court reflected in early 2005 that the process of connection reports being received and evaluated by states seemed virtually quasi-judicial in nature:

> A practice has grown up between parties, principally between state parties and applicant parties throughout Australia, whereby the state requires and the applicants comply with the provision of detailed evidence to prove the various elements of the claimed determination . . . I have come to the clear view that such processes do not fall within the description of 'mediation' as used in the act. They in effect amount to an out-of-court rehearsal of a trial . . .[26]

Underlying the rigidity was the statutory position that even if a particular government was inclined to agree to a lower evidentiary threshold, the proposed determination could be effectively vetoed by a third party or might even be rejected by the Federal Court as inappropriate (a critical point which is discussed further in Chapter 8). A state would have to be confident that the connection material which had been provided would satisfy the other respondent parties, as well as passing the test of judicial oversight. As Deputy Premier Eric Ripper, the minister with responsibility for native title under the Gallop government, observed at one point:

> The State is not responsible for the 400-page NTA, nor is it responsible for the recent outcomes of the Ward and Yorta Yorta High Court cases that have narrowed the scope for native title [and] all native title consent determinations have to win the support of other parties and conform to the law if they are to be ratified by the Federal Court.[27]

Some years later, Ripper acknowledged that the guidelines the Western Australian Labor government had set would be 'sometimes challenging for claimants', but asserted that the challenge emerged 'from native title law, and not government caprice'.[28] There were still leeways of choice available to state governments who wanted to more actively guide claim groups in how to best present their evidence and to assist with persuading other respondents that settlement out of court was the fair and sensible option and Ripper's public disclosure, shortly before the WA Labor government lost office, that only a single connection report had been rejected because it did not meet the guidelines was perhaps testimony to the reasonableness of their application.[29] However, for all state governments the opportunities were always narrower than in an open field of action; anchored to the necessity of evidentiary foundation, the burden of proof was never replaced by unfettered opportunity for the discharge of ideological conviction or a straightforward weighing up of the balance of political convenience.

A brief history of the states and native title[30]

Between the *Mabo* decision and the downfall of the Keating government in 1996, state and territory jurisdictions that were controlled by non-Labor parties provided reliable and often bitter opposition to the NTA. In Western Australia, after having its attempt to legislate native title out of existence ruled out as unconstitutional, the Court Coalition government began to pour tenement applications into the future act system with vindictive enthusiasm, attempting to demonstrate the 'unworkability' of the Commonwealth's legislation. The backlog of unprocessed tenements that quickly built up was a ready statistical indictment for use in native title debates.[31] Joining Western Australia in outright antagonism were the conservative governments of Rob Borbidge in Queensland (1996–98) and Shane Stone in the Northern Territory (1995–99). Whatever other observations are made, it was doubtless the unceasing campaigning of conservative state governments, in lock step with primary industry, that formed a major part of the push that resulted in the 1998 Amendments' weakening of Indigenous rights. The reaction of the Western Australia–Northern Territory–Queensland trio can in some respects be interpreted as classic backlash politics: each of the jurisdictions is large, sparsely populated and heavily dependent on primary industry. Opinions in Perth, Brisbane, Darwin and smaller regional centres were undoubtedly afflicted by the parochialism associated with the 'us and them' mentality characteristic of outlying units in a federal system. In Richard Court's case, opposing Indigenous rights also looked like part of the family business: his father, Sir Charles, who had been Premier in the 1970s, had led the controversial crushing of Aboriginal protest in the Noonkanbah dispute, while one brother of the Premier led the state pastoralists' organisation and another was involved in the mining industry.

Yet if political culture contributes to an account of the peculiar vehemence of opposition to native title in Queensland and Western Australia, it must be acknowledged that historical and economic circumstances meant that native title genuinely was a more significant issue in those jurisdictions. Native title claims appeared more obviously likely to succeed in the larger, more sparsely populated, later-settled and peripheral jurisdictions which, combined with the dependence on primary industry, made matters innately more politically and practically complicated. The political economy of Western Australia and Queensland in particular was simply not conducive to easy acceptance of the native title system. The contrast was with Victoria, New South Wales and Tasmania, which share long colonial histories, comparatively large percentages of land covered by freehold tenure and limited current minerals prospectivity. Indeed, the threshold question in Australia's south-eastern triangle was whether there was any native title at all. The combination of a smaller mining industry, much greater levels of extinguishment of any native title that might exist by the grant of adverse tenure and the destruction and displacement of so much traditional Indigenous culture made native title piety a good deal simpler. In New South Wales, from at least 1995, the Labor government adopted a position of ostensible preparedness to resolve native title claims by mediation.

The Court government's heavy lobbying in the lead-up to the 1998 Amendments seemed rewarded when the changes to the NTA permitted state governments to pass their own legislation watering down the right to negotiate. However, the much-anticipated state regime that Western Australia then introduced was thwarted at the last hurdle through a peculiar provision in the NTA that gave a final right of disallowance to the Commonwealth Senate, which was then controlled by non-government members. The Court government never got the state system it craved. A similar pattern occurred in the Northern Territory.[32] However, the neat story of the 'progressive' south-east and the 'reactionary' north-west also began to become more complicated once the political opportunities for wholesale change had passed. In 2000, Richard Court did his own version of 'Nixon going to China' by agreeing to the first really big consent determination of native title anywhere in Australia, settling a second large claim in the middle of a trial and signing a cooperative planning agreement with an NTRB.[33] The turn was not complete, though: the Court government was, for example, still quite prepared to make use of such loopholes as appeared to push through tenement applications without having to observe procedural niceties.[34]

Meanwhile, over in Brisbane, new Labor Premier Peter Beattie, elected in 1998, began advocating what he called the 'Queensland solution' to the problem of native title, which would be 'centred on consultation, not confrontation'.[35] Thereafter, Queensland's approach to the settlement of native title claims quickly gained the reputation then as the most conciliatory in the country, including an unprecedented level of cooperation in conducting research into evidence of historical connection. Controversially, though, in the sphere of future acts the Beattie administration sought to take full advantage of the potential under Howard's 1998 Amendments to reduce the procedural rights of native title claimants and holders. The result was a protracted struggle over the instrumental meaning of the 'Queensland solution', as QIWG battled the Beattie administration in media, court and conference room over the ensuing years.[36] In 2003, the Queensland State Government eventually reached agreement with industry and QIWG to a modified version of the future act scheme initially favoured by Beattie's administration.[37]

In the interim, the *Yorta Yorta* result cast the shadow of suggestion that perhaps no native title claims would succeed in the 'settled south'. Certainly, in Tasmania it had become apparent that the wholesale destruction of Indigenous society in the nineteenth century raised insurmountable barriers to the prosecution of native title. In New South Wales, the apparent willingness of Bob Carr's Labor government to negotiate seemed confirmed to an extent when the first consent determination of native title anywhere in the nation was achieved over a small parcel of land at Crescent Head on the mid north coast.[38] However, the terms of the determination required the immediate surrender of the native title in exchange for a fixed sum of compensation. Under development pressures, the claim had been resolved almost like a future act deal. No other determinations have followed in New South Wales and the overall strategic situation in the state became much harder for claimants when the High Court ruled in *Wilson v Anderson* that it was the only jurisdiction in which the main form of pastoral tenure extinguished native title.[39] On the other hand, in Victoria, despite the evidentiary difficulties foreshadowed by *Yorta Yorta*, the incoming Labor government of Steve Bracks, elected in 1999, indicated a new willingness to seek negotiated outcomes. Two consent determinations have subsequently been achieved, Wimmera in 2005 and Gunditjmara in 2007.[40] Even the Yorta Yorta have been recognised in an agreement with the state of Victoria as 'traditional owners', if not native title holders.[41] In the Australian Capital Territory, a non-native title agreement negotiated under the Labor government of John Stanhope over the Namadgi National Park estate resolved a number of outstanding claims.[42]

Back in Western Australia, the Labor Party under Geoff Gallop was elected in March 2001. No doubt learning from Queensland, the new Labor administration in Perth vowed a native title policy of conciliation and negotiation, but without seeking to establish an alternative regime for future acts.[43] Similarly, when Labor won office for the first time in the history of self-government in the Northern Territory in 2001, the new Chief Minister Clare Martin adopted policies more conducive to the settlement of claims. In general, though, native title in the Northern Territory has always been overshadowed by the statutory land rights system, which created rights in land much more powerful than anything afforded to traditional owners under the NTA.[44] More than fifteen years' experience with land rights also meant that even the Northern Territory government in its strongest anti-native title phase could be quite muted—as, for example, in its restrained participation in the Alice Springs native title claim in 1996.[45] In contrast, in Western Australia, with no land rights regime and a history of strong political resistance to the NTA, the election of the Labor government was heralded as a sea change. After some initial administrative hiccups, the Gallop administration introduced a highly successful policy framework that yielded a regionalised system for dealing with minerals exploration without denuding the procedural rights of claimants and a process for claims that led to a series of large consent determinations before Labor lost office again in 2008.

A different story altogether emerged in South Australia, where a combination of political economy and that state's particular heritage of liberality and social experimentation, including the 'myth' of having always taken 'a leading role in the recognition and protection of Aboriginal customs and traditions', contributed to the development of a unique approach to native title.[46] In 1999, South Australia adoped an ambitious strategy, seeking a statewide settlement of all native title issues in a single process, a massive undertaking to be facilitated by the government providing substantial additional funding to the state's solitary NTRB.[47] The radical difference of Adelaide's 'special way' took that state out of the mainstream of native title debates to a considerable extent.[48] The South Australian process involves a 'main table' forum for direct discussion between the state, the South Australian Aboriginal Legal Rights Movement rep body (later succeeded by South Australia Native Title Services) and respondent peak bodies. More detailed work is then undertaken at 'side tables' on a sector or issues-related basis.[49] Within the overarching framework, individual negotiations must still take place on specific native title claims. After a strategic review conducted in 2007, the 'statewide negotiating parties . . . confirmed that their focus is on native title claim resolution' and the process was renewed.[50] The South Australian government has committed to resolving 75 per cent of all claims in the state by 2014 through negotiation, but so far has agreed to only one consent determination of native title, in August 2008, while another achieved through litigation was contested all the way to the High Court.[51]

Convergence and its discontents

Putting to one side the historical anomaly of Tasmania and the comparatively tiny ACT, a variety of general observations may be made about the performance of all the remaining states and the Northern Territory. First, although they did not all start out in the same direction, there has been a considerable degree of convergence on a common approach. Whatever their politics and declarations of intent, all of the jurisdictions in question have fought at least one native title claim through to the High Court on issues of connection or extinguishment or both. Yet each and every one has arrived at the view that negotiation is preferable to litigation of native title claims and successfully settled at least one matter by consent determination. All have now introduced formal connection report guidelines except New South Wales, but the latter has indicated that the submission of similar material to other states is still likely to be required in relevant circumstances.[52] The mainland states and the Northern Territory have come together on a common position in relation to native title, characterised by a professed commitment to settling claims by consent determination where sufficient traditional connection can be demonstrated, while still maintaining an actual willingness to litigate on points of controversy. Ironically, when native title determinations have been reached by agreement, states have been swift to then claim a share of the credit, notwithstanding that by their own guidelines settlements can only be reached on the basis of traditional evidence rather than governmental intervention.[53] The tendency to seek acclaim for consent determinations no doubt contributes to the inflation of expectations about what states can and will do.

In 2002 Hal Wootten, casting a cold eye when addressing the plenary session of the third annual native title representative body conference in Geraldton, argued that there had been 'an opportunity when mediation of claims began' under the NTA, for a system 'more flexible and imaginative than the judicial process can be', but the chance was missed:

> Instead governments invariably sent their lawyers along, hugging their cards to their chests, in effect saying to the claimants: 'If you can convince us that it is 100% certain that we will lose if we go to court, we will be prepared to settle'.[54]

Certainly, in the period after *Mabo* and even the first enactment of the NTA, things had been genuinely fluid. A state government could indeed have taken a path outside of the judicial process, not waiting for the law to be clarified or taking the part of the prudential land manager, but instead choosing a more visionary road. So long as it was consistent with the Commonwealth Constitution, what a more expansive approach might have entailed was limited only by ideological imagination, but conceivably any state government could have chosen to pursue wide-ranging regional settlements dealing not only with native title, but also embracing economic, social and cultural matters, perhaps implemented through legislation. It was common enough for Indigenous representatives to urge governments to take precisely that kind of broader approach. The WAANTWG, for example, in its 1999 position paper *Reaching Agreement: A Better Approach to Native Title in Western Australia*, urged wider 'negotiations at the regional, local and project-specific level', including matters as broad as employment and training, economic development, provision of public and essential services and the resolution of Indigenous disputes.[55] As discussed in Chapter 6, the NNTT also fostered notions that a more all-encompassing method might be preferable. Indeed, it was often assumed that the premium policy position for state governments would be to seek what were dubbed as 'comprehensive agreements'.[56]

Putting to one side South Australia, it is probably Western Australia that has shown most interest in a comprehensive approach. In the latter, *A Statement of Commitment to a New and Just Relationship between the Government of Western Australia and Aboriginal Western Australians* was signed by Premier Gallop and senior state and national Indigenous leaders in October 2001.[57] The *Statement* outlined a set of principles and a process for a state-wide partnership framework to support the negotiation of regional and local-level agreements in the areas of health, housing, essential services, native title, justice and other issues. The fine words of the *Statement*, however, remained largely unrealised in practice, not least because of the denouement of ATSIC, which was to be the major agent on the Indigenous side of the deal.[58] Western Australia, along with Victoria, also demonstrated an active tendency towards negotiating 'alternative settlements', which might be defined broadly as agreements finally disposing of native title issues and arising from the NTA process, but which do not consist of a formal determination of the existence of native title. However, although alternative settlements are by definition not limited to the terms of a consent determination, far from being 'comprehensive', they are more likely to be in the realm of a consolation prize: a gesture acknowledging 'traditional ownership' where native title is extinguished or cannot be established. Finally, there were some isolated examples of states bringing a broader approach to resolve disputes over particular flagship future act matters, but those occasions were rare and owed more to the anomalous degree of bargaining power held by the native title parties in such instances. As Wootten wryly commented, claimants found that government was more likely to become flexible if they had it over a barrel than when they appealed to its sense of justice or its imagination.[59]

That state governments rarely entertained an all-inclusive agreement approach to dealing with native title was often seen, either implicitly or explicitly, as a failing of policy. Perhaps, though, both the convergence and limitations of the states' approach to native title are best explained, not through the lens of absence of courage or vision, but more mundanely through an analysis of underlying government imperatives. Some of the commonality was no doubt a consequence of the preponderance of Labor governments over the period in question, suggesting shared ideological precepts and leading to easier information and skill sharing among advisers. However, it is significant that for all his historic antagonism to native title, Richard Court's government eventually adopted many features of the same policy formation. Underlying the variations in approach that are observable between jurisdictions and in different political contexts since the native title legislation was created, state imperatives have remained constant. So, for example, state interests expressed publicly by South Australian Liberal and Queensland Labor governments two years apart, in 1996 and 1998 respectively, in substance contained very much in common.[60] Understanding the point is a matter of turning the case for comprehensive agreements on its head by asking not what the state might have done for Indigenous people, but what government desired from the native title process.

Reasons of state

The essential state interests pursued within the native title system are as follows.

(1) Regularising dealings in land

The catchcry of all state governments has been the need for 'certainty' in dealing with land tenure, an aim which is not unreasonable given the extent to which prosperity in an advanced economy relies on a smoothly operating real property system. In order for security in tenurial dealing to be assured, it has been necessary for native title to be integrated reasonably well into the existing land management system.[61] Accordingly, all state and territory governments have shared the objective of wanting to regularise and systematise dealings with native title to the extent necessary to be able to administer dealings in real property in a timely and orderly fashion.

(2) Securing capital investment and development expansion

In order to facilitate growth, governments must ensure that capital investment is not discouraged through the creation and maintenance of institutions to solve dilemmas of cooperation and problems of time inconsistency. Investors must have confidence that their returns will not be unreasonably jeopardised by shifts in administrative practice. States have been particularly concerned with ensuring that tenements are processed with some expedition because of the longer-term consequences for investment obviously associated with any decline in levels of exploration. It is critical that reasonable expectations of tenure being granted are in fact met in order to encourage further outlay. State governments have been prepared to take extraordinary action in order to make certain that flagship projects proceed, both to secure the immediate economic benefits of the scheme in question as well as to send a broader signal about the safety of future ventures.

(3) Securing other state priorities

Good government entails a wide range of public works and every administration shares the imperative of being able to proceed with building and repairing infrastructure without undue hindrance. Other relevant state priorities include maintenance of the conservation estate (an aim that may appear more rhetorical than actual at times) and natural resources including water, flora and fauna, all of which have some potential to be impacted upon by native title.

(4) Minimising state exposure to compensation claims

The upshot of *Mabo* and the NTA was that government was liable to pay compensation for acts that had extinguished native title that took place after the passage of the Commonwealth's Racial Discrimination Act in 1975. All states and territories were keen to minimise their exposure to paying such compensation, wherever possible. Premier Beattie put the matter in a typically voluble fashion in 1998, telling a media conference that he was 'concerned about the level of compensation for which we might be liable' and that he did not want 'Queensland to be paying millions of dollars in compensation which could be spent on schools and hospitals'.[62]

(5) Resisting Commonwealth cost-shifting

While the NTA is Commonwealth legislation, there is no constitutional obligation for the federal government to fund the system to an optimum level. Indeed, as described in Chapter 3, the rep bodies in particular have been actively deprived of adequate resources. Given that the states have a more immediate vested interest in seeing native title processes operate efficiently (as a consequence of their responsibility for the land titles administration) than the Commonwealth, there is a substantial incentive to redress any funding shortfall. In general, though, states have been wary about providing extra finances for the native title system because of another key aim, which is to avoid federal 'cost-shifting' whereby the regional jurisdictions become responsible for paying for

Commonwealth responsibilities.[63] Despite wanting Canberra to pick up the tab, a number of state governments of both political affiliations have nevertheless in practice stepped into the breach, making some additional funding available to NTRBs in particular.

(6) Identifying where native title exists and to what extent

All governments would consider knowing the precise confines of where native title exists and details of the specific rights and interests it entails as an asset in state planning. Under the NTA system, the lodgment, processing and determination of claims will eventually deliver a more or less complete map of the extent of native title in Australia, as well as a clear indication of the content of the title from place to place. State governments then, as respondents, actually have to do little (in a proactive sense) to establish where native title exists, because the desired clarity will simply come to pass eventually as a consequence of the efforts of claimants and the functioning of the system. Nevertheless, it has been common for state administrations to frame their willingness to engage in the process of recognition as a virtue. Then Premier of Victoria, Jeff Kennett said in 1998, for example, that his government 'accepted the need for laws to recognise and protect native title'.[64] Similarly, a few years later, on the other side of politics, Deputy Premier Eric Ripper said that the government recognised that Western Australia needed an approach which respected 'the legitimate desire of indigenous people to have their native title rights recognised'.[65] The point about a state government promoting the recognition of native title as a policy aim is not that it is bad or disingenuous; it simply doesn't say very much. The functioning of the NTA means that state administrations must recognise native title where it exists, whether they like it or not.[66]

(7) Achieving maximum stakeholder support

In general, governments will want broad community support for state initiatives. In the context of native title, state Labor governments in particular have tended to emphasise the extent to which their policy approach involves building consensus across stakeholder groups. In contrast, Coalition administrations have tended to be more prepared to alienate Indigenous people and their supporters with policy that more openly favours resource development interests. The desire to account for all stakeholders has a particular application to Indigenous parties. No state government has been prepared to pick winners, by explicitly preferring to deal with one registered native title claim group over another. Similarly, states have been reticent to take a policy approach that appears to favour native title holders over 'historical people' in relation to any issue other than the recognition of traditional land tenure.[67]

(8) Orderly conduct of government

The standard interest of good governments in ensuring economic, efficient and methodical administration, regardless of the substantive policy objectives, also applies to native title.

(9) Strategic behaviour for electoral gain

In addition to the eight imperatives already listed, there is a ninth objective that is more covert and analytically elusive: the elected arm of government will seek partisan advantage with a view to retaining power, even at the risk of clashing with one of the previous matters listed above. As Jon Altman pointed out long ago, native title organisations can engage in 'strategic behaviour' designed to achieve advantage by wilfully distorting the system.[68] How the political inclinations of the elected arm impacted upon the actions of the executive is a vexed matter. Public servants and ministers in the conduct of their ministerial duty should be oblivious to electoral concerns. However, in an era of the centralisation of power and the increased politicisation of the executive, the electoral imperatives of the government of the day are a considerable and growing factor in policy implementation. Identifying strategic behaviour is complicated because politically influenced performance of public duties is, of its nature, usually undeclared and clandestine. Words and deeds do not always match and in a time when political discourse is rife with 'spin' and the dark arts of tactical communication, there may be a substantial and deliberate disjunction between the plain meaning of what is being said and the real intent of that which is being done. What is in truth engineered for partisan political advantage will inevitably be justified in the language of principled undertaking.

Assessing state performance

Taking the comprehensive agreement path to dealing with native title issues has never been necessary to satisfying essential state interests. It was not, in other words, that state imperatives could not have been satisfied through expansive approaches, but that it was inessential to do so. Most fundamentally, in terms of political economy, it is hard to see in what economic circumstances individual states and territories would have favoured comprehensive agreement-making in response to native title. The NTA processes have functioned to give private interests a certain regulatory framework providing access to land and waters, and government the capacity to engage in infrastructure development: with those needs already met, there was little to be gained in economic terms by adopting a broader approach to native title issues. A more visionary response to native title would also necessarily involve higher political risk and perhaps greater expense, both of which hardly made comprehensive agreement-making an attractive policy option.

Other structural and historical circumstances also rendered a more ambitious agenda unlikely. Perhaps above all, after 1998 in particular, the states overwhelmingly responded to the native title system as it was, rather than as it might have been. The NTA casts the states and territories not as polities engaged in dealing with Indigenous societies, exercising broad political agency on a comprehensive range of matters, but as litigants contesting the existence of a property right. The native title system frames Indigenous peoples as no more than civil petitioners, entitled to take their chance in a court of law like any other plaintiff in order to establish the existence of a disputed title. Faced with a system that rendered Aboriginal claims to land as *sub judice*, states and territories simply behaved like the litigants that they were.[69] Governments eventually tended towards a position that allowed for negotiated consent determinations of native title, but only to the extent provable on the facts as disclosed in a connection report. The result, as Justice Tony North of the Federal Court observed, is that the state's response to native title claims became 'characteristically rights based', reducing the ambit of the discussion to '"What legal rights have you? What legal rights are we prepared to recognize?"'[70] The structure of the native title system has been conducive to a legalistic state response.

Also lacking was any push in the direction of broader agreement-making from the federal government. The election of the Howard administration in 1996 meant an end to the doctrine of self-determination and an increasing tendency towards the 'mainstreaming' of Indigenous issues, both of which were quite contrary to the kind of assumptions that necessarily underpin calls for the commencement of comprehensive agreement-making. The reality, too, is that for the reasons described in Chapters 2 and 3, the Indigenous leadership lacked the necessary muscle to effectively expand the horizon towards greater political settlements. Clark's efforts to launch treaty talks were a particularly conspicuous failure. In any event, there must also be some doubt as to whether sufficient cohesion and clear lines of authorisation would have existed on the Indigenous side to have made dealings effective.[71]

Mapping and explaining the broad convergence of the state politics of native title is not to argue that there haven't been important differences at work. For one thing, the advocacy and public campaigning of conservative state governments was crucial to building political momentum for the 1998 Amendments. Further, just because all state governments eventually came to embrace the connection report leading to a consent determination model, it did not mean that there were not still substantial gradations in how things were handled. State governments could be more or less antagonistic within the confines of the NTA's processes. As Eric Ripper noted, the distinction between his approach and that of the previous government 'boiled down to its central theme—was about agreement rather than argument'.[72] The law had not changed, but the government could be nicer, more constructive and facilitative about the system as it stood.[73] However, constructive engagement within the process was not to be confused with any relaxation in observing the letter of the law, a duality that explains why the Western Australian Government could find itself committed to 'agreement not argument' yet pursuing native title claims through litigation when principle was at stake, all the way to the High Court. As Ripper told a conference in 2007 in relation to the controversial decision to appeal the Noongar people's unexpectedly successful native title win in the Federal Court over the south-west of Western Australia including Perth:

> It was necessary to appeal the decision because the State Solicitor's advice was that Justice Wilcox's decision contradicted the principles established by the High Court in Yorta Yorta to guide recognition of native title. Consequently, the initial decision created a high level of uncertainty for future native title negotiations, and may have adversely affected the achievement of consent determinations elsewhere in the State. The State's appeal sought clarity in respect of the application of High Court principles by the Federal Court. Since our Connection requirements are based on these very same principles, it was imperative that the Government sought this legal clarity. We now have that. Our preference is to resolve claims by agreement, and accordingly negotiations with the South West Aboriginal Land and Sea Council in relation to six claims that underlie the Single Noongar Claim have been underway since the appeal was lodged.[74]

It might have seemed perverse to the Noongars that the state wanted to simultaneously negotiate and litigate, but the approach was not at all unusual for a government thinking like a courteous litigant. Even in the anomalous case of South Australia, after years of negotiations there was still little to show in the way of any 'concrete gains', with the 'distinctive approach' instead said to be marked above all by an 'emphasis on *process* as a vehicle for exercising Aboriginal self determination'.[75]

The practice of resolving claims on the basis of evaluating connection reports did not fulfil all hopes and expectations of speed, informality and efficiency, but it was on balance probably still strongly preferable to trial on all these grounds. Though not as ambitious or radical as comprehensive agreement-making, the significance of fair, transparent and orderly process should not be diminished as a reasonable expression of good government. Indeed, accepting that states are unlikely to be interested in 'comprehensive agreements', for reasons that are not explicable or perverse, raises the bar for procedural courtesy, reasonableness and fairness. State governments that do not go beyond native title are choosing a path that may be disappointing to some, but which is understandable. However, states that participate safely under the processes of the NTA and the Federal Court but do so as less than exemplary actors can be regarded as egregiously failing.

5

MINING RULES AND THE SHEEP'S BACK

Non-government third party respondents

Caught between the drill and the plough

Native title began life with potent enemies. The mining industry, by far the most dominant sector of the Australian economy, was implacably opposed to the NTA from the outset. The pastoral industry was more ambivalent about the passage of the legislation, but only because the majority of legal opinion guessed that native title had probably already been extinguished by pastoral leases. Once the NTA had been passed, apart from pressing for amendments, resistance to native title could only be articulated within the system. The NTA allowed any 'person' (whether human or corporate) whose interests might be affected by a determination of native title to become party to a claim and the result was that thousands of individual non-government respondents became involved in various proceedings.[1] It was not uncommon for a single native title claim to have hundreds of respondent parties.[2] The most prominent and powerful came from primary industry, including miners, pastoralists, petroleum producers, resource explorers, fishing interests and aquaculturalists, but even minor concerns like recreational shooters, tour operators and jetty licensees could and did become involved.[3] In a political context, respondents with common interests (like 'mining lease holders' or 'pastoral lease holders') tended to be represented collectively by industry-based peak bodies.[4] Outwardly, the respondent peak bodies lobbied government, made submissions to relevant public inquiries, participated in various consultative forums organised by the NNTT and the Federal Court, provided 'industry perspective' speakers to innumerable conferences and issued regular streams of media comment. Inwardly, the role was to provide information and support to the constituent members of the organisation in question, as well as to formulate positions and strategies.

The focus of this chapter is on the mining and pastoral industries, which were represented by various national and state associations and were by far the most politically and economically significant of the organised respondents. All production requires land (or water) on which to operate, but the kind of permission that is required varies greatly, depending on what activities are involved. All industry shares the basic requirement for tenure that is both sufficiently certain to secure investment and robust enough to permit the business to be carried on without impediment. However, different enterprises require varying types of tenure, from the intensive long-term needs of heavy industry to the temporary and shifting rights of more transient activities like fishing or early minerals exploration. There are numerous kinds of legal relationships with land in Australia, from the absolute beneficial ownership comprised by freehold to the flimsiest of licences and permissions to collect wood or for recreational fishing. After *Mabo* and then the enactment of the NTA, the fundamental dilemma of how native title interacted with these different permissions was not answered all at once, but incrementally on a case-by-case basis. The process was pivotal in determining how respondents would behave within the overall native title system. As the former President of the NNTT later recalled, '[t]here was never going to be any real prospect that these respondents would agree to native title determinations without a clear understanding of the impact of those determinations on their interests, whether as land managers, holders of tenements or as leaseholders'.[5] Only as the case law unfolded would particular industries know precisely where they stood.

Although this chapter concentrates on mining and pastoralism, other sectors also faced their own peculiar concerns in relation to native title. The fishing industry, for instance, was not an insignificant political player and had very specific reason for nervousness. Guy Leyland, long-standing native title spokesperson for the Western Australian Fishing Industry Council, admitted in 1994 that it was 'true' that the fishing industry was 'paranoid' about native title, but for 'very good reason', because his constituents only ever possessed 'very weak rights' to conduct their business activities on the water.[6] Fishing interests merely held commercial licences to operate and to take certain species in line with government limits. Given that *Mabo* had been confined to land, the fishing industry was concerned about whether native title could even exist over the ocean and, if so, with what effect. The NTA did not decide the matter but permitted claims to be made over water as well as land, to which in due course fishing interests became party. The fishing industry received the comfort that it craved when the courts eventually ruled that existing commercial fishing rights could not be displaced and that it would be difficult to establish any exclusive native title rights anywhere over the ocean.[7]

There will always be limits to the cooperation that occurs within industry peak bodies, because businesses are also in competition with one another. A leading mining spokesperson explained the duality in 1996:

> We have a role and a duty to ensure that the people who make the rules that govern us all understand what is important to our industry . . . The other role we have is as business people, that is, within the rules whatever they are we negotiate our position in order to enable projects either to continue or proceed, that is new projects. This of course includes notions of clarity of conditions of operation, confidence in contracts, whatever contracts are entered into or agreements, and of course, an expectation on return of investment . . . The first one again is participation in the debate over the rules and the second one is as business people negotiating our position for long term businesses that have to be profitable.[8]

All firms in a particular sector will share some common imperative, but at any time the overall 'industry position' is subordinate to the commercial self-interest of each individual business. The moment that a collective stance ceases to be of benefit to a particular firm, the standpoint will be swiftly abandoned by management, though the shift may occur clandestinely. For instance, while the mining industry's formal position was to deplore the proliferation of overlapping claims in minerals-rich areas of Western Australia in the mid-1990s, the phenomenon was actually fed by individual miners being prepared to enter into multiple arrangements with different groups as an expedient way of resolving their own approval delays without regard for the precedent being created. In one notable instance, each time a new claim was lodged the company in question simply made a further payment, merely encouraging yet more claims to follow. The firm's own tenure needs were eventually met, but a mess of overlapping claims was left behind. A decade later, while 'the industry position' was to keep a cap on the daily fees charged by native title claimants conducting heritage assessment surveys (which had remained, with some exceptions, largely static at $300 per day for Indigenous participants for around a decade), inflationary pressure was created by one company which took the initiative of offering larger than usual payments as an incentive to secure the participation of traditional owners outside of native title representative body processes and in preference to alternative work with other developers.[9] One particularly extreme case of an individual company purporting to act in its own interests but contrary to the broader cause of industry involved a firm actually paying for the lodgment of a number of overlapping claims.[10]

A senior case manager at the NNTT noted in 1998 that representative organisations often entered the native title process 'with policy agendas' that had the capacity to 'get in the way of the actual interest holder being able to effectively enter into the process and to progress'.[11] It is likely that industry associations did instil some discipline among their membership, at least through the promulgation of certain norms and ideas about how the system should work. The sharing of lawyers and other technicians also no doubt contributed to a harmonising of approach. Throughout the history of the native title process, the large commercial law firms have almost invariably acted for non-government third party respondents. On some occasions there was even dialogue and cooperation between the peak bodies of different industries because of the political advantages to be obtained from a common front.[12] Nevertheless, cooperation across industry peak bodies should not be exaggerated and at times gave way to outright hostility or antipathy, particularly when larger and richer interests contemplated arrangements untenable to smaller concerns. In Western Australia real tensions existed between the top end of town represented by the Western Australian Chamber of Minerals and Energy (WACME), the middle to smaller companies which tended to join the Association of Mining and Exploration Companies Inc. (AMEC) and the long-suffering non-corporate economic minnows eligible to belong to the Amalgamated Prospectors and Leaseholders Association (APLA). In Queensland, Frank Brennan recalled that a heads of agreement reached by environmentalists, Aboriginal groups and local pastoralists represented by the Cattlemen's Union up on Cape York was regarded as suspect by the National Farmers' Federation, who were worried that the broader strategic position had been compromised and 'smelt a rat'.[13]

Mining I: The hard approach to hard legislation

In Australia all minerals are owned by the state, which then grants tenements to those who wish to mine and explore, with the right to sell the material that has been extracted. The state is paid rent for all tenements, as well as receiving royalties based on what is actually produced. The overall principle behind Australian mining legislation is to maximise the amount of exploration that occurs by requiring minimum amounts of annual expenditure on all tenements, which are held for finite periods of time and progressively reduced in size.[14] Where the requisite expenditure does not take place, tenements may be resumed by the state. The land requirements of the resources industry itself are multidimensional. Mining companies need security of tenure and freedom to conduct and vary operations according to technical and commercial imperatives, but the industry as a whole constantly craves access to new ground to regenerate the pool of commercially viable deposits. Vast programs of exploration have to be completed, most of which will ultimately prove to be fruitless, because to some extent it is only through sheer quantity of geological investigation that new resources are uncovered. Accordingly, after *Mabo*, the minerals industry was not only concerned to shield existing mining tenements from any consequences, but to ensure that it remained easy to get access to exploration areas. Mining and exploration tenements can be granted over other land holdings, meaning that the interaction of native title and other tenure types—including particularly the vast pastoral leasehold estate—were also of interest to the extractive industries. Many of Australia's most lucrative mining operations are found within the boundaries of pastoral leases.

Historically, the resources sector had relied on a 'hard' public approach to Indigenous affairs, crashing through (sometimes literally) any Aboriginal opposition to mining or exploration, usually with the tacit or even explicit support of the relevant state government.[15] Initially, the mining lobby responded to native title in much the same way, adopting remorseless and denunciatory positions on the *Mabo* decision and the native title legislation.[16] The Minerals Council of Australia (MCA) did not support the original NTA, writing off the new system as 'unworkable' because it had 'created considerable uncertainty about acquisition of future titles and security of past and future titles'.[17] The most volatile point of discord was the operation of the right to negotiate, which industry detested as an obligation to 'negotiate economic benefits with unspecified groups of people with unproven claims involving unproven rights'.[18] The miners collectively despised the extent to which the right to negotiate encouraged and rewarded overlapping claims, a trend that reached its zenith in the debacle of the Goldfields in the mid-1990s. Even where individual companies were successful in reaching agreement with all existing claims, there was no mechanism in the NTA to prevent further claims by new (or newly splintered) groups on the next occasion the firm in question required additional tenure. A company might reach agreement with a dozen overlapping claim groups over known tenure requirements but then a year later have need of another lease, inviting further claims by new groups. In practice, the unamended NTA demanded extraordinary efforts be made before a resource company could determine with any confidence that it had resolved all native title questions over a project. Rio Tinto's audacious Yandocoogina agreement with native title groups in the Central Pilbara in 1997 was one of a small number of deals that showed it was possible to get through the morass in orderly fashion, but the resources, effort and risk involved were very considerable.[19]

The question of precisely how damaging native title was to industry in the early years of the NTA is a matter of considerable professional, scholarly and political debate.[20] It does seem likely that the disruption to normal business marked by the introduction of the NTA would have caused at least some downturn, because—politically motivated exaggeration aside—companies truly did 'face an unpredictable future for their development plans'.[21] The NTA was, after all, by any measure a long and confusing item of legislation and native title was a new thing in Australia. Nevertheless, the interpretation of domestic productivity data is contested and complicated by global economic trends.[22] There is also the question of strategic behaviour: a more cooperative approach by state governments in the early years of the Act would doubtless have made for a significant qualitative improvement in the functioning of the legislation.[23] Even the 'backlog' of applied-for-but-not-yet-granted tenements in Western Australia—so often adduced as one of the principal indications of the 'unworkability' of the future act system—is a highly questionable indicator, because of the practice of 'tenement parking'.[24] Indeed, an accumulation of unprocessed tenement applications could actually be of significant pecuniary benefit to mining companies.[25]

Mining II: The soft approach to seeking softer legislation

The passage of the NTA no doubt came as a shock to the mining industry: the fact that the legislation had got through at all marked a very considerable political defeat. Clearly, a new public and political approach was warranted.[26] According to AMEC's George Savell, speaking at a conference in 1996, the sector had been 'slow to grasp the concept of collective action' and had found itself at a disadvantage because the 'public affairs debate' over native title had 'been skewed by a whole range of issues which [had] their genesis in social justice questions'. According to Savell, '[c]ommercial reality [was] a dry subject' and did not easily achieve 'the sort of exposure in the media which human interest issues attract'.[27] Notwithstanding the shortness of Savell's memory in relation to the effectiveness of the anti-land rights campaigns of the 1980s, his words nevertheless signify recognition within the mining peak bodies that the packaging of their policy agenda merited an overhaul. In July 1996, senior political journalist Michael Gordon reported on a general change in tactics on the part of the mining lobby to 'an emphasis' on 'persuasion, rather than attempting to bludgeon opponents into submission—or secure victory over their heads'.[28] The approach was 'essentially one of seeking to persuade government and community to the position that the industry would judge in its own and the community's best interests'.[29]

The hallmark of the new softer style was the pairing of overt 'acceptance', 'respect' and 'recognition' of native title with renewed insistence that the system must be tooled to suit the needs of the resources sector. Indicatively, in 1997 the MCA's annual survey report, which had previously carried an uncompromising case against native title,[30] now described

> a growing acknowledgement within the broader community of the need to put in place effective and efficient legislative mechanisms to support the interaction of the resource industry and indigenous interests. The Minerals Council is maintaining a longer-term perspective on the issue and recognizes that industry and indigenous people will need to form co-operative partnerships. All arrangements, however, need to be underpinned by effective legislation that produces workable outcomes within realistic time frames.[31]

Critically, then, the softening of the mining industry's position did not mean any abandonment of calls for the procedural rights of native title groups to be weakened; the hard approach had simply been padded. Dick Wells, the Executive Director of the MCA, exemplified the new pattern when he quoted Paul Keating to a summit meeting in early 1997, claiming that industry's 'twin goals' were 'to do justice to the *Mabo* decision in protecting native title and to ensure workable, certain land management'.[32] The disingenuousness in claiming that the resources sector had any interest at all in 'protecting native title' is obvious, but the charade was played with growing heartiness even as the campaign to secure the abolition of the right to negotiate was pursued with unrelenting vigor. While lobbying for statutory protections of native title to be substantively weakened, industry representatives were increasingly inclined to express warm support for the process of reconciliation,[33] or earnestly attend conferences to talk about how to 'do business with Aboriginal communities' or even to express generous concern about whether native title was benefiting Indigenous people themselves.[34]

The shift in the way in which mining industry opposition to the workings of the NTA was communicated oddly coincided with political shifts in the Indigenous position. The peak representatives of the minerals sector and the Aboriginal leadership found themselves appropriating one another's arguments so as to ward off potential attack. As described in Chapter 2, particularly after the Howard government was elected in 1996, ATSIC and NIWG began adopting the language of economic progress as a rationale for not abolishing the right to negotiate or any other radical amendment to the NTA. On the other hand, the resources industry sought to argue that its support for native title was rock solid, but as a fuzzy rhetorical prelude to suggesting that significant changes to the legislation were thoroughly necessary. 'It was not,' the MCA argued in 1998, 'the concept and recognition of native title that was the core issue', simply the procedural rights granted by the NTA that were the problem.[35] In 1998, in answer to the question 'does the minerals industry support native title?', WACME asserted that '[t]he answer' was 'an unequivocal "Yes"', before offering the equivocation that industry was also 'proactive in promoting the need for a workable NTA and consistent and sensible administration of that Act'.[36]

Mining III: The softer approach under softer legislation

The enactment of the 1998 Amendments fundamentally transformed the strategic situation for mining interests.[37] Even greater hope was invested in the opportunity created by the Amendments for the procedural rights of native title claimants to be further weakened by the creation of alternative state regimes.[38] No longer was the NTA the problem: after the 1998 Amendments were passed, the mining sector not only 'respected' native title, but in an ironic turn now called for full and respectful observance of the legislation via the implementation of weaker procedural rights for claimants by the states. The MCA argued in 1999 that

> The native title processes must be allowed to operate to the fullest extent available in the legislation. This is necessary for the benefit of all the stakeholders.[39]

Ultimately, the failure of the states to do away with the right to negotiate in favour of frailer alternatives proved to be a considerable disappointment to industry.[40] However, the changes that were achieved as a consequence of the 1998 Amendments were still a significant prize. Prior to the Amendments, although it was technically possible, the feat of obtaining security of tenure and freedom to operate was extremely difficult. On the other hand, after the 1998 changes to the NTA had been introduced, there were far fewer overlapping registered native title claims, more certain processes and even the ability to secure whole areas through new Indigenous Land Use Agreement provisions that had been introduced. It no longer took trail-blazing by Rio Tinto; it was becoming clear that almost anyone could do it. The prospect was made even rosier as the NNTT demonstrated a complete reluctance to ever make an order that mining not proceed, meaning that if negotiations with native title claimants were forced to arbitration, the resource interest could be well confident of the result.[41] An increasing spread of experience within industry also meant that there was a growing practical sense of how 'doing business with Aboriginal people' was best conducted. Sitting in obscure community halls with groups of Aboriginal people and their advisers was losing its novelty. Indeed, as the heat of the 1998 Amendments died down, the process by which individual resource interests resolved native title issues began to look increasingly familiar. Miners could get their security of tenure and freedom to operate through the same mechanism as when they purchased machinery or hired labour; that is, a private contract in the form of an agreement with the native title group in question. After the 1998 Amendments, the 'problem' of native title had been reduced to the more or less mundane business of wrangling over the terms of specific transactions.[42] Global economic conditions also increasingly favoured industry equanimity, at least until the abrupt slowdown following the financial crisis in 2008. While the 'rise of China' and the associated commodities boom had put pressure on firms to reach accommodation with native title claimants as quickly as possible so as to make the most of the favourable economic conditions, the general liquidity also meant the availability of plenty of financial capacity to provide the kind of 'process funding' described later in this chapter, as well as often substantial valuable consideration within the negotiated agreements themselves.

The Amendments also ended what remained of the national debate between the Indigenous leadership and the mining industry. Once the modifications to the NTA were passed and the efforts to see alternative regimes established in the states and territories petered out, there was little left to argue about. The espousal of the idiom of economic liberalisation by the Indigenous peak bodies themselves meant that any argument of principle with industry was essentially over, providing an ideological convergence. The evident practical and political reality was that, with few exceptions, the ghost of Noonkanbah had been laid to rest by Aboriginal leaders speaking the language of growth and productivity and even adopting the logic of economic rationalism.[43] By 2005 the establishment of a national Indigenous mining association was being touted.[44] Such debates as remained were not a struggle over the rules of the system, but negotiations in relation to particular future acts. Project-specific deliberations were localised, likely to take place under the confidentiality cloak of contractual negotiations and rarely the concern of anyone outside of the immediate parties. The ideological positions of miners and Indigenous people had come together in the common acceptance that contract was the appropriate means of governing the relationship and it was just a matter of getting the deal done. The various negotiating parties could be left to work out the details.

Mining IV: Soft and hard approaches to rep bodies and representation

Choosing the optimum mechanism for dealing with native title claimants represented a perpetual dilemma for mining companies. Industry lobbyists had been among those most antagonistic to the prospect of a national system along the lines of the Northern Territory model when the form of the NTA was being negotiated. The mining industry was naturally disinclined to support anything that looked like collective bargaining or the creation of so-called 'gate keepers' between companies and Aboriginal communities and was apprehensive even about the level of power that was eventually given to NTRBs.[45] Nevertheless, despite the historic misgivings, there was an increasing awareness that rep bodies could play a very useful role for industry as the deal brokers that could intermediate the relationship with native title claimants, including the messy business of locating traditional owners, arranging meetings and advising on cultural protocols.[46] Big mining also began to openly recognise the reality of rep body under-funding. In 2004 the MCA told an inquiry that

> The experience of the minerals sector to date is that NTRBs are chronically under resourced, and in order to meet the requirements of the NTA, minerals companies are obliged to meet the resourcing gap. Despite the best endeavours of individuals working within NTRBs, the lack of resourcing means that they are incapable of effectively carrying out their broad responsibilities.[47]

Accepting the existence of the Commonwealth funding shortfall, and with their own development timelines in mind, it even became the practice of those miners that could afford it to provide 'process funding' to native title representative bodies in order to progress negotiations at a speed that better suited corporate expansion plans. Naturally, no government minded the development of what was in effect a successful exercise in privatising part of the cost of the native title system; if a particular company needed an NTRB to work faster than Commonwealth funding allowed, then the developer could pay for it.[48] The introduction by stealth of user-pays funding for rep bodies was not lost on the MCA, which protested to an inquiry in 2004 at what was going on:

> The result of this chronic under resourcing is that minerals companies are often asked (obliged) to pay for a service that is clearly the responsibility of government. It is simply unacceptable that the private sector is put in a position where it must meet the costs of doing business with the public sector because governments have failed to adequately fund organizations to deliver services that they are legislatively required to provide.[49]

By 2007 the reticence appeared to have lessened as the MCA openly acknowledged the existence of what it termed miners' corporate 'responsibilities in funding Indigenous engagement in specific commercial negotiations' as standard practice.[50]

Mining firms providing funding for rep bodies to undertake core functions more quickly undoubtedly created distortions in the system as commercial-style negotiations could be prioritised while claims languished. The inevitable effect was that NTRBs began to program their work in order to discharge the functions that industry was paying for. At a systemic level, while the NTRB system had been established to provide representation to claimants, it was now being subtly re-tooled to meet the needs of the minerals industry. There is nothing on the face of the public record to indicate anything as vulgar as a rep body coming to regard itself as existing to do the bidding of mining companies and no doubt the aims of staff remained as ambitiously on the side of their clients and constituents as ever. So long as there is full transparency and disclosure—sometimes even the direct instructions of client groups—there is nothing unethical about process funding. Yet there is also little doubt that NTRBs had their operational priorities dictated by the availability of funding and when the money came from industry to progress negotiations, that is where effort would be directed. Whenever process funding was accepted, it implicitly became the function of rep bodies to facilitate industrial development through the timely enabling of transactions. It was a fact not lost on the smaller-scale end of the industry which by the second half of the 2000s was complaining that, while the big side of town could provide resources to rep bodies, process funding was a luxury that the junior firms could not afford. The solution, according to AMEC, was to quarantine a percentage of Commonwealth support for rep bodies that would have to be spent on facilitating transactions:

> Our understanding is that at present NTRBs are not required to allocate a percentage of their funding to conduct future act negotiations for their claimant groups. The result is that they use their majority of allocations to progress native title claims. This means that proponents are expected to provide the funds required by NTRBs to conduct future act negotiations as well as funding their own involvement in the future act process. A number of very large resource developers have been prepared to provide considerable financial assistance to NTRBs to facilitate their own negotiations (hundreds of thousands of dollars in some cases) . . . For small to medium sized companies . . . funding NTRBs in addition to their own negotiation cost is often not financially possible when they are trying to get new projects up and running.[51]

Even for the larger companies that formally accepted the institution of process funding arrangements, there was always the nagging temptation in corporate minds that perhaps a company might get a better and faster agreement if dealings occurred direct with a claimant group rather than through an NTRB. Giving voice to the enticement, AMEC's George Savell claimed as late as 2003 that '[t]he benefit of going around the Act and the NTRBs is usually a reasonable agreement concluded'.[52] Despite Savell's upbeat bravado, the dilemma was basically a choice between speed and greater security. Decision-making for both resource companies and NTRBs was complicated by the ongoing reality of a range of actors often simultaneously claiming to represent a particular group or area of country. A miner could be faced not only with a chorus of overlapping claims, but offered different kinds of decision-making structures by multiple voices, each asserting the strength of their own right to speak. Unquestionably, in most instances the statutory qualifications of the NTRBs offered greater certainty of dealing, but perhaps an agreement could be reached more quickly and not actually breach the letter of the law if a consultant were to ride into town with a stuffed brown paper bag and some pre-prepared waiver documentation. At the level of the industry peak body, the position became one of supporting the proper functioning of the NTRBs, but implicitly still defending each company's freedom of action to go around the back if they wished.

Pastoralism: From axe to grind to access protocols

Around half of mainland Australia has been covered in pastoral leases of various kinds at one time or another, which partly explains why the question of the impact of the tenure on native title was of such great significance.[53] The enormous cattle and sheep stations were historically crucial to the development of Australia's economy, but even as the industry became relatively less lucrative, the myth of the pastoral industry and, rather more prosaically, rural vote-weighting in some jurisdictions ensured that the sector continued to exercise substantial political and cultural influence. Unlike the exploration needs of the minerals industry, the land requirements of the pastoral community tend to be relatively fixed, entailing a 'clear title for sustainable land management and as a basis for sound long term business decisions'.[54] When the NTA came into effect in January 1994, the collective position of pastoralists' organisations was that the industry had no reason to be concerned because their leases extinguished native title.[55] Certainly, the preponderance of legal opinion at the time favoured the view that pastoral leases did obliterate any underlying customary tenure. Indeed, in an act of stunning political compromise, the National Farmers' Federation had actually agreed to the original NTA on the basis that the question of the extinguishment of native title by pastoral lease should be largely left to the courts.[56] While the pastoralists would no doubt have preferred legislative confirmation that their tenure extinguished native title, the leadership was prepared to simply bet on the weight of legal opinion being right and to wait for the court cases to confirm the wisdom of their wager. Consequently, once the legislation was in operation, the pastoral industry took every opportunity to argue that native title had been wiped out by their leases and did not want to participate in the 'costly, complex and inequitable mediation' of claims which they hoped and anticipated would not ultimately be of concern to them.[57]

The Tribunal, faced with legal uncertainty and political intransigence, attempted the line of reasoning that even if, as a strict matter of law, pastoralists did not need to deal with native title claims, there were still advantages to be had in these two sets of parties coming to terms. In particular, the NNTT advocated the development of pastoral access protocols as a way of settling matters and avoiding litigation, regardless of the existence of native title.[58] In 1995, for example, Justice French asserted that there was 'a need for a new relationship between Indigenous people and the pastoral industry which moves out of the post-colonial twilight and into an era of real mutual recognition and respect', which could be achieved in part by the elaboration of 'rules for access and use of traditional country'. According to the President, if native title was 'found to exist on land covered by a pastoral lease it would be necessary to agree upon a code of conduct and rules for access to the land and enjoyment of native title rights and interests consistently with the rights of the pastoralists'.[59] Equally, though, if native title did not exist, given that many pastoral leases were already encumbered by a statutory right of access for Aboriginal people, it could be argued that a formal set of documentation to regularise and particularise arrangements was advisable anyway. The alternative presumably would be to simply allow ordinary social interaction to take place, with each party relying on their rights, but in the hope that the people involved would treat one another with ordinary courtesy.

The early cases before the Federal Court and the Tribunal seemed to vindicate that the legal punt had been well made, with a number of decisions indicating that pastoral leases did indeed extinguish native title.[60] However, when the matter finally came before the High Court in *Wik*, a majority of the judges informed a shocked Queensland pastoral industry that their leases only extinguished native title to the extent of any inconsistency, but that otherwise Aboriginal customary tenure survived to coexist with the lessee's rights. The pastoralists' peak bodies expressed outrage, asserting that the industry had been tricked and that the National Farmers' Federation (NFF) had only accepted the NTA on the basis of assurances about extinguishment. According to the pastoral lobby, in order to make good on the original legislative bargain the Commonwealth must now move to legislatively do what the High Court had failed to achieve and blanket extinguish native title on pastoral leases.[61] Although in strict legal terms, *Wik* only applied to Queensland tenure, it appeared likely that the result would be the same for similar tenure elsewhere in Australia and accordingly the reactionary campaign that followed was conducted on a national basis.[62] The pastoral industry's peak bodies openly advised their members not to take part in any mediation processes, insisting on a 'return' to the law as they believed it to have been.[63] In the stormy climate, the Tribunal again attempted to soothe the water by returning to pastoral access protocols as a way of resolving matters. In the period when statutory extinguishment of native title on pastoral leases by the Commonwealth seemed like a very real possibility, advocating the negotiating of access protocols constituted a de facto argument for legislative restraint.[64]

In the event, the 1998 Amendments did not blanket extinguish native title on pastoral tenure, but pastoralists were rewarded with new statutory comfort that any native title that might exist on their leases could not interfere with any of their activities.[65] The Prime Minister himself went to some lengths to explain to a gathering of pastoralists that by any real measure, native title was something that would not worry them and indeed that their rights were to be enhanced:

> [Y]ou can't have your title in any way diminished or affected by a native title claim. You can't be put off your property. You can't be stopped from carrying on your pastoral activities on your property. Your right to do that will be fully confirmed. No pastoral titleholder

> can have their title in any way affected or diminished, but most importantly of all, you can go away from this meeting safe in the knowledge that when this legislation is passed in the national Parliament, you will have the full and unfettered capacity to run your property. You will not only be able to carry on pastoral activity, but you will be able to diversify into all aspects of primary production. You will even be able to carry on an incidental tourist business, a farm-stay business, if that is what you want. And while ever the dominant purpose of the use of the land remains one relating to pastoral or primary industry activity, you will be able to do that without getting the say-so, the permission, the beg-your-pardon or whatever of anybody else.[66]

As Howard indicated, the 1998 Amendments were to be an outstanding victory for the pastoral industry. Not only had native title been wholly negated as an issue, but pastoralists achieved a substantial increase of their tenurial rights. If the bet on the original legislation had been lost on the *Wik* case, it was a gamble that paid out richly in 1998. After the Amendments were passed, no pastoralist in Australia had anything at stake in whether native title claims succeeded or failed: they had effectively won.

Curiously, though, despite their lack of any real interest in the outcome of claims following the 1998 Amendments, pastoralists retained the right to party status. The consequence was that the claim mediation process which had once been dismissed as a nuisance and then a threat now became an opportunity for pastoralists to even further improve their position. When it came to settling a claim by consent determination, the objections of some minor recalcitrant might be procedurally overridden, but the opposition of the pastoral industry would inevitably mean substantial litigation in which states and other parties could mostly be expected to adopt default positions contesting the claim. If pastoralists had to pay for their own participation in mediation or litigation the cost would still have been an important disincentive, but to further sweeten the situation the Howard government had generously increased the level of funding to respondent parties. The scheme, administered by the Commonwealth Attorney General, imposed no financial hardship test and far less rigorous monitoring and regulatory requirements than on the funding provided to NTRBs.[67] The provision of financial resources negated the last possible disincentive for pastoralists to use the process for gain. As Noel Pearson memorably put it:

> if there is a third party that (a) has all of his rights and interests already guaranteed at law—and therefore he can never lose anything, and (b) has all of his costs paid for by the Attorney General of the Commonwealth—then of course these third parties are not going to be amenable to negotiated settlement of claims, and will resist recognition until the cows come home, or the native titleholders have surrendered most of their rights.[68]

In the event, pastoral access protocols proved to be the bell that reliably brought the cows home. The *Smith* consent determination in 2000 in particular had demonstrated emphatically the reality of what favourable access protocols could deliver to pastoralists.[69] The protocols in question require any native title holder wishing to access their land to give the lessee at least 72 hours notice containing detailed information about the number of people who wish to enter, the number of vehicles, the places that will be visited, the length of stay, the camping locations and details about the kind of hunting that will take place on the station and to comply with numerous other conditions. If permission to enter is obtained, a multiplicity of rules apply that the persons can be excluded from the property for breaching.[70] The pastoral lessees may at any time unilaterally prescribe further restrictions that must be obeyed.[71] After the determination but before entering any of the leases in question, native title holders were also obliged to take out public liability insurance premiums to cover up to $5 million but an inability to obtain funding for the policy effectively barred their access to the properties for some time.[72] All of these conditions under the Smith pastoral access protocols applied to properties to which, before the consent determination had been reached, the then claimants had enjoyed a statutory right of access. Shortly after the protocols were negotiated, Henry Esbenshade, Director of Native Title for the Pastoralists and Graziers Association of Western Australia, commented that:

> A lot of pastoralists might well be more than happy to arrive at a similar agreement . . . This would be almost too good to be true . . .[73]

The protocols sent the native title group's rights backwards and increased the power of the pastoralists.[74] In August 2002, the Pastoralists and Graziers Association of Western Australia claimed that 'for years the pastoral industry has been working within the Native Title Act to formalise access agreements with applicants known to them, thereby recognising the High Court in *Wik* findings of co-existing, shared rights' and, strictly speaking, the assessment was correct.[75]

With their position not only secure but capable of betterment through negotiations, the pastoral industry now had every reason to respect and accept the native title system and all that it offered. The industry that had formerly wanted to stay out of the claims system altogether suddenly developed an enthusiasm for the mediation process. If both the pastoralist and the native title holder have something at issue, then it is easy to imagine that right of entry protocols might represent a compromise. However, given that pastoralists had nothing at all to lose after the 1998 Amendments, the negotiation of pastoral access agreements became a free hit: the price that claimant groups would have to pay in order to secure the consent of the lessees to a determination.[76] The significant shift in the balance of legal power underlying the relationship between native title groups and pastoral lessees eluded the Tribunal, which continued to agitate about access protocols as if they operated neutrally.[77] On the fifteenth anniversary of the *Mabo* decision the Tribunal released a promotional DVD, featuring a pastoralist who agreed to participate in the filming because 'he wanted people to know that for him native title provided security':

> I still think there are a lot of myths out there about land use agreements. It's ridiculous because when you work out an agreement it's a bonus not an impediment.[78]

Despite their rights being cosseted, legal costs being paid by the Commonwealth and having the ability to improve their position still further when negotiating access protocols, in the course of various submissions in the second half of the 2000s, the pastoral industry still called for the NTA to be tightened. Pastoralists, the NFF claimed with unwitting irony, were still not being afforded 'the same respect and importance as claimants'.[79]

Certain and workable

The mantra of business voluntarism, sometimes manifested as a commitment to 'corporate social responsibility' or, in the specific context of Indigenous affairs, professed adherence to 'reconciliation' and 'respect and recognition' for native title, enjoys widespread currency. The familiar tale has it that initially suspicious industries eventually came round to the realisation that native title should be respected and that it is optimal to resolve matters with Aboriginal people by agreement. The narrative is in many ways correct, but in conflating description with explanation it does little to account for why the transformation occurred, premised on a proper appreciation of commercial imperatives. In purely economic terms, the very best outcome for private enterprise may well be no native title at all because, for business, any extra imposed process adds to transaction costs, detracts from flexibility and is sub-optimal. The function of corporations is to optimise profit for shareholders, not to respect native title or anything else. As American political economist Robert Reich has amply demonstrated, except as a strategy for increasing profit, there is no such thing as corporate social responsibility where the obligation exists to maximise returns to shareholders.[80] Corporate social responsibility (or a mining industry entirely reconciled to native title) is not false, but it is a myth that tells only a part of the story.[81] Steps may be taken by firms that are socially worthwhile, but they will be done so in order to reduce costs. Leon Davis, one of the pioneers of the ground-breaking 'progressive' corporate approach to native title adopted by Rio Tinto, when discussing what motivated the huge change in attitude undergone by his company acknowledged that the problem was fundamentally one of economics, not values: '[t]he mining industry's adversarial operating environment was measurably eroding performance and profitability'.[82]

Prior to *Mabo* and the Native Title Act, except where there was land rights legislation, the mining industry did not offer recompense or agreements to Aboriginal groups. The so-called 'culture of agreement-making' that has arisen is solely a product of the doctrine of native title and the expectations that have accompanied it. Yet, the public posturing of industry has often been to shroud the link. Prior to the 1998 Amendments in particular, one of the tactics of the resources sector was always to try to obscure the fact that any changes in business attitude were related to shifts in the power possessed by native title groups under the NTA. If miners and pastoralists were 'doing the right thing' anyway, then what need was there for pesky legislative rights? Conspicuous corporate voluntarism is a vital tactic in avoiding increased regulation.[83] Both the mining and pastoral industry argued that strong procedural rights were actually antithetical to good 'practical' relations with Aboriginal people.[84] The native title system could be contrasted with industry's preference for what it called 'practical processes which address native title equitably without creating a barrier to development and communication'.[85] For example, it was '[o]utside of the Act', WACME claimed in 1997, that industry was really 'striv[ing] for meaningful and rewarding relationships with Aboriginal communities'.[86] Even when agreements began to be reached under the native title legislation, the organised face of the mining industry insisted that the deals were 'voluntary', as if the right to negotiate did not provide any impetus or compulsion.[87]

After the Amendments were passed, the situation changed again. Now, pastoralists could indeed participate in mediation and agreement-making on a willing basis, secure in the knowledge that they could only gain from voluntary participation. The minerals industry, on the other hand still laboured under statutory pressure to reach agreements. Yet with relations increasingly comfortably within the realm of contractual negotiations pursuant to reasonably certain timelines, mining firms found that their future dealings with native title groups had become a not too inconvenient way of managing certain externalities. Under the future act system after the 1998 Amendments, the routine functioning of the system involved native title groups trading their permission to resource interests in exchange for valuable compensation. What had been an unpredictable and multifaceted contest between resource interests and native title groups had been transformed into a market, with the rules of the exchange governed by the NTA. In their new willingness to reach agreement, the mining industry had not undergone some ideological or cultural conversion but had simply reached the general view that making contracts with native title groups was an economically feasible impost.[88] Native title was just one transaction cost among many to be resolved, as Savell put it, 'reflecting commercial values and an atmosphere of goodwill'.[89] The balance of rights and power that eventually crystallised within the native title system meant that both the pastoral and mining industries were once again able to rest easy and secure.

6

POETS AND SLAVES

The National Native Title Tribunal

Confusing beginnings

If the history of the National Native Title Tribunal has a single motif, it is captured in the very incongruity of the organisation's title. The discursive connotations of the name suggest a powerful decision-making body, but in actuality the Tribunal had few such powers. The first full-time President of the NNTT, Justice Robert French, often reflected that the designation 'Tribunal' was ill-suited because the NNTT was never 'empowered to hear cases and make decisions about the existence or non-existence of native title'.[1] From the outset, it was the Tribunal that couldn't. Rather, the principal functions of the Tribunal were to mediate native title claims and to assist in resolving future act matters through a mixture of alternative dispute resolution and arbitration.[2] In the first year of his presidency, French, while characteristically attempting to 'make it so', suggested that the 'Tribunal might more accurately and appropriately have been called "The National Native Title Dispute Resolution Service"', a suggestion that was never taken up.[3] The Tribunal's title was the organisation's foundational irony.

French was an astute choice as the first full-time President of the Tribunal; a Western Australian Federal Court judge with a formidable reputation and a background that included both participating in the establishment of the WA Aboriginal Legal Service and as a parliamentary candidate for the Liberal Party, he would be a difficult target for opponents of native title.[4] The second President, Graeme Neate, appointed from 1999, was not a judge but had impeccable technical credentials, having been a part-time member of the NNTT for some years and serving otherwise as the chairperson of the Aboriginal and Torres Strait Islander Lands Tribunal in Queensland. Though no doubt accentuated by the changes in native title law and practice, the difference in presidential styles was marked.[5] Both men were willing participants in public debate and evinced Trojan work ethics, but while French strove to catalyse, Neate, lacking the stature, profile and statutory powers of his predecessor, was more inclined to earnestly catalogue.[6]

Apart from the President, the NTA also allowed for deputy presidential and ordinary members of the Tribunal, to be appointed on either a part- or full-time basis to preside over mediation and arbitration. Despite the ostensible hierarchy, individual members possessed very considerable autonomy in conducting their work.[7] The result was that, for all of the Tribunal's eventual emphasis on process, the effectiveness of the NNTT as a mediator was often arbitrarily contingent on the ability, training and inclination of the particular member dealing with the matter in question.[8] Relatively flexible statutory criteria meant that members have been appointed with a wide array of qualifications and experience, but lawyers have dominated.[9] Notable early appointees included Fred Chaney, Hal Wootten, Ian Viner and Paul Seaman, all of whom were significant public figures with established reputations in Indigenous affairs.[10] Very few members have been Indigenous themselves.[11] Curiously, as the Tribunal itself would eventually point out, there was no requirement that members have any expertise in mediation.[12]

The Principal Registry of the NNTT was located in Perth, far from the usual centres of national power, in consideration of the importance of Western Australia to the contest over native title.[13] The Tribunal's first years of operation were characterised by rapid staff and budgetary growth, amid operational confusion engendered by the innate opacity of parts of the NTA accompanied by jarring clarifications from the courts.[14] Each new judicial interpretation of the NTA required (often substantial) change in the way the Tribunal operated, contributing to a climate of some administrative instability.[15] Most significant was confusion over what powers the Tribunal possessed in relation to the regulation of claims at the front end of the process. The NNTT initially adopted a restrictive interpretation which gave some order and restraint to the spread of claims, but the approach was thoroughly rejected by the High Court as a misapplication of the relevant law.[16]

The Tribunal and the future act system: emancipating the mining industry

Conscious of the possible tensions between the two roles of dealing with future acts and mediating native title claims, early in 1995 the Tribunal divided its principal operations between 'claims' and 'future acts' units which ran quite distinct operations.[17] The most obvious manifestation of the partition was that neither of the presidents played much part in the administration of the Tribunal's future act role, which was instead led for most of the organisation's history by former state Labor Attorney General from South Australia, Deputy President Chris Sumner, who was left to get on with it. Although the NTA created the basic parameters, the Tribunal played a critical role in deciding precisely how the rights of the parties were to be weighted within the future act system, through both formal arbitral rulings as well as bureaucratic decisions about how procedures should operate. The Tribunal was not required to exercise its responsibilities in relation to the future act system until 1995, when the Western Australian State Government suddenly began issuing large numbers of notices of intention to create mining rights.[18] In what became one of the first key litigation battlegrounds under the NTA, the State of Western Australia insisted that every exploration tenement attracted the 'expedited procedure', a statutory euphemism meaning that native title claimants would get no right to negotiate. Various native title groups were quick to challenge the designation and the Tribunal was required to arbitrate. In the first hearings, former Western Australia Supreme Court judge Paul Seaman presided and took an approach (later wholly endorsed by Sumner) that resulted in the objections being dismissed. Other objections followed in which it became clear that not all members accepted the Seaman approach, leading to indecision that was resolved through appeals to the Federal Court that eventually went the way of the claimants.[19]

Fracas over the expedited procedure was followed by the first referrals of full future act matters to the Tribunal. In these cases, the NNTT was required to decide whether certain mining leases could be granted or not and, if so, under what conditions. One of the principal technical issues to be resolved was how the Tribunal should address the discrepancy between what, at law, the mining leases permitted the company in question to do and the activities that, as a matter of fact, would actually be undertaken.[20] Complicatedly, the structure of the Western Australian mining legislation meant that it was common for a lease to be granted, but for no actual commercial mining to ever be undertaken.[21] Placed in the invidious position of knowing what was legally permissible but not necessarily what would really happen, in each instance the NNTT allowed the tenements to be granted but attempted to place some conditions on any mining that actually might take place. On appeal, the Federal Court rejected the Tribunal's approach as legally impermissible.[22]

After the 1998 Amendments the Tribunal was faced with a recalibrated future act system, in which claimants' access to procedural rights had been considerably reduced.[23] The amended Act made it considerably harder, for instance, to sustain an objection to the application of the expedited procedure, largely in keeping with the original interpretation taken by Seaman and Sumner.[24] Success in objecting to the expedited procedure became much harder.[25] It was also becoming clear that winning a broader future act matter before the NNTT—actually gaining a ruling that mining should not go ahead because of the importance of the interests of a claimant group in a particular area—was well nigh impossible. In the history of its existence, when arbitrating on the main future act processes, the Tribunal has never once ruled that a resource company should not get its mining leases. The inevitable effect has been to reduce the value of the right to negotiate to registered claimants, while resource firms have been able to engage in bargaining, increasingly secure in the knowledge that it is unlikely that if a matter goes to inquiry, the consequences will be anything more onerous than the additional delay occasioned by the hearing.[26]

In addition to the formal exercise of arbitral power under the Act, the NNTT has also actively influenced the balance within the future act system through decisions on administrative policy. Importantly, the Tribunal moved to a fully fledged outcome and output accounting structure in accordance with accrual budgeting arrangements after the Amendments were passed in 1998.[27] Under the new system, the Tribunal was required to come up with quantitative ways of measuring success through the achievements of outputs and sub-outputs, said to flow from stated corporate goals. In designing a numerical basis for gauging how well it was administering the future act system, the NNTT made a clear value judgment. While 'corporate goals' still remained neutral or indeed designed to address the interests of Indigenous people, the achievement of these objectives was determined by reference to criteria that seemed to favour the resources industry. In measuring productivity, the Tribunal relied on statistics dealing with the number and speed of mineral tenements that were passing through the process and being granted. Perversely, for example, the Tribunal represented that the number of times a native title group missed out on the right to negotiate because the expedited procedure was applied acted as a measure of 'the cultural and customary concerns of Aboriginal and Torres Strait Islander people' being successfully addressed.[28]

The Tribunal's effectiveness in managing the future act system came to be defined by how quickly and efficiently it was servicing the needs of industry. In various submissions to parliamentary inquiries, the Tribunal used the available statistics to show that the NTA was mining-friendly: tenements were described in positive terms as being 'cleared for grant', and in one particularly striking effort the NNTT boasted that '70,000 square kilometres of land [had] been approved for mining exploration' in the previous year.[29] The deemphasising and sometimes diminution of claimant interests cannot simply be explained by reference to an adjustment in the balance of the right-to-negotiate system caused by the 1998 Amendments because the Tribunal went beyond what was required by the Federal Parliament.[30] In part the NNTT's course in dealing with the future act system might be read as reflective of the more general shift to the right in Australian political culture in the Howard years, but a fuller explanation lies in the underlying structure of the national economy. The Tribunal often accurately noted the immense value of the resources sector to the nation's ongoing prosperity, making it perhaps unsurprising that the organisation's future act unit became increasingly inclined to do its bit for the country.[31] In its administration of the future act system, the NNTT came to reflect the central priorities of the Australian economy.[32]

The Tribunal and the claims system: What was the dispute about?

One of the central statutory puzzles that the Tribunal had to solve was what, exactly, the resolution of native title claims was really all about.[33] The NTA in its original form provided only a very general basis for the Tribunal's central function of mediating native title claims, referring sparingly to a 'conference of the parties . . . to help in resolving the matter'.[34] The early years of legal flux over the content and extent of native title meant that what was actually being claimed was a subject of considerable doubt. Yet even more fundamentally, given that at no stage did the NTA ever allow traditional owners to claim rights owned by others, what was actually in dispute? A native title claim was not a contest of the asserted rights of traditional owners against those of other interests, because nothing could be claimed from anyone else. There was, for example, no contest with pastoralists about their rights, merely an assertion by claimants that there might be some residue of native title that could continue to co-exist. Ironically, then, the Tribunal was meant to conduct mediation between parties that were, on the face of it, not in disagreement in respect of competing claims of current rights. Nevertheless, the whole machinery of the Act contemplated native title claims as being decided by alternative dispute resolution: so what was mediation actually to be about? It was the NNTT's existential question.

The Tribunal was able to deal with the fundamental quandary of how to approach mediation in part through professed adherence to a particular school of alternative dispute resolution practice that placed the primary obligation for defining the dispute on the parties themselves. What was variously known as the 'interest-based', 'principled' or 'Harvard' model of alternative dispute resolution required the parties to identify their own interests, after which options for resolving matters could then be developed.[35] However, underpinning the parties' expression of their own interests were certain broad suppositions held within the Tribunal itself that provided a set of wider paradigms for interpreting what was going on in mediation. These assumptions constituted a set of ways of explaining what the 'dispute' was really all about. The Tribunal's collection of ideas of the dispute (none of which was exclusive of the others and indeed were often mutually reinforcing) provided a de facto answer to the basic ambiguity created by the statute as to the purpose of mediation and informed the organisation's perspective on how particular matters should be resolved.

i. The dispute as expression of broader 'grievance' to be addressed

In historical terms, every Indigenous society in Australia has experienced some form of past dispossession or intrusion on their traditional country, commonly in association with violence, indignity and racism. Accordingly, it was assumed that the making of a native title claim, whether wittingly or not, marked the existence of a wider set of feelings of anger and resentment about past and present wrongs that had been suffered. Wootten, for example, argued that every individual claim signalled 'a community with a grievance about its past treatment',[36] while French described native title as 'an element of a broader range of issues between Aboriginal and Torres Strait Islander people and wider Australia' from which it could not easily be disentangled.[37] The idea of a native title claim as signifying a wider set of grievances was to implicitly interpret the application process set out in the Act as potentially impoverished if broader matters were left unaddressed. The President's conception of the task at hand was that, whatever the inadequacies of the doctrine of native title might be, they could be addressed through the creative application of alternative dispute resolution. The parties, French urged, should seek agreements 'rooted not in the strict letter of the law, nor concessions made under an imperial approach to land management but in the recognition of substantial justice'.[38] The NTA was there to sew up the cut, but perhaps the mediation process might be used to treat the infection too.

The proposition that every claim was a sign of wider grievance supported an ideal of the native title process that might be described as 'mechanistic', implying that mediation could be used as a constructive and multifaceted instrument with which to begin tackling the full suite of (post)colonial discontents. Native title applications could lead to what one lawyer described as a process of 'manufacturing' not only determinations of rights and interests, but socio-economic and political outcomes.[39] French himself talked of the 'sculpting' of agreements.[40] The overriding principle was that the parties need not be confined to legalistic outcomes, but might apply their collective will and imagination to developing more ambitious compacts. Interpreting each native title claim as signifying expansive grievance also had consequences in terms of scale. French argued in December 1994 that '[t]he fact that native title is an element of a wider range of issues, and cannot really be extracted neatly from them, points to the need to consider and develop an intellectual framework for regional and local agreements, and more comprehensive settlements of questions about land use and management'.[41] Building on some statutory encouragement, the Tribunal explicitly encouraged regional agreements that would be more likely, in financial and logistical terms, to include provision for significant socio-economic outcomes.[42] In the mid-1990s in particular, the Canadian tradition of regional agreements seemed to offer an example of the road that Australia might take.[43]

ii. The dispute as 'knowledge deficit' to be remedied[44]

In attempting to realise both the narrower objective of resolving individual claims and the broader purpose of achieving acceptance of the precepts of the legislation, the Tribunal operated under the critical assumption that, at least in part, the intransigence of parties was based on an information deficit capable of redress through education and liaison.[45] Once the parties understood the limitations and potential of the process, so it was believed, matters would be bound to progress and be resolved. Understanding the dispute as being a matter of information deficit had the appeal of explaining why parties could appear to be at loggerheads when, as a matter of legal reality, there was nothing at issue between them. It was all just a misunderstanding; people only thought that they were in dispute and once they'd formed both a proper appreciation of their own interest and a better understanding of the law, matters would be resolved. Once a party realised that there was nothing to lose and that its interests could be satisfied, it would settle or withdraw. It was a classic application of liberal faith in progress through the spreading of knowledge and reason.

There clearly was a great deal of initial confusion and uncertainty surrounding the NTA—difficult legislation to begin with that was made tougher in the comprehension by some wilful misinformation.[46] Reflecting back, French observed that from 'the first day of the Act, there was an overwhelming need to communicate as widely as possible with that part of the general community affected by native title issues' and, accordingly, the 'Tribunal became a major provider of information and education'.[47] The NNTT's community liaison policy was broad indeed and had a clearly instrumental purpose, with one of the principal objectives being to '[f]oster a positive understanding of the native title claims process and relevant interests' to 'engender a constructive approach to the mediation of claims'.[48] One of the 'performance indicators' of specific liaison campaigns in claim areas was said to be the 'ability of parties to participate in constructive mediation'.[49] Fresh information needs were identified each time there was a change in procedures, a new case handed down and obviously when there were amendments to the NTA. Indeed, as a way of explaining disputes, the notion of a knowledge shortfall never really went away, no matter how much explanatory material, education and liaison the Tribunal provided. The purported information deficit acted like Norman Lindsay's Magic Pudding: the flavour might change, but the bulk never diminished and the NNTT's communications and liaison plate always remained full. From the Tribunal's perspective, the idea of an abiding information deficit became one of the operative truths about the process.[50]

iii. The dispute as moral or spiritual deficit to be overcome as part of 'reconciliation'

The idea of a transcendental national 'journey' of redemption between Indigenous and non-Indigenous people was officially initiated in the 'reconciliation process' launched by the Hawke Labor government in 1991.[51] Given the redemptive narrative that was attached to *Mabo* and the rhetoric of justice in which the enactment of the NTA was ordained, it was perhaps inevitable that the procedure for resolving native title claims came to be understood as part of reconciliation. Tribunal member Sean Flood, for example, felt that *Mabo* had acted to 'show the way to a new respectful relationship between indigenous and non-indigenous Australians'.[52] French recalled the High Court's decision as generating 'existential discontinuity—when a choice is made which is life altering and seems to have little connection with what has gone before'.[53] Native title was interpreted as a vehicle of epiphany, capable of manifesting a kind of deep realisation to those who opened their hearts. The words 'reconciliation' and 'resolution' are, after all, close to synonymous, and idealised imaginings of the native title process, in which parties came together and talked openly and honestly about how to share land and waters before resolving their differences, looked very much like reconciliatory behaviour in practice.

Sometimes, coming to grips with native title was evoked as a complex and morally loaded affair requiring something in the nature of bearing witness. Flood claimed that through 'millions of words' and '[h]undreds of discussion groups across Australia', the nation was engaging in a 'journey of the spirit' through which 'we might receive forgiveness' and become 'reconciled with each other, old citizens and new'.[54] The 'dispute', then, became a matter of the transcendental, in which parties could either be implicitly lost or saved as part of a more expansive narrative of national redemption. As French told a major conference in late 1995:

> The events of the day, whether they be particular funding decisions or changes in the law, however, must be seen in an historical perspective. One way or another, indigenous peoples who have been agitating for recognition of their rightful place in Australian society and for social justice will continue to do so . . . There can be no restoration, but the repair of the damage is a task for all of us without which our whole society is flawed. It is a task which requires pragmatism and determination. We must find in ourselves the courage, the spirit, the ingenuity and the goodness to keep the process of reconciliation and this necessary repair of our society alive.[55]

Native title mediation was not only a matter of remedying gaps in technical knowledge, but also addressing a spiritual and moral challenge that surpassed the materialism of interacting legal interests. Indeed, the two could be brought together under a single educative rubric:

> The positive aspect of the process upon which the Tribunal has embarked, and on which wider Australia is launched as a result of native title and its recognition, is that . . . [it] . . . does provide an opportunity to educate and introduce people to a new way of looking at Aboriginal and Torres Strait Islander and wider Australian relationships.[56]

If *Mabo* had been a revelation, the personnel of the Tribunal saw themselves as the bringers of good news to friends. Having witnessed and understood, it became the role of the men and women of the NNTT to proselytise, banishing fear and prejudice and engendering the 'understanding' that mediation bore the truth and shone the way to salvation. Once the parties understood the path elaborated by the NTA and became conscious of their own and each other's real interests, native title might be resolved by common consent, liberating all from earthly conflict and contributing to the building of an Australian Jerusalem. Although the origins of the doctrine of native title were embedded in the solemn observance of the Dreaming, followed by the fall encapsulated in the immutable darkness of colonial dispossession, the NTA offered a path to reconciliation and redemption. Those who embraced what Flood intoned as the 'spirit of *Mabo*' and accepted the word of the NTA joined a community of the uplifted. The Tribunal's functional preoccupation with a perceived information deficit about statutory process became overlaid with a more evangelical concern about moral ignorance associated with a failure to 'accept' native title in a deeper sense.

iv. The dispute as a set of relationships requiring practical solutions 'on the ground'

The fourth way in which the Tribunal conceived of the 'dispute' was as a practical question arising from the social relationships between the parties. Whatever the law might say, the NNTT reasoned, in actuality people needed to share land. The neatness of the conceptualisation of the issues to be resolved as being more 'practical' than legal' was that it sidestepped both outstanding legal questions, as well as broader questions of politics and ideology. Indeed, it was argued, one of the great advantages of mediation over litigation was that the parties could themselves determine detailed arrangements to govern their 'relationships' into the future.[57] For example, in the case of pastoral leases, whether there was native title or not lessees still needed to work out how they would deal with Aboriginal people who possessed various other rights to come onto their property, even if they were no more than public rights of traverse. Chaney and French both addressed the problem of resolving the dispute between pastoralists and native title groups as consisting of a range of practical questions to be solved in their presentations to the *Wik* summit held in Cape York in 1997 to discuss ways ahead from the High Court's decision. The emphasis of Chaney's presentation was on 'practical solutions', whether issues had arisen 'because of native title or indeed because of the operation of state law'.[58] Similarly, French argued that 'whether it is native title or statutory access rights which are contemplated, there is a need for rules or codes of practice to regulate the management of the relationship between those rights and the rights of the pastoral lessee'.[59] Both men then talked of the need for greater information about the kind of practical solutions that had proven to be effective. The dispute, then, was really a question of how in real life the parties in question were going to get on with each other.[60]

The idea of native title disputes as being all about relationships had particular implications for how mediation should be conducted. The clear connotation was that matters could be sorted out with some good old earthy common sense if only there could be some plain and unadorned communication between those directly involved. The Tribunal's rhetoric tended to cast other actors in the native title system as being implicitly resistant to the special knowledge that direct communication could be helpful. Ultimately lawyers and peak bodies created unnecessary barriers to real people talking with each other about how to sort out practical issues—a kind of idealisation of the 'wisdom of folk'. Yet the Tribunal knew there would come the moment when the parties would realise the truth; that their differences were fundamentally about practical questions that could be resolved with the kind of good pragmatic sagacity that is legion in the Australian bush. If positions, ideology, politics, rights and tactical manoeuvring could all be put to one side, then, with the lawyers out of the room, the parties could push back their chairs, pour the tea, talk openly and work out how things should be between them in the future, in practice, 'on the ground'.

v. The dispute as a more than mere forensic inquiry

In addition to the positive ways in which the Tribunal conceived of the dispute, there was a negative possibility that the organisation attempted to limit and discount. The statute was clear that the end result of the claims process was meant to be a determination of fact and law as to who held any native title that might exist and how it interacted with the rights of others.[61] Curiously, given that the end result of the claims process was meant to be a declaration of the state of things, it might have been guessed that the optimal approach for resolving matters would be adjudicative or inquisitive; after all, '[m]ediation is a process not adapted to "proving" claims'.[62] In order for alternative dispute resolution to have any work to do, there would have to be something involved beyond an argument over facts and law. The difference between native title being declared after investigation or mechanistically constructed through compromise was fundamental. If there was not sufficient flexibility to permit negotiation and dialogue, allowing native title to be what the parties agreed, then the point of the process as it was seemed altogether uncertain.

As French noted, '[c]ourts offer principled answers to particular problems' while mediation plays an altogether different role.[63] The various ideas of the dispute elaborated by the Tribunal all clearly extended the ambit of native title mediation beyond what could be dealt with through an adjudicative process. Yet at no stage did anyone within the Tribunal discount the importance of knowing at least some facts; indeed, by fostering the concept of the connection report as described in Chapter 4, the NNTT actively promoted the notion that it was reasonable to expect some forensic presentation by the claimants in a mediation context. Some factual information could be helpful (and would eventually be needed to satisfy the Federal Court at the final point of a consent determination anyway, as described in Chapter 7), but to insist on searching for too much would necessarily make a mess of mediation and lose out on the benefits of the process. The result of the logic was necessarily hybrid; under the model pursued by the NNTT, native title was to be both found and made.

Resolving native title claims by agreement

In his opening address to the Tribunal's first public conference of stakeholders in December 1994, French acknowledged that 'entrenched prejudice and cynicism', as well as unresolved political legal issues 'affecting the extent to which native title survives', were formidable obstacles to be overcome.[64] As the chief organisational incarnation of the NTA, the new Tribunal was the direct target of considerable antipathy.[65] Nevertheless, the Tribunal steadfastly evinced confidence in the face of the storm. In an interview given one month after the NNTT's first formal effort at mediation in mid-1994, in relation to a claim over 180 hectares of commons with a mere handful of parties, French boldly forecast that matters of that kind might well be 'resolved one way or the other within two or three months'.[66] Throughout the early years, the Tribunal's talk remained focused on what could be possible with the right will. French argued in 1996 that

> If we wait for the courts to answer all the unresolved questions of extinguishment and the other legal issues related to the establishment of native title we will be waiting a long time. It will mean that opportunities for the resolution of native title claims may be missed.[67]

In the first years of the NTA's operation, and in the face of much obstinacy, the NNTT continued to argue that if the parties were satisfied within basic standards of reasonableness and accountability, there was no reason why agreements could not be reached, notwithstanding legal uncertainties. It was a brave attempt. The reality, however, was that the barriers to the consensual resolution of claims were insurmountable.[68] As described in earlier chapters, the state of the law was so fluid that hands were sat on and cards were played close to chests in the claims process, while parties contested the rules of the broader framework in the hope of improved positions. Then again, even if the law had been clearer, without a functioning statutory filter the sheer proliferation of overlapping claims in many areas meant that few would have progressed beyond interminable intra-Indigenous dialogue.[69]

In simple quantitative terms the results of native title mediation prior to the passage of the 1998 Amendments made for sobering reading, with only two actual consent determinations having been achieved.[70] The NNTT's *Annual Report 1997–1998* recorded a total of 227 documented agreements accumulated over the preceding four years which were hopefully branded as 'related' or 'leading to' future determinations of native title, with the overall agglomeration optimistically interpreted as evincing 'a developing culture of negotiation'.[71] Yet close inspection of the case studies emphasised in the *Annual Report* revealed the limited nature of what was being achieved. Among the 'highlights' of the 1997–98 financial year were the 'Quandamooka Process Agreement', which created a communications protocol accompanied by an unenforceable consultation arrangement about municipal administration, and the 'Beekeeping Associations Agreement Queensland/New South Wales', an unbinding memorandum for further talks between apiarists and native title claimants.[72] The boasts of the claims resolution process in the middle of 1998 were clearly modest. Gradually, though, as the structural impediments to resolving native title claims by agreement disappeared, the tally of consent determinations steadily began to climb. As discussed elsewhere in this book, the development of law and policy was not neutral in terms of its impact on the distribution of rights and power, but conditions within the native title system doubtlessly did become objectively more conducive to agreements being reached. The cumulative consequence was a clear trend upwards in the rate of resolving native title claims by consent.

The credibility gap

The growing number of agreements, including actual consent determinations, represented a striking evolution of the native title system. The overall total of five claims that had been resolved by common concurrence of all the parties by the end of 1999 had more than doubled to twelve by the end of 2000 and increased twofold again to a total of 24 by the end of 2002. The NNTT claimed that the long-anticipated take-off in numbers of consent determinations, as part of the growth of a wider 'culture of agreement-making', was a sign of the organisation's own success. In a 2002 submission, the Tribunal described the increasing willingness of parties to resolve matters by accord as the 'most precise indicator' of its own 'particular contributions and effectiveness'.[73] However, other actors were much less inclined to attribute the transformation of the native title landscape to the Tribunal. Rather, there was an increasing tendency to see the NNTT as irrelevant or out of touch.

In February 2002, the Parliamentary Joint Committee on Native Title and the Aboriginal and Torres Strait Islander Land Fund began an inquiry into the effectiveness of the National Native Title Tribunal.[74] The tone of the submissions made by various parties to the inquiry was not overwhelmingly negative (and as might be expected was largely positive in relation to the performance of the 'information and assistance' function), but responses to the Tribunal's efforts at conducting mediation were mixed and there was a distinct lack of enthusiasm about the NNTT's general 'effectiveness'.[75] Often, it seemed to the parties and bodies making submissions that the Tribunal was not helpful in progressing mediation or it displayed flawed situational analysis. Expressing the point with force, the Cape York Land Council submitted that if 'the flurries of activity, meeting tensions, and mounds of tracking documents' were stripped away, then it became starkly apparent that the 'NNTT ha[d] been unable to influence the operating environment'.[76] '[A]t times', the Cape York Land Council noted, 'the NNTT appear[ed] to over-estimate its own relevance to negotiations, resulting in overspending and inefficient use of resources'.[77]

The decline of trust in the Tribunal's capacity as a mediator was most starkly reflected in the mounting tendency of key parties to actively exclude the organisation from the process.[78] The Queensland Government regarded 'the manner in which the Tribunal ha[d] conducted the mediation of some matters' as not 'conducive to the resolution of the issues between the parties' and accordingly had begun selectively excluding the NNTT from meetings.[79] The same phenomenon occurred in Western Australia, where the view had developed that the 'absence of the NNTT from any process of negotiation was . . . not to be crucial to the process of reaching consensual agreements'.[80] Unlike earlier periods in the history of the NTA, when the anger of parties had been directed at the Tribunal in lieu of the native title schema as a whole, later resentment was not always directed at the system at large so much as at the NNTT in particular. Both the states of Queensland and Western Australia were demonstrably committed to the functioning of the NTA and to resolving native title claims by agreement, yet neither considered the Tribunal to be a particular asset to making progress. Senior NTRB lawyer Paul Hayes perhaps reflected the kind of frustrations that led to some parties trying to exclude the Tribunal in an excoriating article published in 2002. According to Hayes:

> All too often, NNTT mediations involve:
>
> - Sessions where an array of parties discuss what action they will take before the next mediation session;
> - The next mediation session involving the same parties discussing why they have not met any of their commitments;
> - A further flurry of commitments then being made for the next session which will be equally unfulfilled;

- The NNTT after each session circulating a reasonably content free report on the 'outcomes' of the last session; and
- An array of lawyers then billing their respective clients.[81]

Often, Hayes thought, meetings served 'no purpose other than to inform the NNTT of what is going on', indulgences which could be actively 'detrimental to the progress of negotiations'.[82]

Importantly, it was not just individual native title lawyers or rep bodies and state governments, but also industry peak bodies that viewed the effectiveness of the Tribunal with scepticism. In January 2007 the NFF opposed giving the Tribunal more power, noting that the organisation did 'not have a good track record in resolving mediation issues'.[83] The MCA was similarly cautious, citing productivity statistics as raising doubt over 'the issue of the NNTT's capacity in mediation of native title claims'.[84]

There were no doubt also strategic reasons why various parties were critical of the Tribunal at times. However, underlying any tactical rationales that were in play, it is possible to isolate some clear grounds for disquiet at the NNTT's claims and performance. The most obvious source of dissatisfaction was the drastic over-funding of the NNTT relative to the rep bodies, a radical disparity that was widely apprehended though not definitely conceded by the Tribunal itself.[85] NTRBs themselves perpetually protested the injustice of the allocations, while state governments and mining companies increasingly resented that they were making up for rep body shortfall through their own revenue while the Commonwealth continued to fatten the Tribunal. At times, the disparities were the stuff of parody. While the likes of the Kimberley Land Council were forced to retrench staff and sell assets to pay for litigation, the Tribunal promoted the achievements of native title by issuing a range of commemorative glossy bookmarks.

However, the widespread dissatisfaction with the NNTT was not only a product of inequitable funding arrangements. More broadly, a profound credibility gap had emerged between the official pronouncements from the Tribunal about itself and the native title process at large and the perceptions held within other organisations about what was going on. For example, by 2002 the Tribunal was describing the claims resolution enterprise as 'cross-cultural, multi-party mediation in relation to areas of land or waters, using a primarily interest-based model in a rights based context',[86] which differed in important respects from the connection report-based bilateral settlement negotiations predominantly between states and claim groups leading to determinations of rights that had come to dominate the system. Significantly, the 1998 Amendments had substituted the original version's vague and general references with an explicit reference to the Tribunal conducting 'mediation' for the 'purpose' of assisting 'the parties to reach agreement' on 'whether native title exists or existed' and how it interrelated with other interests, though under other sections of the Act it was permissible for broader matters to be brought in with the agreement of the parties.[87] On the face of it, though, the new clarity given to the meaning of the dispute seemed to make clear that what was at issue was, above all, forensic: the dispute was as to whether native title existed or not.

Despite the fact that the process that it imagined scarcely existed, the Tribunal continued to evince an ongoing preoccupation with mediation design. In 2002 one member of the Tribunal, Geoff Clark (not the same person as the ATSIC Chair Geoff Clark), described his 'single most significant contribution to the overall mediation process' as being 'to design an appropriate "space" within which persons with different landscapes can feel confident and secure'.[88] It was like a defeated general moving a fantasy army over a map. Similar make-believe attended the Tribunal's ongoing imagining of the parties in curiously idealised anthropomorphic and naive terms. Many, perhaps most, respondent parties were not humans but abstractions, including corporations and state parties. Yet the Tribunal persistently cast the process as one revolving around individual people. According to Clark, each of the parties would bring to the mediation a set of values and standards that would differ as a result of their upbringing, experience, perception and social mores, informing their comprehension of and willingness to partake in the mediation process.[89] In the same paper, Clark argued that mediation offered the parties 'an opportunity to express their individual perspective on the dispute'. Mediation could be, speculated Clark:

> the first opportunity that a party has had to express to the other party how the conflict has affected them and how they feel about the situation. Storytelling can be cathartic because it allows an opportunity to vent frustration, express concerns [and] release stress. Extreme emotions are often expressed in storytelling.[90]

The kind of dynamic described by Clark is simply inapplicable to corporations and state actors and even problematic in relation to native title claim groups. Clearly, a group cannot have an 'upbringing' and is likely to experience a varying set of values and perceptions, given differences between individual lives. Neither was each mediation, as some within the Tribunal seemed to imagine, a *tabula rasa* of angry innocents, but most often an exchange between professional representatives from a small number of readily identifiable sectors whose interests were largely structurally pre-determined.

The Tribunal successfully fights back

The NNTT had always engaged in some self-promotion, but the nature of the exercise changed significantly with context. In the period of volatility between the passage of the NTA and the 1998 Amendments, when the future of native title seemed far from secure, defence of the Tribunal was almost one and the same exercise as defending both the doctrine and the legislation. However, once the NTA had begun to garner widespread acceptance and constructive participation, the functioning of the Tribunal's image management took on an altogether different character. The NNTT responded to the credibility gap engulfing its performance by forcefully touting the organisation's usefulness. In the course of the parliamentary inquiry into the NNTT's effectiveness, the organisation energetically defended itself.[91] The Tribunal had begun spending considerable resources on sampling 'clients' on how well it was doing and the poll results provided a significant plank in its self-promotion. In 2002 the Tribunal paid $99,990 to a consultancy firm to undertake a 'client satisfaction survey' and, as Neate was proud to tell an audience in Singapore in November 2003, '[o]verall the survey showed that 65% of those surveyed were satisfied or extremely satisfied'.[92] In 2007, one of the chief components of the Tribunal's claims to efficacy was again that market research had

> shown generally high levels of satisfaction . . . in all cases the majority of people surveyed found the Tribunal had met or exceeded their expectations for each criterion. Mediations were seen in the main to be conducted fairly and to be effective in delivering an outcome.[93]

More subtle than peddling survey results was a range of impressive public communications that the Tribunal published in which the organisation featured in a starring role. Following the earlier audio-productions *Yarning about Native Title* and its sequel *Yarning about Indigenous Land Use Agreements*, in 2002 the NNTT released its first film, entitled *Native Title Stories: Rights, Recognition, Relationships*, narrated off-screen by the Aboriginal actress Ningali Lawford. The movie depicted a number of case-study disputes described by representatives of some of the major participants. In each of the settlements portrayed in the show, it was heavily implied that the Tribunal had played a key role in ensuring that agreements were reached.[94] The same implication—that the NNTT played a decisive role in deals being made—could be drawn from the multitude of press statements that the NNTT released over the years, narrating the story of agreement-making in the organisation's carefully developed patois. After reporting what it wished of the parties' own statements (which may have been drafted with the assistance of the NNTT's communications team), the Tribunal could then editorialise about the importance of agreement-making and the nature of its own role. These media releases, though no doubt intended to spin out 'top lines', were also honestly reflective of the Tribunal's corporate view: that every agreement achieved was indicative of the organisation's success, regardless of its actual operational involvement.

The outward buoyancy and promotional efforts of the Tribunal were not simply a matter of being Panglossian. In light of the increasing marginality of the NNTT's role, image management had become more vital, both as a way of enabling the organisation to defend its existence and effectiveness, and to secure a disproportionate share of the available funding from the Commonwealth. Faced with a credibility gap in real terms, the Tribunal determined to present a plausible artifice: a mythologised version of the native title claims process featuring the NNTT 'ready, willing and able' at the centre of interest-based mediation.[95] Understanding that the Tribunal had become preoccupied with self-preservation helps to explain the particular idiom that came to dominate its public representations. Tightly drafted bureaucratic summaries were accompanied by a pastiche of feel-good sentiment and folksy expressions such as 'yarning about native title', which might not evoke many people's lived experience of the system but with which it was hard for anyone to really disagree.[96]

The Tribunal's fight-back was remarkably successful. Not only did the organisation retain extraordinary levels of funding, the report of the 2003 parliamentary committee into the organisation's effectiveness ended up being blandly complimentary. More remarkably still, following a further review of the functioning of the statutory machinery in the 2007 Amendments to the NTA, the Commonwealth legislated to actually increase the powers of the Tribunal, in part at the expense of the Federal Court. The shift in functions is discussed further in Chapter 7. In political terms, the NNTT had successfully iterated the organisation's functioning in terms appealing enough to the Howard government to be rewarded with expanded authority. Treating native title groups as simply one of a range of 'clients' to whom the Tribunal provided services (which was, for instance, how the methodology of the 'client satisfaction survey' operated, putting native title holders at the same level as any other party) was no doubt quite in keeping with prevailing government ideology and policy formations. In increasing the Tribunal's powers at the expense of the Federal Court the government had ignored a wide range of views, including those of the rep bodies and native title services, the MCA, some states and the Federal Court. The Howard government's rewarding of the Tribunal also stood in considerable contrast with its harsher treatment of numerous other organisations, including in a native title context, ATSIC, the rep bodies, the Human Rights and Equal Opportunities Commission and even the Federal Court itself.

Native title stories

The metaphor of 'poets and slaves' in the title of this chapter is meant as an evocation of the contrast within the Tribunal between those who advocated broad visions and others who understood their role in more constrained terms, serving the interests of the organisation in implementing a particular policy conception of the statute. The poets were not legal radicals in favour of activist law-making; indeed, contributing to their dreams of an expansive program of regional settlements based on substantive justice was positivist acceptance that doctrine has limitations. The mindset was exemplified in one of French's early judgments when, after ruling against the interests of Aboriginal claimants, he provided a short postscript to the judgment that lamented the 'significant moral shortcoming in the principles by which native title is recognized'.[97] The alternative, encapsulated in the fundamental argument made by French and others in the early years of the Tribunal's operation, was that agreement-making could genuinely substitute for the kind of legal and political conflict over native title that was so characteristic of the period before the 1998 Amendments were enacted. Counter-factualism can be anodyne, but there was a chance in those early years that something approaching interest-based, open-ended dispute resolution might just have come into being had the trajectory of Australian cultural and political life been other than that which transpired. The visionaries of the Tribunal had not been wrong at the time, but were wrong-footed by the course of history. What seemed possible, or even the prevailing tendency, after *Mabo* in Paul Keating's Australia was left floundering by the 'long 1998'.

The route proscribed by the poets was not followed by any of the principal actors; instead, stalemate ensued until the late 1990s. When agreement-making did begin to take off within the claims process it was not 'mediation' in any meaningful sense, because the procedures that developed were more in the nature of a cooperative inquiry into the actual state of facts and law, to be settled by court adjudication if common understanding could not be reached. The chasm between the way the native title process was rendered and what actually ensued left the Tribunal's various conceptions of the dispute, as described earlier in this chapter, floundering in irony. As time wore on and the opportunities of the early years became temporally and discursively ever more distant, buried under newer dominating political motifs, the moral iteration of the NTA by the Tribunal took on a different character. The system had been proven to be profane rather than sacred, narrow not broad and marked more by an ethic of commoditisation than deliverance, through agreements steeped more in mammon than any god. A willingness on the part of the Tribunal to interpret Indigenous participation in statutory processes beyond their formal meaning, once enlivened by emancipative ideals, became a device apt for exculpation. The 'spirit of *Mabo*' remained, but had come to function as a legitimating justification for an organisation which was now regarded with resigned disappointment and frustration in the Indigenous sector.

The poetic fluidity of native title did not survive '1998' but some of the verbiage did, albeit in increasingly stylised form, becoming progressively more empty. When reading the Tribunal, it is critical to appreciate the nuances of context. In their own mouths the language and imaginings of the poets was one thing; but when reiterated later or standardised as part of image management by a bureaucracy, it was quite another: visceral engagement with one of the great issues of the day became reduced to the routine utterance of cloying sentiment. When deployed to justify the maintenance and increase of statutory powers and budget share for a Commonwealth agency of doubtful utility, the 'spirit of *Mabo*' had become reduced to little more than the legitimising ideology of a particular form of path dependency.[98] Rhetorically, conceptually and operationally, the Tribunal's approach to the claims resolution process had come to lack basic credibility in the eyes of the principal parties. The poets had mostly long gone, replaced with a well-meaning slavishness that rarely entailed looking up from the careful operation of a machine that had taken on its own purpose.

As it turned out, the native title claims process had not provided the catalytic effect for achieving 'substantial justice' as hoped and advocated by French and others. The disjunction dashed anticipations and exposed the Tribunal's early ambitions as starkly unfulfilled. In their submission to the inquiry on the Tribunal's effectiveness, the Cape York Land Council gave voice to the disparity:

> But where are the just agreements? Where are the fair outcomes? Nothing.[99]

Significantly, even some Tribunal members began to publicly lament the failures of the mediation process.[100] Fred Chaney, one of the last of the Tribunal's poets, noted in 2004 that all of the consent determinations achieved to that date were 'limited in their scope' and had 'not amounted to broad political settlements based on an assessment of what might be a desirable outcome balancing Aboriginal and non-Aboriginal interests . . . aiming at the social and economic integration of the disparate communities'.[101] The radical asymmetry was abundantly clear. The ambit of the dispute, it had turned out, was actually narrower than the broadeners at the Tribunal had once believed; the stream of the claims resolution process lacked the propulsion to rise above its source.

7

YOU CAN TAKE THE JUDGE OUT OF THE COURT . . .

The Federal Court of Australia

Going to court

It was judges, not politicians, who decided that native title existed in Australia. Among settler societies, Australia is an anomaly in relying on the judiciary to act as the principal 'recognition agent' of Indigenous polities on behalf of the state.[1] That it was the High Court's decision in *Mabo (2)* that created the political and legal fact of the doctrine of native title in Australia gave rise to a cultural impression that the judiciary was the guardian of Indigenous rights against governments that had failed to recognise traditional property interests in the past and may well try to extinguish them in the future. When the High Court quashed the State of Western Australia's attempts to wipe out native title and held that pastoral leases did not have an extinguishing effect, the perception was underlined. Under the NTA, the judiciary were cast as sentinels of the overall process given the responsibility for issuing the final determination as to whether native title existed and for exercising oversight of the NNTT. Although the schema of the NTA allocated much of the work to other actors, from the outset the legislation confirmed that the formal act of acknowledging the existence of native title belonged to the judges.

The Federal Court of Australia is a superior judicial body established under Chapter III of the Constitution, with general jurisdiction over civil matters arising under Commonwealth law.[2] Established by the eponymous Commonwealth *Federal Court of Australia Act 1976*, the new institution began operation on 1 February 1977.[3] At its inception the Federal Court had twenty members and a fairly narrow jurisdiction, evolving, by the year 2000, to a court with 50 judges exercising power under 125 different statutes.[4] Appeals from a decision of a single justice of the Federal Court are made to a full bench of three judges and from there to the High Court of Australia. The addition of the native title jurisdiction to the Federal Court created considerable and unusual challenges for the administration of justice; as one judge put it with typical curial understatement, land claims are 'not conventional civil proceedings'.[5] In order to prove a native title claim, it is necessary to give compelling evidence of the internal functioning of a society as well as demonstrating around 200 years of socio-historical continuity, generally requiring testimony from numerous Aboriginal witnesses as well as anthropologists and historians, possibly accompanied by archaeologists, linguists and experts from other more arcane disciplines. The scale and complexity of native title litigation was brought home by *Yorta Yorta* and *Ward*: in the former, the Court sat for 114 days and heard 201 witnesses, while the latter took less time, coming in at 83 days, but also with large numbers of people giving testimony and often in the challenging terrain of the far north of Australia.[6]

The changing role of the Court

Under the original NTA, although the Court was required to make the final orders giving force to any consent determination that was reached, the Tribunal held responsibility for the overall management of the claims process. Being 'referred' to the Federal Court was a fate to occasion apprehension, which parties were strenuously encouraged to avoid where possible. Against the preferred option of mediation under the auspices of the Tribunal, litigation was conceived in an inherently negative light as an expensive, time-consuming, inflexible and impractical option of last resort for applications that had 'failed' to be resolved through mediation. In the event, only three claims were determined by the Federal Court in the period between 1994 and 1998. As early as 1995, French pointed out that the NTA placed 'the NNTT and the Court end to end in an inflexible "series" arrangement' and suggested amendments to the Act, allowing for a more supple relationship between the bodies.[7] The 1998 Amendments largely took up French's suggestions, and 'effectively transferred the overall management of native title cases from the NNTT to the Federal Court'.[8] All new claims were also to be filed with the Court, to then refer across to the NNTT for registration testing and mediation, while retaining judicial oversight. Parties could, in theory, now be engaged in interlocutory litigation on particular issues of law or fact while still continuing with mediation. The statutory redesign of institutional responsibilities made the Court a 'driver' of the native title process with significant instrumental power to 'propel claims down critical paths'.[9] The Court even possessed the power to order its own mediation of native title matters as an alternative or in addition to that conducted by the Tribunal, at least until the further Amendments described at the end of this chapter.

In addition to substantially increasing the Court's workload, the expanded native title jurisdiction also posed an unusual challenge in terms of judicial administration. The common law legal system proceeds on the general basis that actions are discrete from one another. However, in the context of native title, not having regard to regional, state and national linkages and considerations would have led to the complete dysfunction of the system; not only did many native title claims partially or wholly overlap one another geographically, but parties, peak bodies, lawyers, expert witnesses and crucial issues recurred across cases within an overall context of a limited pool of resources. In recognition of the peculiar interconnectedness of the native title jurisdiction, the Court established a number of mechanisms for considering the conduct of claims on a collective basis. In the course of the 1997–98 financial year, Chief Justice Michael Black directed the establishment of a 'Native Title Coordination Committee' to assist with the administration of the Court's newly expanded jurisdiction.[10] Later, the Court established national, state and territory 'User Groups' to 'explain its procedures to the people who use the Court; and to allow the users to explain to the Court their requirements and the extent to which the procedures can be modified to work better'.[11] Early in the new millennium, the Court also initiated a practice of conducting regional case management conferences 'to hear from applicants and respondent parties on a range of matters, including the strategic listing of matters, the prioritising of cases, and the role of mediation', which allowed 'parties to re-define their priorities on a regional, rather than on a case-by-case, basis'.[12]

When the Amendments came into effect on 30 September 1998, the 58 claims that had already been referred to the Court were joined by another 778 native title determination applications.[13] The transfer required a considerable effort of judicial administration as the Court brought order to applications that had often been drafted rather lazily under the loose terms of the unamended NTA. The Court had to organise matters into appropriately configured directions hearings, as well as dealing with the numerous parties to claims. In order to meet the exacting standards of Federal Court proceedings, all claim documentation required substantial redrafting and supplementation with affidavits and other materials. The Court organised the new work by introducing 'a national allocation protocol for the case management and listing of native title matters', under which each claimant application was assigned to a 'Provisional Docket Judge' who, with the assistance of a Deputy Registrar, would be 'responsible for managing the case' unless and until 'substantive action' was required, such as the hearing of a contested interlocutory application or a 'main hearing', at which point the matter would be 'referred to the Court's Native Title Secretariat for substantive allocation to a trial judge'.[14] The initial appearances before the Court sometimes tended towards the chaotic, as parties that were more used to the lackadaisical approach of the Tribunal administering the unamended NTA became exposed to judicial dispensation. Gradually, the bedlam was reduced to an orderly process and the parties adjusted to the new formalities.

The need for speed

It was hoped and anticipated that the changes to the native title system brought in by the 1998 Amendments would increase the speed with which claims were resolved. In general, the Federal Court prided itself on the expeditious determination of matters brought before it and had adopted case-flow management principles as a way of guiding the timely administration of the judicial workload. The intention behind case-flow management is that 'courts take over from lawyers much of the responsibility for controlling the course taken by litigation' so as to avoid the kind of Jarndycean saga that drags on interminably.[15] The adoption of managerial principles by a court is explicitly intended to influence the conduct of both judges and parties, by setting out a clear standard of 'best practice'. The prevention of delay and the general reduction in the length of litigation is one of the fundamental aims of a more managerial approach to judicial administration. One of the 'key case-flow management principles' adopted by the Federal Court was 'the establishment of a time goal' within which cases would be disposed, necessitating 'the implementation of practice and procedure' designed to achieve the specified disposition rate.[16] The Court adopted the laudable aim of having 98 per cent of cases concluded within eighteen months of commencement.

The Federal Court recognised that a 'key factor' in keeping to the eighteen-month 'disposal rate' was 'the mix of cases', because 'some matters, such as bankruptcy proceedings, were innately faster to deal with than others'.[17] The acquisition of the native title jurisdiction was quickly identified as a hazard to maintaining the average pace at which matters were being concluded. In the course of the 1999–2000 financial year, the Court expressly recognised that the resolution of native title claims could be expected to be unusually lengthy and adopted 'a time goal of three years from commencement' for the completion of both pending and new matters: double the period allowed for 'normal' litigation.[18] The Court's own calculations for 1999–2000 indicated that the 'average time span from filing to disposition for native title matters determined by consent' was '3 years and 5 months' and 'for matters determined by a trial judge' the less precise '4 to 5 years'.[19] Nevertheless, it was believed that the 'time goal of three years from filing to disposition of native title matters' would be achieved 'through the active case management of matters, and the implementation and refinement' of various related initiatives.[20] As Graeme Neate observed, the Court would 'not allow parties to delay indefinitely'.[21]

It goes without question that the Federal Court intended the time goal of three years to operate neutrally, not favouring any one party over another.[22] Intuitively, it might be thought that the more swiftly claims were determined, the more 'just' the process would be for Indigenous people who had waited so long for the doctrine of native title to be recognised at all. ATSIC, for example, was fond of lamenting that justice delayed was justice denied.[23] Ironically, though, because of the operation of the future act system, the procedural rights of native title claimants are in most cases stronger before their application has been determined. In one sense, then, the longer that the process of determining a claim takes the better it is for the claimants. In contrast, though respondents may be relieved of procedural obligations if a claim is dismissed, their existing interests are not devalued as a consequence of an application remaining on foot. As barrister Susan Phillips said in 2001:

> It must be born in mind that future act procedures and non-claimant applications as well as compulsory acquisition procedures allow non-Indigenous parties to acquire new interests or change uses without native title causing undue delay. The claims themselves do not create a prejudice to any interests with which they at best co-exist.[24]

The adoption of a three-year time goal, although formally neutral in effect and intended to be fair, did not affect all parties equally.[25]

Each year after the time goal was adopted, the Court's *Annual Report* noted the various 'initiatives' that had been tried in a bid to see native title claims determined in accordance with the targeted disposition rate. Some mechanisms, such as the use of videoconferencing and the timetabling of related matters for directions on the same day, were easy and obvious timesavers.[26] At times the Court's desire to be seen as proactive in trying to encourage swiftness seems to have led to just a touch of administrative overstatement. In 1999–2000, for example, the Court asserted that the 'combining of applications' as an initiative of its own, notwithstanding that the combination of native title claims was, from 1998, specifically provided for in the NTA and could only occur on the applicants' motion.[27] Similarly, in its 2000–01 *Annual Report*, the Court claimed that '[a]ctive judicial case management of native title cases' had 'led to a substantial number of claimant applications being amended, combined, withdrawn or discontinued', a relationship of cause and effect that seems again overestimated, given that it was the force of the new registration testing regime under the amended NTA that was far more likely to have produced the result in question.[28] On other occasions, the Court's 'initiatives' appear little more than dressing ordinary professional conduct in the brogue of managerialism. The 'use of extensive consultations and information sharing', for instance, sounds suspiciously like a gilded description of the act of ordinary professional engagement.[29]

Co-existent with 'doing better justice' as a reason for resolving litigation more quickly were certain efficiency imperatives that followed the Court's adoption of an outcome and output accounting structure in accordance with accrual budgeting arrangements. Beginning in 1998–99, the Court's 'management of cases and deciding disputes according to law' was characterised as 'Output Group 1' in end-of-year accounting.[30] Key performance information about 'Output Group 1' included the number of 'cases disposed' and the average cost of disposition.[31] In order for the Court to demonstrate organisational effectiveness, the 'price' of 'cases disposed' would need to be reasonable and, presumably, in order to demonstrate improvements in efficiency, the average cost of determining matters would need to decrease year by year. The complexities of the native title jurisdiction were a threat because a few long native title cases could significantly raise the average unit cost of determining cases, making the Court appear as if it was becoming less productive. Speed, then, had become an end in itself, a proposition borne out by the Court's claim in 2000–01 that one of the benefits of the three-year target was that it acted 'to attribute responsibility to those who can contribute to, not only the resolution of the [native title] matter, but the achievement of the time goal'.[32] Ideas of justice had become at least to some extent conditioned by the ideology of productivity.

When, by the close of 2000–01, there was yet to be a single claim resolved by substantive determination at the Court's nominated disposition rate,[33] the Native Title Coordination Committee still defended the three-year disposition target 'as a reasonable working estimate' but was forced to concede that 'a number of practical limits' were likely to get in the way of 'achieving the goal', even if only 'in the short-term'.[34] In August 2001, the Federal Court remained 'optimistic that the publication of a time goal' would 'focus the minds of Government, applicants and others on the need to resolve native title matters within a time frame that will be acceptable to their respective constituency and related stakeholders'.[35] However, shortly afterwards and following a meeting of the National User Group in October 2001, the Court's Native Title Coordination Committee commenced a further review of the disposition target, noting that there were 'strong contrary views on the three-year disposition target, with some parties and interest holders believing it is too short and others believing it to be too long'.[36] By the end of the 2001–02 financial year the Committee was 'still considering the issue', but maintained the view that it was 'desirable to keep a national target' even if 'noting that this may be varied at a regional level in light of information provided by relevant user groups or case conferences'.[37] Stubbornly, the average disposition rate was refusing to move.

The Court's preoccupation with time targets was viewed with considerable apprehension by the NTRBs in particular. Although it was stressed on the part of the Court that it was 'not the intention to place unreasonable pressure upon the applicants and parties', the rep bodies experienced genuine anxiety about the possible operational impact of an enforced disposition schedule.[38] In the absence of any increase in the level of funding, the Court's emphasis could well achieve what the Kimberley Land Council's Peter Yu called 'extinguishment by stealth' if matters were pressed to trial without the time or resources for proper preparation.[39] Although the reality of rep body under-funding was publicly recognised by more than one judge, communicating with the Court about concerns in relation to the disposition rate required delicacy; after all, it would be improper to try to influence how specific matters were dealt with outside of curial processes.[40] In the event, the various forums for dialogue that had been established by the Court were used extensively to try and convey the extent of the under-funding and the strategic complexity in a respectful and open manner. In addition, ATSIC had facilitated representations to the Court by instructing a firm of solicitors to engage a leading senior counsel to write directly to the Chief Justice.[41]

In practice, the Federal Court bench did not rigidly apply the three-year time target and individual judges often exercised considerable tolerance of delay.[42] In an interlocutory matter decided in 2001 Justice Paul Finn gave curial expression to the importance of restraint, emphasising that 'the public interest in the early and expeditious resolution of disputes' was 'not necessarily secured by an inflexible adherence to the particular case management procedures (by way of timetabling and otherwise) that had been put in place to bring about the resolution of a dispute in a given case'.[43] On other occasions, though, and perhaps influenced by what was regarded as the 'reasonable' disposition rate, individual judges lost patience with the pace of mediation and referred claims for substantive hearing or refused further applications for adjournment or the vacation of trial dates.[44] However, making any overall assessment is difficult, because in the end the onus is on individual parties to provide adequate reasons for adjournments, supported by appropriate affidavit evidence. Indeed, given particularly the overall strains on the representation on offer, based on an assessment of the general trend, it seems likely that individual judges largely exercised an abundance of caution to ensure that injustices were not done.

In August 2002, a meeting of judges concluded that the three-year time goal for the disposition of native title matters should henceforth be treated as no more than 'a desirable objective for the time elapsed between substantive allocation and final determination, subject to factors beyond the control of the Court including resource limitations of the parties and related to the need to establish regional priorities for mediation and litigation of applications'.[45] More frankly, in June 2003, Chief Registrar Warwick Soden made a point of telling a conference that the Court had 'hear[d] the criticism that its procedures may lead to the extinguishment of native title', censure which was 'a concern to many'. The Chief Registrar then went on:

> Indeed our time goal was seen as contributing to this imperative. Whereas the Court's intention was to attempt to progress cases within a reasonable timeframe having regard to the expectations of the native title applicants . . . the Court has substantially amended its time goal in response, in part, to this concern.[46]

Eventually the language of the Court mellowed considerably, referring to 'an appropriate balance between the litigation process, the scheme of the NTA and the resource demands placed upon applicants and others'[47] and emphasising the importance of 'transparent processes for prioritising native title matters in each state, territory and region' in line with 'general acceptance of the need for a more systematic approach to ensuring appropriately resourced native title claims can be progressed to trial or consent determination in a timely manner'.[48] Meanwhile, the question of maintaining the Court's overall disposition rates had been resolved in another manner: native title claims were simply excluded from the general productivity figures.[49]

Adapting to the work

The unamended NTA directed the Federal Court to be 'fair, just, economical, informal and prompt' in hearing native title matters, as well as to 'take account of the cultural and customary concerns' of Indigenous people.[50] The Act in its original form also relieved the Court of the obligation to comply with 'technicalities, legal forms' and 'rules of evidence' in determining native title claims.[51] In addition to directions made under certain inherent powers, the Federal Court is permitted to issue general rules by agreement of a majority of the judges.[52] The Court produced a variety of new rules to deal specifically with native title proceedings, which were eventually consolidated in June 1997 as well as being subject to later addition and alteration.[53] Importantly, the Amendments changed the way the Court was to handle the evidentiary process in native title claims. After 1998 the Court was bound by the rules of evidence, except to the extent specifically ordered otherwise.[54] Taking into account the cultural and customary concerns of Indigenous peoples was now only discretionary and was not permitted if it would have the effect of prejudicing any other party to the proceedings.[55]

In order to facilitate the hearing of native title claims in accordance with statutory directives, the Court developed a variety of novel practices and procedures.[56] The hearing of claimant evidence often occurred in situ on the land subject to claim in the vicinity of particular sites or areas of significance. As Chief Justice Black explained, the practice of 'on country' hearings constituted

> a recognition that, for many claimants, their relationship to country is not able to be explained in the abstract, and that it is necessary to be on country to gain a true appreciation and understanding of that relationship and the claimants' evidence about it.[57]

Witnesses were sometimes permitted to give evidence in groups[58] and culturally restricted information might be provided under the cover of orders restricting access on the basis of gender or traditional propriety.[59] The Court might also observe the use of basic Aboriginal cultural protocols, including the avoidance of using certain words or the names of the deceased.[60] Nevertheless, there were limits to what was allowed and modification of the ordinary way of doing judicial work could not be assumed: applications for exceptional orders still had to be made by counsel for the applicants, usually supported with affidavit evidence.[61]

Where necessary, interpreters could be called upon to assist with translating the language of witnesses. Even when interpreters were not used appearances could be deceiving, as one judge observed:

> The ability of an Aboriginal person, who was born in the Outback and who has lived and worked in the Outback all of his or her life, to comprehend questions that are presented in English has to be assessed with care. Even though a witness might speak English with an apparent degree of fluency there are competing factors which could affect the accuracy of the answer of a witness if he or she were required to answer in English. In the first place, there is the problem of comprehension: does the witness truly understand the questions that have been asked, particularly those that are couched in idiomatic

> English or those that are couched in terms that are not restricted to plain every day words? The second great area of concern is the witness' ability to think in English in order to answer accurately in English.[62]

In addition to difficulties associated with language and culture, Indigenous witnesses were also statistically more likely to suffer from ill health or infirmity, while the necessary emphasis on giving evidence of the content of law and tradition meant that testimony was often given by the very elderly.

Aside from the formal practices and procedures adopted by the Federal Court to handle native title claims, judges and registry staff were not immune to the general trend to cross-cultural education. In 1995 the Federal Court was reported to be 'developing an Aboriginal awareness program for registry staff and, in due course, for judges',[63] while the Australian Institute of Judicial Administration (AIJA) conducted an 'Aboriginal Cultural Awareness Seminar for the Supreme Court of Queensland and Federal Court', which was held in April of the same year in Brisbane, one of eleven such programs for various sections of the Australian judiciary (not all involving the Federal Court) that were conducted by the AIJA between the handing down of *Mabo* and the end of 1997.[64] In addition to formalised 'judicial education' programs and the cross-cultural training of registry staff, occasionally judges and Federal Court attended broader events with an emphasis on Indigenous sensibilities.[65]

The Court's flexibility in dealing with native title matters was facilitated by a significant investment in infrastructure. According to the teaser for a promotional video released in 2004, '[i]n the mid-1990s, faced with tighter budgets, outdated technology and procedures that desperately required an overhaul, the Federal Court of Australia critically re-evaluated its priorities' and embarked on operational changes 'to achieve its objective of becoming and being recognized within Australia and internationally as a world leading superior court'.[66] It is not unfair to observe that the acquisition of the native title jurisdiction assisted the Court in achieving some of its own institutional aims. According to Chief Justice Black the logistical requirements were 'enormous', because 'providing the same standards for a hearing when on country as in the capital cities' necessarily relied on 'advanced technology', including 'military style' laptops that were 'dust, moisture and shock proof' and networked through 'a desert intranet', 'world first' daylight data projection and the short-range radio transmission of proceedings.[67] Technological innovation was not confined to proceedings on country. In the course of the 2000–01 financial year, the Court developed an 'information kiosk, being a stand-alone touch screen interactive system' using 'text, images, videos and a voiceover to explain the role of the Court in particular areas of law'.[68] The Court also invested heavily in videoconferencing and other facilities.[69]

The significance of the measures taken by the Court attempting to ameliorate the difficulties for claimants giving evidence in native title proceedings should not be underestimated. In the context of Australian judicial administration, the practice directions and rules the Court established for native title hearings were 'revolutionary'. As Chief Justice Black told an Aboriginal festival in August 2001, the mere 'acknowledgement that the Court ought to hear from the claimants on their land' reflected 'a large shift' because previously 'it was very rare for judges to hear cases away from the familiar environment of their courtrooms'. In the past, it would have 'been unthinkable for judges to sit in the desert under trees or in tents for 4–6 weeks at a time to hear evidence, with limited facilities and very few formalities'.[70] Nevertheless, while the adaptation of the Court's procedures was remarkable, it is important to recognise the limits of the reforms. A court cannot stop being judicial in nature: the modified practices and procedures were designed to achieve a measure of fairness and informality, not to ensure that the claimants always won. Justice Anthony North pointed out at a conference in 2000 that while the Federal Court could 'be proud of its achievements', he nonetheless recognised that 'the management of cases [was] very much a secondary concern for native title claimants' whose 'primary interest is in achieving a favourable result in their cause'.[71]

The function of the Court

In 1992, the interpretation of the courts as the protectors of Indigenous rights was near axiomatic, given that at that stage native title in Australia consisted solely of the jurisprudence of *Mabo*. It was not simply the result, but the vivid and dramatic language of some members of the Court that invited more expansive iterations of the meaning of the judgment. In one of the most often quoted passages, Justices Deane and Gaudron said that a 'conflagration of oppression and conflict' had 'spread across the continent to dispossess, degrade and devastate the Aboriginal peoples', leaving 'a national legacy of unutterable shame'.[72] In the lead judgment Justice Brennan, with whom Chief Justice Mason and Justice McHugh agreed, said that it was 'imperative in today's world that the common law should neither be nor seen to be frozen in an age of racial discrimination'.[73] Interpreting the judiciary as the emancipators of the Aborigines in the mid-1990s was also linked to wider trends, including the recognition of implied rights within the Commonwealth Constitution[74] and accepting that international obligations played a role in the interpretation of domestic law.[75] Between 1992 and 1998, the courts so consistently went the way of the Indigenous litigants, particularly on appeal, that any incongruity between the interests of Aboriginal People and Torres Strait Islanders and the role of the judiciary went largely unexposed. However, in December 1998 the decision at first instance in the *Yorta Yorta* case shattered the fiction that it was the function of the judiciary within the native title system to emancipate Indigenous peoples.

Yorta Yorta, the first native title claim to be heard by the Federal Court under the NTA, was made over land and waters in New South Wales and Victoria. Justice Howard Olney, who decided the case, determined that there was no native title in existence on the basis that documentary evidence showed that, as long ago as the 1880s, the native title of the Yorta Yorta people had been 'washed away by the tide of history'.[76] In two crucial passages, Olney stated that:

> It is unnecessary to comment further upon the mechanisms of determination adopted by the Court in order to fulfil its statutory obligations. However, it is appropriate to observe that the special procedures that were previously ordained by s 82 do not authorise the Court to depart from two basic principles of litigation in this Court namely that the standard of proof is on the balance of probabilities and that the Court

> will have regard only to evidence which is relevant, probative and cogent. In particular, pure speculation, of which there has been much, must be disregarded. Nor is there any warrant within the NTA for the Court to play the role of social engineer, righting the wrongs of past centuries and dispensing justice according to contemporary notions of political correctness rather than according to law.
>
> . . . The oral evidence of many of the applicants' witnesses was in some respects both credible and compelling. This was particularly so with the more senior members of the applicant group. Regrettably, this was not always so. In one instance two senior members of the claimant group were caught out telling deliberate lies, albeit about a relatively minor matter, but nevertheless incidents of that nature tend to cast a shadow over the other evidence of those witnesses. The testimony of some of the younger members of the claimant group was less impressive than their senior colleagues. Evidence based upon oral tradition passed down from generation to generation does not gain in strength or credit through embellishment by the recipients of the tradition and for this reason much of the testimony of several of the more articulate younger witnesses has not assisted the applicants' case. Another unfortunate aspect of much of the applicants' evidence was frequent, and in some instances, prolonged, outbursts of what can only be regarded as the righteous indignation of some witnesses at the treatment they, and their forebears, have suffered at the hands of the colonial, and later the various State, authorities. As I have commented earlier, this case is not about righting the wrongs of the past, rather it has a very narrow focus directed to determining whether native title rights and interests in relation to land enjoyed by the original inhabitants of the area in question have survived to be recognised and enforced under the contemporary law of Australia.[77]

The *Yorta Yorta* decision was deeply confronting: it was the first native title claim to be lost under the NTA and carried potentially ominous implications for the likelihood of applications succeeding elsewhere in the 'settled south'. The tone and language of the judgment were also in severe relief to the generous language of *Mabo*; an argot redolent of condolence and atonement had been replaced with blunt statements about how the law worked. Justice Olney made it plain that the judiciary did not have the role of 'redeeming the nation' by attempting to remedy the effects of colonisation, except to the incidental extent occasioned by the recognition of traditional property rights where they continued to be exercised according to law and custom. That it was the acts of the colonisers that had deposed the traditional owners or wrecked their society was of no probative interest to a Court trying to ascertain a state of facts, except to the extent that it might be prejudicial to the claimants' chances. Whatever the political or historical implications of the recognition of the doctrine of native title in *Mabo*, the function of the Court as explained in *Yorta Yorta* showed that the role of the judiciary was to decide cases, not to try and make whole that which had been smashed.[78] The decision was the subject of withering condemnation from Yorta Yorta spokespeople and was much criticised in scholarly and academic circles for alleged misapplications of the jurisprudence and unthinking adherence to colonial ideology.[79] The discontent was both fed and expressed by overstatement about the formal meaning of the case, which some Aboriginal leaders described as 'genocidal'.[80] However, Justice Olney was fully vindicated on appeal when the decision was upheld 2:1 at the Full Court of the Federal Court and 5:2 before the High Court of Australia.

This book is not preoccupied with the complexities of the content and evolution of the law of native title in Australia or the tactical acumen of the litigation strategies pursued by particular parties over time. However, *Yorta Yorta* requires some discussion because of the case's particular ideological implications in the context of the functioning of the native title system. After *Yorta Yorta*, it was no longer possible to maintain adherence to the cozy myth that the courts were there to act as guardians or promoters of an Indigenous rights agenda. *Yorta Yorta* made it abundantly clear that it was not the role of the Federal Court to decide cases in accordance with any broader ideas of justice; the role of the judges was limited to proper judicial administration and the adjudication of disputes. Arguing against the tide of attacks on *Yorta Yorta* and other judicial setbacks to native title groups, Wootten commented that:

> In the courts, issues of justice are necessarily replaced by strict legalism. Indigenous people who claim native title have to come as individuals

> or groups into the courts of the wrongdoers, carrying all the burdens of the plaintiffs in adversary proceedings . . .[81]

If governments did not initiate political solutions to broad-scale questions then the courts could not be expected to intervene; disappointment that broader political conceptions of justice had not been realised should be saved for the legislature and the executive, not the judiciary. Responding to criticism of Olney in particular, Wootten wrote that *Yorta Yorta* marked 'a bona fide and reasonable attempt by a sympathetic but "black letter" lawyer to apply the *Mabo* decision to a situation of severe social disruption'. Taking a different view would necessarily involve a departure from the ideal of courts seeking to exercise neutrality to the extent humanly possible and 'which for all their shortcomings remain the best guarantor of a rule of law that is a necessary support for all democratic struggles'.[82]

One of the principal doctrinal criticisms made of *Yorta Yorta* was that the judge had applied an incorrect understanding of the level of 'continuity' that was required in order to found a determination of native title. The argument was put at its most intellectually forceful by Noel Pearson in June 2003:

> [T]he Yorta Yorta had proved that a native title burdened the radical title of the Crown at the time of sovereignty. Native title came into existence. They had proved that these occupants included two ancestors of the claimants. They had also proved their descent from these two elders. They had proved their case.[83]

A blunter formulation of the position was put by ATSIC's Geoff Clark, who argued that the Yorta Yorta claimant group had 'mounted a strong case for native title, including the establishment of bloodlines that date back to the time of settlement'. Culture, Clark said, actually lived 'within the people who stood outside that court room'.[84] Radicalised by what he understood to be the failure of all three arms of the Australian Government to protect Indigenous rights, Clark had departed on a more fundamentalist trajectory of support for native title, in which the source of legitimacy lay in a unity of culture, blood and soil in the primordial past.[85] Within academia, Indigenous whiteness studies scholar Aileen Moreton-Robinson stated that '[d]espite the High Court's decision, the bloodline to country of the Yorta Yorta continues to carry their sovereignty'.[86]

After *Yorta Yorta* it was clear that the foundation of native title was a matter of contemporary social realities, not merely inheritance (or for that matter the unification of descendants). Whether native title existed or not depended on the continuous existence of a system of normative rules. As the majority of the High Court said on appeal in *Yorta Yorta*:

> To speak of rights and interests possessed under an identified body of laws and customs is, therefore, to speak of rights and interests that are the creatures of the laws and customs of a particular society that exists as a group which acknowledges and observes those laws and customs. And if the society out of which the body of laws and customs arises ceases to exist as a group which acknowledges and observes those laws and customs, those laws and customs cease to have continued existence and vitality. Their content may be known but if there is no society which acknowledges and observes them, it ceases to be useful, even meaningful, to speak of them as a body of laws and customs acknowledged and observed, or productive of existing rights or interests, whether in relation to land or waters or otherwise.[87]

Ironically, given the outrage and protest that *Yorta Yorta* engendered, in eschewing the possibility of legal entitlement based only on descent, in favour of title requiring the recognition of social practices, the courts had articulated a basis for native title that, in conventional terms, could be seen as more ideologically progressive. The right to property demanded normative reality, rather than just the romantic assumption of a particular group's 'blood' being inextricably bonded to certain territorial soil.

Consent determinations: reality and rhetoric

Section 87 of both the original and amended NTA gave the Federal Court power to make determinations with the consent of the parties where it was satisfied that an order in, or consistent with, those terms was within power. The critical question was always the extent to which the Court would seek to scrutinise the basis of the declaration that it was being asked to make: the more cursory the assessment by the judges, the greater flexibility available to the parties not to be constrained by facts and law. The judicial die was cast in April 2000 when Justice Doug Drummond, in refusing to make orders consistent with a settlement proposed by the main parties, stated:

> It seems to me that notwithstanding the consent of the state, there are real problems in trying to push the envelope of any native title rights you might be expected to be able to prove out beyond the ambit of those rights. Maybe you can but I'm not prepared to accept that at the moment.[88]

Even with all the parties in agreement, the Federal Court could refuse to make a determination of native title in the absence of sufficient evidence. Drummond's ruling, subsequently followed and applied in other cases, made it abundantly clear that there were limits to the extent to which parties could 'sculpt' or 'manufacture' agreed determinations of native title that went beyond what a judge could order on the basis of the available factual material.[89] In 2007 Justice North expressed the same principle, albeit in more generous terms and circumstances, saying that:

> when the Court is examining the appropriateness of an agreement, it is not required to examine whether the agreement is grounded on a factual basis which would satisfy the Court at a hearing of the application. The primary consideration of the Court is to determine whether there is an agreement and whether it was freely entered into on an informed basis. Insofar as this latter consideration applies to a State party, it will require the Court to be satisfied that the State party has taken steps to satisfy itself that there is a credible basis for an application. There is a question as to how far a State party is required to investigate in order to satisfy itself of a credible basis for an application. One reason for the often inordinate time taken to resolve some of these cases is the overly demanding nature of the investigation

> conducted by State parties. The scope of these investigations demanded by some States is reflected in the complex connection guidelines published by some States . . . The Act does not intend to substitute a trial, in effect, conducted by State parties for a trial before the Court. Thus, something significantly less than the material necessary to justify a judicial determination is sufficient to satisfy a State party of a credible basis for an application.[90]

In order for a native title claim to be resolved by consent, the law requires that the content of the determination correspond to an actual state of social facts that can be demonstrated at least on a credible basis. In making consent determinations as much as in deciding litigated matters, the function of the Federal Court is not to right the broad wrongs of the past but has the narrower focus of determining whether native title rights and interests in relation to land have survived to be recognised albeit by agreement.[91]

Curiously, though, there is one particular class of judicial activity where judges of the Federal Court frequently do make statements that suggest that they have been engaged in an exercise broader than simply determining property rights under statute. When a matter has been resolved, after either negotiation or litigation, the practice has developed for the Court to convene a 'ceremonial sitting' somewhere within the traditional country of the successful applicant group. The function of these sittings is explicitly ritualistic; they don't serve any particular instrumental purpose that could not be carried out in a courtroom. The judge reads out a statement with some solemnity, and counsel for the parties will perhaps add a few submissions suited to the occasion. Local media are likely to be invited and representatives of the claim group themselves may be given leave to address the Court. Often, the successful claim group will perform a dance or other cultural activities for the occasion and the whole thing may be followed by a barbecue to which everyone is invited.

Where members of the bench have found themselves making consent determinations they have apparently felt able to engage much more freely with grand language, rhetorically assuming the kind of attitude that is explicitly disavowed in *Yorta Yorta* and is unusual in the discharge of the judicial role. So, when making the consent determination in *Nangkiriny v State of Western Australia*, for example, Justice North stated that:

> Today is the day of formal recognition under the laws of Australia by all the people of Australia of the ancient rights and interests of the Karajarri people in their land. It is a moment of celebration and joy for all Australians. This act of recognition is a foundation upon which reconciliation is being built. I am immensely proud that my signature on these orders will carry the message of the Australian people to the Karajarri people that justice is now being done.[92]

In similar tones, in *Clarrie Smith v Western Australia* Justice Madgwick said that he wished to 'express the Court's congratulations' and he was 'sure, those of the Australian community as a whole, to those who made this settlement possible', before going on to adumbrate and thank by name and at some length many of the witnesses, lawyers, court officials and others whom he considered to be 'responsible' for the settlement.[93] Justice Lockhart, in making consent orders associated with a group of five small determinations, contextualised the matters in long-historical context, noting that '[t]he law which came to this country in the wake of Captain Cook, the common law of England, now the law of Australia, today by order of the Court acknowledges that the Kaurareg claimants, as the descendants of the men and women who lived on these islands when Captain Cook sailed these waters, are the traditional owners'.[94] In *Clarke v Victoria*, Justice Merkel no doubt had an eye back towards *Yorta Yorta* in stating that:

> The orders I propose to make are of special significance as they constitute the first recognition and protection of native title resulting in the ongoing enjoyment of native title in the State of Victoria and, it would appear, on the South-Eastern seaboard of Australia.[95]

At the second consent determination of native title in Victoria in 2007, Justice North offered the concluding remark that:

> This day therefore marks a special achievement for the Gunditjmara People. They have won another battle to cement their place in this

> country and in history. But their success is a shared victory. By doing justice to the Gunditjmara People, the State, the Commonwealth and the other respondents have taken a step to right past wrongs and lay a basis for reconciliation between indigenous and non-indigenous Australians. In this respect the agreement is a major achievement taken on behalf of and for the benefit of the people of Victoria, in particular, and for the people of Australia, more generally. To the extent that our society acts justly it is enhanced. This proceeding and its resolution has thrown light on the rich reality of Gunditjmara society in this place stretching back into the mists of time. The case has provided the means by which we may all recognise the rights and interests of the Gunditjmara People.[96]

The language, style and tone of consent determinations indulges the type of expectations of the judicial role that the Federal Court normally seeks to disabuse. The kind of ceremony that takes place seems far more in keeping with forms of grander political justice than an end to legal proceedings. Ceremonial sittings are suggestive of reconciliation and redemption: the parties and their legal champions, formerly at odds, now meeting at peace before the law-giver, with the occasion solemnified by an observance of rites under both legal systems. Every participant implicitly becomes entitled to a share of the available moral capital, 'to be immensely proud'. There is no doubt that the practice of ceremonial sittings emerged with the most gracious of intentions, but the hazard is further perpetuation of unrealistic expectations of the judicial role. Like many other forms of ritual observance, the practice of convening ceremonial sittings to commemorate determinations of native title functions to propagate a myth. It is, of course, not that the content of ceremonial consent determinations propagates falsehood or smacks of insincerity, because clearly the parties have come to terms and the occasions are of historic significance, but there is myth-making at work to the extent that the story evoked at such occasions is an exaggerated and idealised version of reality.

One perhaps less obvious dimension of the mythic function of ceremonial sittings is the extent to which the occasions are expressions of the Federal Court's broader organisational nationalism. In its corporate publications the Court often stresses its 'national-ness' (perhaps to be contrasted with an implied parochialism and occasional fustiness on the part of state supreme courts) as well as, implicitly, a project of 'nationalising' through the uniform application of Commonwealth laws. As the adjudicator of native title claims, the Federal Court became legitimately able to appropriate images of Indigenous people, rural industry and 'the outback' to an institutional iconography steeped in mythic images of the nation. In a promotional video from 2002, for example, the Court is depicted as mobile and airborne, with a continental map showing the far-flung locations where judges have sat.[97] In travelling around the country with tents and technology, the Court was self-consciously delivering justice to the nation. Yet, if the Court's identity was bound up with an idea of the nation, the vision was one that was intrinsically cosmopolitan, accepting of diversity and technologically savvy, what one judge dubbed '[f]rom the internet to the outback—a world class court'.[98] Ritual sittings for consent determinations not only legitimise the native title process, but enhance the broader nation-building credentials of the Federal Court itself.

Mediation turf wars

In 2005, secure in the knowledge that it could pass whatever reforms to the NTA it wanted without any hindrance from the Senate which it now controlled, the Howard government initiated a Native Title Claims Resolution Review, that examined the roles of the Tribunal and the Federal Court and considered measures for greater efficiency within the existing framework of the NTA.[99] The appointed reviewers travelled the country meeting with key stakeholders including the Federal Court and later reported to the Commonwealth. The final report of the Native Title Claims Resolution Review was a matter of disappointment because it recommended the consolidation of the Tribunal's mediation powers at the expense of the Court. When the Commonwealth Government announced its intention to implement the recommendations of the review and introduced the Native Title Amendment Bill 2006 into Parliament, the Federal Court felt bound to make a submission to the

Senate Legal and Constitutional Affairs Committee Inquiry into the proposed legislation. Soden introduced the submission by saying:

> The comments that follow reflect, in general the views that were expressed by me and by other representatives of the Federal Court to the consultants engaged to conduct the Native Title Claims Resolution Review. As much of what follows was not ultimately highlighted in the consultant's final report to Government, I thought it appropriate to make the comments again.[100]

The submission then contained a description of the measures taken by the Court to deal with native title matters, followed by some expressions of concern about the constitutional and administrative appropriateness of the proposed Amendments. Other submissions tended to support the view of the Court, including those of the MCA, the NNTC, the NFF and the states. There was, in other words, little stakeholder enthusiasm for any reduction in the Federal Court's powers, particularly if they were to be reallocated to the Tribunal.[101] The NNTT gave a typically robust response to the array of doubts and criticism that had been submitted, including a hearty rejoinder directed at the Federal Court. The Tribunal described some of the concerns as 'unfounded', before hitting out at the Court's overall record in dealing with native title cases in language that bordered on the petulant:

> In fact, the history of the Federal Court native title litigation in the rest of Australia over the past five years shows no significant improvements in terms of costs or length of trial time.[102]

In the event, the Howard government exercised its policy preference and strengthened the NNTT's role at the expense of the Federal Court's jurisdiction. Justice French, no longer president of the NNTT but soon to be elevated from the Federal Court bench to become the twelfth Chief Justice of the High Court of Australia, described the changes as 'a partial return to the pre 1998 NTA in that the Tribunal is again given exclusive authority in relation to mediation while mediation is on foot'.[103] In organisational terms, the Tribunal's triumph over the arguments of the Court was emphatic. However, the victory proved to be short lived as the Rudd government quickly moved to reverse the NNTT's exclusive jurisdiction over mediation.

The Court succeeds

In many ways, the Federal Court's performance within the native title system can be seen as a genuine triumph of institutional adaptation. In an adjudicative sense, individual judges have not—of course—always made the correct decisions; the system of appeal courts exists precisely in order to address such mistakes as they occur. However, in terms of overall judicial administration, in the Federal Court's case, ubiquitous organisational buzz words like 'innovative', 'proactive' and 'flexible' are well deserved and take on their true meanings in describing the procedural measures implemented, as well as the sensitive manner in which, for example, the question of timeliness was ultimately dealt with. It is ironic, given that the whole structure of the NTA was premised on the undesirability of claims being handled by the judiciary giving rise to the need for an alternative specialised institution, that it should be the Federal Court rather than the Tribunal that came to be seen by so many parties as the preferable option for dealing with matters. It has been argued here that although the judicial rhetoric associated with consent determinations is no doubt a sincere and well-intended expression of feeling, the result may be to inflate expectations of what courts can do in relation to native title, reviving memories associated with the high oratory of the *Mabo* judgment itself. In another sense, though, in innumerable small and largely unnoticed ways the Federal Court has aptly and amply proved to be the right and proper heir to *Mabo* properly understood; by demonstrating consistent and transparent application of the rule of law in as impartial manner as possible.

8

THE END OF UNCERTAINTY

The native title system in retrospect

After fifteen years of the NTA, the NNTT could announce some impressive-sounding figures:

> In fifteen years, more than one hundred decisions have been made about where native title exists. Three quarters have found that Indigenous people have native title over their land and waters, with almost eighty percent made by agreement. Agreements now exist all around Australia.

In February 2008 the Tribunal headlined these statistics in a 24-minute film, *15 Years of Native Title*, in which an off-screen narrator, Indigenous actress Ursula Yovich, provided a potted history accompanied by mood music, maps, graphics and a range of excerpts from interviews. In addition to archival footage of Eddie Mabo himself, a variety of talking heads provided their overwhelmingly positive testimony of the native title system in operation. Even a Yorta Yorta man was featured, talking about the benefits of the process, as was the claimants' lawyer in a separate interview. The overwhelming theme of the show was that, no matter how fractious or litigious relations were in the past, the only wise course in the end was to proceed with agreement-making, a now widely shared understanding as demonstrated by the testimonials of satisfied participants featured in the film. The take-away message was that native title had clearly arrived in an age where claims were commonly resolved by negotiation, with the implication that although there was still more to do because many claims remained outstanding, the system could already be considered a success.

Fundamentally, this book argues against the grain of the story iterated in *15 Years of Native Title*; not as being wrong, but as the expression of a myth of how consensus was arrived at—an account denuded of politics and the application of power. The view of the history of native title in Australia that the film represents is accurate to the extent that there is now little momentum for fundamental change to the system, near unanimity that agreement-making is the optimal way of resolving matters and in that the number of actual negotiated outcomes continues to increase. In stylised form, it is a narrative of how the various 'stakeholders'—Indigenous people, governments and industry—have come to 'accept' native title. Even the government of John Howard, in those hubristic days of complete Coalition control of the Senate, 'accepted' native title sufficiently to revisit the statutory framework with only comparatively minor adjustments, rather than the 'bucketloads of extinguishment' promised by then Deputy Prime Minister Tim Fischer less than a decade earlier. We all 'respect' and 'recognise' native title now.

However, the configuration of native title that has emerged is not the product of cultural revelation; actors within the system have not simply learned that agreement-making is the wiser choice. Rather, the present policy consensus on native title in Australia is predicated on a distribution of rights and power, supported by a common set of normative assumptions about how things work, that was only settled after bitter and protracted contest. Indigenous groups claiming customary interests were only admitted to the negotiating table because the judicial recognition of the doctrine of native title and the passage of the NTA gave them a measure of enforceable rights. Yet no agreement-making really followed until, after an uncertain start, the balance of power and convenience within the native title system had been reordered sufficiently in the direction of state government and primary industry that the respondents became prepared to deal. The post-millennial consensus that agreement-making is the optimum way of resolving native title issues does mark a cultural shift, but the origins and momentum of the transformation lie in politics and political economy.

The overwhelming view that native title issues are best resolved through reaching agreements is a product of hard-fought contests having been played out. 'Practical experience' may well demonstrate the benefits of negotiation, but these relationships are developed on a stage that is constructed atop a legal, economic and political landscape determined at a more fundamental level. The same interests and parties that bitterly clashed in the political sphere and the courts, in attempting to refashion the system to their advantage, have come to embrace negotiating over their differences, but only because of the form in which the strategic terrain has settled and in some cases the absence of realistic alternatives for seeking further change. The deal-making that is now so prevalent reflects underlying power relationships; it does not alter them.

The struggle over the fundamentals of native title in the appellate courts within the legislatures and in public discourse seems sometimes regarded almost as having been an inconvenience to the real business of getting on with mediation and agreement-making; it is an inversion that borders on the fantastic. As one legal academic has argued:

> In the real world, conflicts arise which are valid, and cannot be resolved by everyone being 'nice' to each other, or talking through the issues 'reasonably'.[1]

Native title is an arena of political conflict in which competing actors have striven against one another for fundamental economic and ideological reasons; the great game for the parties was the tussle over how rights and power would be allocated by the parliaments and the judiciary. The agreement-making that proliferated after the big battles were decided was not something that spontaneously generated in a bell jar but occurred as a direct consequence of key political and legal engagements having been decided; or, as Neate put it in 2002, the 'ground rules' becoming 'set'.[2] Consensus was founded on the weakening and disappearance of strategic options for some and the strengthening and sufficient satiation of the economic and ideological interests of others. For one thing, the rise of the culture of agreement-making was fuelled on the combustion of what once seemed like the possibility of stronger Indigenous rights. Fifteen years of native title is a story of winners, losers and pragmatic settlers, not a castle in the air in which everyone is happy with their lot.

The predication of the common contemporary outlook on native title as a more or less settled issue explains why the public language that is now routinely employed is so often devoid of real meaning. The native title system does not encourage the actors to look back in anger. Indeed, the Tribunal has adopted an approach of actively cultivating retrospective sentimentality. In March 2009 participants in the native title system were asked to:

> Share your favorite native title memories
> With your help, this year *Talking Native Title* will look back over the past 15 years of native title. In each edition we'll publish favourite photos from native title determinations, and we'll also publish these on the Tribunal website.[3]

There is nothing wrong with nostalgia, but in compiling a public scrapbook that only contains happy memories, the myth-making is made explicit and the political contest is forgotten in an application of a selective amnesia.

'Respect' or 'recognition' of native title means no more than a willingness to participate within the rules as they have come to be. Primary industry and state governments broadly 'accept' native title because it has mostly become acceptable to them. There could be no clearer indication that the terms of native title had become good enough for primary industry in general and big mining in particular than the fact that massive influence was not brought to bear on the Howard government to radically revisit the NTA when it had control of the Senate between 2004 and 2007. The eventual 'acceptability' of native title did not happen by chance; the terms of 'acceptance' were politically and legally pursued by the principal respondent parties. Opposition was offered from the Indigenous quarter. If Aboriginal people and Torres

Strait Islanders have come to 'accept' native title it is not because the hopes of 1992–93 have been realised, but because some significant recognition of entitlement remains, combined with a blunt realisation of the paucity of strategic possibilities for doing any better.

The election of the Rudd Labor government to Canberra in 2007 raised questions of to what extent the native title settlement would be revisited. The reality is that the path already taken, with all of its associated institutions, places profound limits on what is politically likely. Perhaps the most significant remaining unknown of the Australian law of native title as it stands at the moment is how compensation might be calculated for the extinguishment of native title since 1975. At present there is no case that deals with the issue.[4] Then again, seismic events like the global financial crisis of 2008 or the urgent imperative of climate change might force broader reconsideration of the native title system for wholly extraneous reasons.

In any event, the trouble with bold new beginnings in Indigenous affairs is that there have been so many of them. It is Aboriginal people themselves who experience the brunt of each fresh start, often accompanied by a new minister, another report, fresh consultations and more promises. Fred Chaney has described the 'start again' or 'shocked minister' syndrome as almost inevitable with each new arrival in the portfolio, leading to reports, reviews, promises and programs that are announced but rarely followed through with until surpassed by the latest new initiative.[5] In relation to the Howard government's theatrical intervention in the Northern Territory, former premier of Western Australia Carmen Lawrence has pointed out that in the previous decade there had been at least 30 reports dealing with child abuse and family violence in Aboriginal communities, each of which no doubt recommended change that had scarcely been delivered.[6] In the arena of native title, as Chief Justice French has observed 'we are beyond the point where the rock is likely to roll down the hill again'.[7] Existing assumptions and patterns of power relations conditioned by economics, ideology, history, society and politics will continue to shape the evolution of the consensus.

NOTES

Prologue

1 See R. Sitch, *The Castle*, Working Dog Productions, 1997.
2 See D. Ritter, *The Native Title Market*, University of Western Australia Press, Perth, 2009.
3 See M.J. Roe, 'Chaos and Evolution in Law and Economics', *Harvard Law Review*, 109(3), 1996, 641–68.
4 See D.C. North, *Institutions, Institutional Change, and Economic Performance*, Cambridge University Press, Cambridge, 1990.
5 R. Bartlett, *Native Title in Australia*, Butterworths, Sydney, 2004; M. Perry and S. Lloyd, *Australian Native Title Law*, Thompson, Sydney, 2003 and G. Neate et al., *Native Title Service*, LexisNexis, Sydney, 1995–2007.
6 L. Strelein, *Compromised Jurisprudence*, Aboriginal Studies Press, Canberra, 2006 and S. Young, *The Trouble with Tradition—Native Title and Cultural Change*, Federation Press, Annandale (NSW), 2007.
7 See, for example, P. Sutton, *Native Title in Australia: An Ethnographic Perspective*, Cambridge University Press, Cambridge, 2003 and G. Bagshaw, *The Karajarri Claim: A Case-Study in Native Title Anthropology*, Oceania Publications, Sydney, 2003.
8 See, for example, C. Choo and S. Hollbach (eds), *Studies in Western Australian History*, 23, 2003 and M. Paul and G. Gray, *Through a Smoky Mirror: History and Native Title*, Aboriginal Studies Press, Canberra, 2003.
9 See, for example, S. Toussaint (ed.), *Crossing Boundaries: Cultural, Legal, Historical and Practical Issues in Native Title*, Melbourne University Press, Melbourne, 2004.

10 See, for example, the journals *Australian Critical Race and Whiteness Studies Association Journal* and *Balayi: Culture Law and Colonialism.*

11 See, for example, D. Ivison, *Postcolonial Liberalism*, Cambridge University Press, Cambridge, 2002; D. Ivison, P. Patton, W. Sanders (eds), *Political Theory and the Rights of Indigenous Peoples*, Cambridge University Press, Cambrige, 2000; and L.P. Hinchman, 'Australia's Judicial Revolution: Aboriginal Land Rights and the Transformation of Liberalism', *Polity*, 31(1), 1998, pp. 23–51.

12 See, for example, M. Langton et al. (eds), *Honour Among Nations? Treaties and Agreements with Indigenous People*, Melbourne University Press, Melbourne, 2004 and P. Kauffman, *Wik, Mining and Aborigines*, Allen & Unwin, Sydney, 1998. More generally, see B. Horrigan and S. Young, *Commercial Implications of Native Title*, Federation Press, Sydney, 1997.

13 M. Goot and T. Rowse (eds), *Make a Better Offer: The Politics of Mabo*, Pluto Press, Leichhardt (NSW), 1994.

14 See http://www.anu.edu.au/caepr/.

15 See, for example, T. Corbett and C. O'Faircheallaigh, 'Unmasking the Politics of Native Title: The National Native Title Tribunal's Application of the NTA's Arbitration Provisions', *The University of Western Australia Law Review*, 33(1), December 2006, 153–76; C. O'Faircheallaigh, 'Evaluating Agreements between Indigenous Peoples and Resource Developers' in M. Langton et al. (eds), *Honour Among Nations? Treaties and Agreements with Indigenous People*, Melbourne University Press, Melbourne, 2004; and C. O'Faircheallaigh, 'Aborigines, Mining Companies and the State in Contemporary Australia: A New Political Economy or "Business as Usual"?', *Australian Journal of Political Science*, 41(1), 2006, 1–22.

16 B. Attwood, *Rights for Aborigines*, Allen & Unwin, Sydney, 2003; M. Belgrave, *Historical Frictions: Maori Claims & Reinvented Histories*, Auckland University Press, Auckland, 2005 and G. Byrnes, *The Waitangi Tribunal and New Zealand History*, Oxford University Press, Melbourne, 2004.

17 Paraphrasing Oliver Wendell Holmes Jnr's famous observation: 'The life of the law has not been logic; it has been experience.'

Chapter 1 Reading the porridge

1 The single anomaly remains John Batman's attempt at purchase from Aboriginal people in Victoria in 1835. See G. Warner and J. Edge-Partington, 'John Batman's Title Deeds', *Man*, 15, 1915, 49–51.

2 See, for example, H. Reynolds, *The Law of the Land*, Penguin, Camberwell (Vic.), 2003; A. McGrath (ed.) et al., *Contested Ground: Australian Aborigines under the British Crown*, Allen & Unwin, Sydney, 1995 and H. Goodall, *From Invasion to Embassy: Land in Aboriginal Politics in New South Wales 1770–1972*, Allen & Unwin, Sydney, 1996.

3 See R. French, 'The Race Power: A Constitutional Chimera' in G. Winterton (ed.), *Australian Constitutional Landmarks*, Cambridge University Press, Cambridge; Port Melbourne, 2003 for a comprehensive discussion. For the meanings of the referendum, see B. Attwood and A. Markus, *The 1967 Referendum, Or When Aborigines Didn't Get the Vote*, Aboriginal Studies Press, Canberra, 1997.

4 *Milirrpum v Nabalco Pty Ltd* (1971) 17 FLR 141.

5 The reasoning was denounced as 'wholly wrong' by the Supreme Court shortly afterwards: *Calder v Attorney General for British Columbia* (1973) 34 DLR (3d) 145 (S.C.), p. 218.

6 Every state and territory except Western Australia now has land rights in some form: see Aboriginal Land Trusts Act 1966 (SA), *Aboriginal Land Rights Act (Northern Territory) 1976* (Cwlth), *Pitjantjatjara Land Rights Act 1981* (SA); *Maralinga Tjarutja Land Rights Act 1984* (SA); *Aboriginal Land (Aboriginal Advancement League) (Watt Street, Northcote) Act 1982* (Vic.); *Aboriginal Land Rights Act 1983* (NSW); *Aboriginal Land Grant (Jervis Bay Territory) Act 1986* (Cwlth); *Aboriginal Land (Lake Condah and Framlingham Forest) Act 1987* (Cwlth); *Aboriginal Land Act 1991* (Qld); *Torres Strait Islander Act 1991* (Qld); *Aboriginal Land (Manatunga Land) Act 1992* (Vic.); *Aboriginal Lands Act 1995* (Tas.).

7 The RDA came into effect on 31 October 1975. The constitutional validity of the RDA was upheld by the High Court in *Koowarta v Bjelke-Petersen* (1982) 153 CLR 168 and *Gerhardy v Brown* (1985) 159 CLR 70.

8 *Mabo v Queensland (No 1)* (1988) 166 CLR 186.

9 *Mabo v Queensland (No 2)* (1992) 175 CLR 1.

10 There are a vast number of commentaries on the case. See, for example, R.H. Bartlett, *The Mabo Decision*, Butterworths, Sydney, 1993; Law Book Company, *Essays on the Mabo Decision*, Law Book Company, Sydney, 1993; M. Kirby, 'In Defence of *Mabo*' in M. Goot and T. Rowse (eds), *Make a Better Offer: The Politics of Mabo*, Pluto Press, Leichhardt (NSW), 1994; M.A. Stephenson and S. Ratnapala (eds), *Mabo: A Judicial Revolution*, Queensland University Press, St Lucia (Qld), 1993; and P. Butt and R. Eagleson, *Mabo: What the High Court Said and What the Government Did*, Federation Press, Sydney, 1996.

11 See R.H. Bartlett, 'Mabo: Another Triumph for the Common Law', *Sydney Law Review*, 15(2), 1993, 178; G. Nettheim, 'Judicial Revolution or Cautious Correction?', *University of NSW Law Journal*, 16(1), 1993, 1; M. Kirby, 'In Defence of Mabo' in M. Goot and T. Rowse (eds), *Make a Better Offer: The Politics of Mabo*, Pluto Press, Leichhardt (NSW), 1994; G.F.K. Santow, 'Aspects of Judicial Restraint', *Australian Bar Review*, 13(2), September 1995, 116–47; S. Churches; 'Mabo: A Flexible Sinew of the Common Law', *Brief*, 20, 1993, 8; and H. Wootten, 'Mabo and the Lawyers', *The Australian Journal of Anthropology*, 6(1 & 2), 1995, 116–33.

12 See, for example, *Utemorrah v Commonwealth* (1992) 108 ALR 225; *Coe v Commonwealth* (1993) 118 ALR 193; and *Ejai v Commonwealth* (WASC, Owen J, No 1744/93, 18 March 1994, BC9401597, unreported).

13 See R.H. Bartlett, *The Mabo Decision*, Butterworths, Sydney, 1993, pp. xx–xxii.

14 See T. Rowse, 'How We Got a Native Title Act' in M. Goot and T. Rowse (eds), *Make a Better Offer: The Politics of Mabo*, Pluto Press, Leichhardt (NSW), 1994 and R. Tickner, *Taking a Stand: Land Rights to Reconciliation*, Allen & Unwin, Sydney, 2001.

15 The 'A-Team' was perceived as the more moderate and representative of northern Australia and included Lowitja O'Donoghue, Noel Pearson, Sol Bellear, Marcia Langton and David Ross. The 'B-Team' was seen as the more radical and included Michael Mansell and Aden Ridgeway.

16 *Western Australia v Commonwealth* (1995) 183 CLR 373.

17 Detailed descriptions of the NTA can be found at R. Bartlett, *Native Title in Australia*, Butterworths, Sydney, 2004; M. Perry and S. Lloyd, *Australian Native Title Law*, Thompson, Sydney, 2003 and G. Neate et al., *Native Title Service*, LexisNexis, Sydney, 1995.

18 (Cwlth) NTA 1993, s. 225(b).

19 Though there were limits: *Bissett v Minister for Land and Water Conservation (NSW)* [2002] FCA 365 and *Walker on behalf of the Ngalia Kutjungkatja People v Western Australia* (2002) 191 ALR 654; [2002] FCA 869.

20 B.A. Keon-Cohen, 'Mabo, Native Title and Compensation: Or how to enjoy your Porridge', *Monash University Law Review*, 21(1), 1995, 84–115, pp. 112–13.

21 See note 15, Chapter 6.

22 *North Ganalanja Aboriginal Corporation v Queensland* (1996) 185 CLR 595. See R.H. Bartlett, 'Undermining the National Native Title Tribunal—Waanyi No. 1 and 2', *Aboriginal Law Bulletin*, 1995, 28.

23 R.S. French, 'A Moment of Change—Personal Reflections on the National Native Title Tribunal', *Melbourne University Law Review*, 2003, 27, 488–522, p. 511.

24 R.S. French, 'A Moment of Change—Personal Reflections on the National Native Title Tribunal', *Melbourne University Law Review*, 2003, 27, 488–522, p. 501.

25 The debates were so lengthy because the Howard government did not have control over the Upper House of the Commonwealth Parliament. See P. Burke, 'Evaluating The Native Title Amendment Act 1998', *Australian Indigenous Law Reporter*, 3(3), 1998, 333–56.

26 *Yorta Yorta Aboriginal Community v Victoria* (FCA, Olney J, No 6001/95, 18 December 1998, BC9806799, unreported); *Members of the Yorta Yorta Aboriginal Community v Victoria* (2000) 110 FCR 244; *Members of the Yorta Yorta Aboriginal Community v Victoria* (2002) 214 CLR 422; *Yarmirr v Northern Territory* (1998) 82 FCR 533; *Commonwealth v Yarmirr* (1999) 101 FCR 171; *Commonwealth v Yarmirr* (2001) 208 CLR 1; *Ward v Western Australia* (1998) 159 ALR 483; *Western Australia v Ward* (2000) 99 FCR 316; *Western Australia v Ward* (2002) 213 CLR 1.

27 *Western Australia v Ward* (2002) 213 CLR 1 at [9] per Gleeson CJ, Gaudron, Gummow and Hayne JJ [76] to [79], [82], [95], [190] to [192], [221], [258] to [260] and [422].

28 *Wik Peoples v Queensland* (1996) 187 CLR 1 at [132–3].

29 *Commonwealth v Yarmirr* (2001) 208 CLR 1 at [70] and [75].

30 *Western Australia v Ward* (2002) 213 CLR 1 at [384].

31 *Western Australia v Ward* (2002) 213 CLR 1 at [60].

32 *Fejo v Northern Territory* (1998) 195 CLR 96, per Kirby J p. 155.

33 Borrowing from E.P. Thompson, *The Making of the English Working Class*, Gollancz, London, 1965, p. 11. More generally, it might be said that all property is 'socially constituted fact' that 'oscillates between the behavioural, the conceptual and the obligational': K. Gray and S.F. Gray, *Elements of Land Law*, Butterworths, London, 2001, p. 111.

34 A point acknowledged right from the outset of the native title process: See, for example, R.S. French, 'Opening Address' in F. McKeown (ed.), *Native Title: An Opportunity for Understanding*, National Native Title Tribunal, Perth, 1994, p. 4 and reiterated *Clarke v Victoria* [2005] FCA 1795.

35 P. Agius et al., 'Comprehensive Native Title Negotiations in South Australia' in M. Langton et al. (eds), *Honour Among Nations? Treaties and Agreements with Indigenous People*, Melbourne University Press, Melbourne, 2004, p. 205.

36 The *Report of the National Inquiry into the Separation of Aboriginal and Torres Strait Islander Children from Their Families*, April 1997 at Recommendation 4.4 of the Reparations Chapter recognised that many 'descendants of those forcibly removed' would 'as a result, have been deprived of community ties, culture and language, and links with and entitlements to their traditional land'.

37 The term is notoriously open to many and competing interpretations. See, for example, the varying emphasis in M. Grattan (ed.), *Essays on Australian Reconciliation*, Black Inc., Melbourne, 2000.

38 N. Sharp, *No Ordinary Judgment: Mabo, the Murray Islanders' Land Case*, Aboriginal Studies Press, Canberra, 1996.

39 S. Flood, '"The Spirit of Mabo"—The Land Needs the Laughter of Children: Native Title and the Achievements of Aboriginal People' in G.D. Meyers (ed.), *Implementing the Native Title Act: The Next Step: Facilitating Negotiated Agreements*, National Native Title Tribunal, Perth, 1996, p. 104.

40 See, for example, J. Winter (ed.), *Native Title Business: Contemporary Indigenous Art*, Keeaira Press, Southport (Qld), 2002.

41 F. Collins and T. Davies, *Australian Cinema after Mabo*, Cambridge University Press, Cambridge; Port Melbourne, 2004.

42 B. Attwood (ed), *In the Age of Mabo. History, Aborigines and Australia*, Allen & Unwin, Sydney, 1996.

43 K. Gelder and J.M. Jacobs, *Uncanny Australia: Sacredness and Identity in a Postcolonial Nation*, Melbourne University Press, Melbourne, 1998, p. 135.

44 In the shape of the organisation Australians for Native Title and Reconciliation.

45 The phrase is from N. Pearson, '204 years of Invisible Title' in M.A. Stephenson and S. Ratnapala (eds), *Mabo: A Judicial Revolution*, Queensland University Press, St Lucia (Qld), 1993.

46 *Wilson v Anderson* (2002) 213 CLR 401.

47 Often more than ten and on some occasions greater than 40. Even if a large applicant group was chosen, often a different collection of individuals became responsible as a matter of practice for giving instructions to representatives or there might be insistence on a particular issue going to the entire claimant group for decision.

48 See D. Eades, *Aboriginal English and the Law*, Continuing Legal Education Department, Queensland Law Society Inc., Brisbane, 1992 and J.M. Arthur, *Aboriginal English: A Cultural Study*, Oxford University Press, Melbourne, 1996.

49 The comments made in this paragraph are from the author's own experience. Not all meetings were like this, of course, but many did have some or all of these features. I'm conscious, of course, of the very real structural limitations on my own field of perception in these circumstances.

50 See, for example, *Daniel v Western Australia* [2002] FCA 1147.

51 Described by Justice French in June 1994 as 'fundamental' to the organisation's operation. Van Hattem and R.S. French, 'New President of National Native Title Tribunal', *Brief*, June, 1994, 12–21, p. 20. See also R.S. French, 'Opening Address' in *Native Title: An Opportunity for Understanding*, National Native Title Tribunal, Perth, 1995.

52 For example, the 'AIC Annual Conferences on Doing Business with Aboriginal Communities', a series that commenced in 1995.

53 H. Wootten, 'Some Thoughts on Native Title and Doing Business' in G.D. Meyers (ed.), *Implementing the Native Title Act: The Next Step: Facilitating Negotiated Agreements*, National Native Title Tribunal, Perth, 1996, p. 52.

54 S. Kee, 'The Process of developing a claim from the perspective of the National Native Title Tribunal' in J. Finlayson and A. Jackson-Nakano, *Heritage and Native Title: Anthropological and Legal Perspectives*, AIATSIS, Canberra, 1996, p. 197.

55 A number of early critics were scathing. See in particular P. Sullivan, 'Problems of Mediation in the National Native Title Tribunal' in J. Fingleton and J. Finlayson, *Anthropology in the Native Title Era: Proceedings of a Workshop*, AIATSIS, Canberra, 1995 and S. Jackson, *When History Meets the New Native Title Era at the Negotiating Table: A Case Study in Reconciling Land Use in Broome, Western Australia*, North Australia Research Unit, Australian National University, Canberra, 1996.

56 Although not in a native title context, see G. Cowlishaw, 'Black Modernity and the Bureaucratic Culture', *Australian Aboriginal Studies*, 1999 (2), 15–24. The phrase 'neo-colonial farce' is employed at pp. 19–20.

57 National Native Title Tribunal, *Talking Native Title*, 15 June 2005, p. 9.

58 Interpreters were rarely (if ever) hired by the NNTT and even when utilised might be found to be less than satisfactory. 'The use of interpreters is either no more than a token solution to the problem of language, or slows proceedings down to a point where they collapse': H. Wootten, 'Mediating between Aboriginal Communities and Industry' in G.D. Meyers (ed.), *Implementing the Native Title Act: The Next Step: Facilitating Negotiated Agreements*, National Native Title Tribunal, Perth, 1996, p. 180.

59 H. Wootten, 'Mediating between Aboriginal Communities and Industry' in G.D. Meyers (ed.), *Implementing the Native Title Act: The Next Step: Facilitating Negotiated Agreements*, National Native Title Tribunal, Perth, 1996, p. 170.

60 See, for example, H. Wootten, 'Mediating between Aboriginal Communities and Industry' in G.D. Meyers (ed.), *Implementing the Native Title Act: The Next Step: Facilitating Negotiated Agreements*, National Native Title Tribunal, Perth, 1996, p. 180 and G. Cowlishaw, 'Black Modernity and Bureaucratic Culture', *Australian Aboriginal Studies*, 2 (1999), 15–24. Wootten reflected in 1996 that the harder he tried 'to manipulate the proceeding to conform to the ideal of an empowering mediation experience' the more it became 'obvious that the Aboriginal participants are being pressured into an alienating and frustrating experience': p. 180.

61 H. Wootten, 'Mediating between Aboriginal Communities and Industry' in G.D. Meyers (ed.), *Implementing the Native Title Act: The Next Step: Facilitating Negotiated Agreements*, National Native Title Tribunal, Perth, 1996, p. 170.

62 Indigenous claims to country in a native title context were often bitterly contested by competing groups in the context of both mediation and litigation: See, for example, *Rubibi Community v Western Australia* [2001] FCA 1553; *Daniel v Western Australia* [2003] FCA 666; and *Bodney v Bropho* [2004] FCAFC 226.

63 The concept of a group bound together by common legal entitlement comes from M. Edele, 'Soviet Veterans as an Entitlement Group', *Slavic Review*, 65(1), Spring 2006, 111–37, p. 132.

64 On 27 October 2006, the Australian Government Attorney General and the Minister for Families, Community Services and Indigenous Affairs released a report examining the structures and processes of native title prescribed bodies corporate: Australian Government, Attorney General's Department, Prescribed Bodies Corporate, accessed 29/11/08 from Attorney General's website, available at http://www.ag.gov.au/www/agd/agd.nsf/Page/Indigenouslawandnativetitle_Nativetitle_Prescribedbodiesco rporate(PBCs). See J. Weir, 'Native Title and Governance: The Emerging Corporate Sector Prescribed for Native Title Holders', *Land, Rights, Laws: Issues of Native Title*, 3(9), 2007, 1–16. In 2006 the Native Title Unit of the Insitute of Aboriginal and Torres Strait Islander Studies noted that there was 'currently no network and little coordinated information about the structure and activities of Prescribed Bodies Corporate' and initiated a major project to study and support such organisations. See http://ntru.

aiatsis.gov.au/major_projects/pbc_rntbc.html#overview. For background see D. Martin and C. Mantziaris, *Native Title Corporations: A Legal and Anthropological Analysis*, Federation Press, Leichhardt (NSW), 2000.

Chapter 2 The dilemmas of the black leadership

1 For some discussion of conflicting sources of authority see J. Finalyson, 'Aboriginal Tradition and Native Title Representative Bodies' in D. Smith and J. Finlayson, *Fighting over Country: Anthropological Perspectives*, CAEPR, Australian National University, Research Monograph 12, 1997. Generally see also S. Maddison, *Black Politics: Inside the complexity of Aboriginal political culture*, Allen & Unwin, Sydney, 2009.

2 H. Wootten, 'Mediating between Aboriginal Communities and Industry' in G.D. Meyers (ed.), *Implementing the Native Title Act: The Next Step: Facilitating Negotiated Agreements*, National Native Title Tribunal, Perth, 1996, p. 178.

3 P. Coe, 'ATSIC: Self-determination or Otherwise' in *Race and Class: A Journal for Black and Third World Liberation*, 35(4), April–June 1994. Individuals, of course, could exercise simultaneous responsibilities as ATSIC officials and under traditional law and custom, though this would necessarily produce its own set of tensions.

4 G Cowlishaw, 'Governing Cultural Difference', *Dialogue*, 23(2), 2004, pp. 47–56, p. 52.

5 G.L. Hand, Minister for Aboriginal Affairs, Second Reading Speech, *Commonwealth House Hansard*, 4 May 1989, p. 1994.

6 Department of Aboriginal Affairs (DAA) staff simply transferred to ATSIC in the interests of continuity of service provision—as well as continuity of employment: G. Cowlishaw, 'Governing Cultural Difference', *Dialogue*, 23(2) 2004, pp. 47–56, p. 51.

7 Discussion of turn-out is limited by the lack of reliable figures as to the potential numbers of voters: W. Sanders, J. Taylor and K. Ross, 'Participation and Representation in ATSIC Elections: A Ten-year Perspective', Centre for Aboriginal Economic Policy Research Discussion Paper No. 198/2000, Australian National University, http://dspace.anu.edu.au/bitstream/1885/41644/1/2000_DP198.pdf, pp. 7–8.

8 Hon. G.L. Hand, Minister for Aboriginal Affairs, Second Reading Speech, *Commonwealth House Hansard*, 4 May 1989, p. 1994.

9 Much of the rhetoric which surrounded the creation of ATSIC invoked 'self-determination' as one of its foundational principles. This view persisted in the words of the Indigenous leadership; Geoff Clark argued

that 'Indigenous self-determination is the foundation stone upon which ATSIC was built when it began 13 years ago': ATSIC, 'A Bump in the Road to Self-Determination', News Room Media Release, 17 April 2003, http://pandora.nla.gov.au/pan/41033/200601060000/ATSIC/news_room/media_releases/archive/2003/Apr/2674.html and K. Palmer, 'ATSIC and Indigenous Representation in Australia: Is There a Future?', *Dialogue*, 23(2), 2004, p. 30. For more sceptical views, see H. Wootten, 'Self-Determination After ATSIC', *Dialogue*, 23(2), 2004, pp. 16 and 23 and G. Cowlishaw, 'Governing Cultural Difference', *Dialogue*, 23(2), 2004, pp. 47–56, p. 51.

10 NTA, s. 203(3).

11 An extra $5 million was allocated in 1998–99: ATSIC, *Annual Report 1998–1999*, p. 131. In 1999–2000, '[b]udgeted funds from the government appropriation were supplemented with other funds from ATSIC's global allocation after it was decided that other priorities would have to be foregone for the sake of the drastically under-funded representative body system': ATSIC, *Annual Report 1999–2000*, p. 112. The pattern was repeated in later years.

12 *ATSIC Act* (Cwlth), s. 7(1)(c). See also ss. 7 and 94, passim.

13 ATSIC, *Annual Report 2000–2001*, p. 71.

14 W. Sanders, *ATSIC's Achievements and Strengths*, Centre for Aboriginal Economic Policy Research, Australian National University, August 2004, p. 2.

15 From the Indigenous Land Corporation and the National Aboriginal and Islander Legal Services Secretariat, as well as the Aboriginal and Torres Strait Islander Social Justice Commissioner. The initial membership of NIWG was Gatjil Djerrkura, Aboriginal and Torres Strait Islander Commission; Geoff Clark, Aboriginal and Torres Strait Islander Commission; David Ross, Indigenous Land Corporation; Mick Dodson, Aboriginal and Torres Strait Islander Social Justice Commissioner; Charles Perkins, National Aboriginal and Torres Strait Islander Legal Services Secretariat; Les Malezer, Foundation for Aboriginal and Islander Research Action; Noel Pearson, Cape York Land Council; Aden Ridgeway, New South Wales Aboriginal Land Council; Ken Saunders, Mirimbiak Nations Aboriginal Corporation; Parry Agius, Aboriginal Legal Rights Movement; Glen Shaw, Aboriginal Legal Service of WA; Peter Yu, Kimberley Land Council; Yvonne Brownley, Goldfields Land Council; Tracker Tilmouth, Central Land Council; Galurrwuy Yunupingu, Northern Land Council: http://www.faira.org.au/niwg/.

16 *Western Australia v the Commonwealth; Woorora Peoples v Western Australia; Biljabu v Western Australia* (1995) 183 CLR 373.
17 See http://www.faira.org.au/niwg/.
18 P. Burke, 'The Native Title Outcome Takes Shape in Queensland', *Indigenous Law Bulletin*, [1999] *Indigenous Law Bulletin*, 4(17), 1.
19 'To ensure maximum participation of Indigenous people in the development of complementary legislation, ATSIC funded State-based Indigenous working groups in 1999–2000' in Queensland and Western Australia. 'Their role was to coordinate the Indigenous response, seek to negotiate directly with . . . Governments and promote awareness within the Indigenous community.' ATSIC continued to fund QIWG and WAANTWG in 2000–01: ATSIC, *Annual Report 2000–2001*, p. 72.
20 M. Dillon, 'Native Title: A View from the Commonwealth' in F. McKeown (ed.), *Native Title: An Opportunity for Understanding*, National Native Title Tribunal, Perth, 1994, p. 208.
21 ATSIC, *Annual Report 1995–1996*, Component 1.5, 'Future Directions'.
22 ATSIC, *Annual Report 1997–1998*, Sub-program 5, Component 5.1.
23 ATSIC, *Annual Report 2003–2004*, p. 54.
24 ATSIC, *Annual Report 1996–1997*, Sub-program 4, Component 4.1. A year earlier, at the end of 1995/96, ATSIC claimed that it was seeking 'a significant reduction in the number of overlapping claims', a claim they also made in the ensuing year.
25 For example: 'ATSIC sees its role in this area as representing and advancing Indigenous interests': ATSIC, *Annual Report 1994–1995*; ATSIC 'has a key statutory role in advocating the views of Indigenous people to the government': ATSIC, *Annual Report 1997–1998*; has a key role in 'putting an Indigenous perspective' and 'coordinating the views of Aboriginal and Torres Strait Islander peoples': ATSIC, *Annual Report 1998–1999*, p. 126; 'ATSIC advocates the Indigenous position in respect of Comonwealth and State/Territory native title and land rights legislation': ATSIC, *Annual Report 1999–2000*, p. 111; 'ATSIC has played a major role in advocating an Indigenous position': ATSIC, *Annual Report 2000–2001*, p. 71 and so on. There were always some strident Indigenous critics of ATSIC; See, for example, I. Watson, 'The Aboriginal Tent Embassy 28 Years After it was Established: Interview with Isobell Coe', *Indigenous Law Bulletin*, 2000(5).
26 For example, ATSIC Commissioner Colin Dillon expressed the casual assumption of pan-Indigenous identity this way: 'Indigenous people are not like everyone else—we are the First Australians'. C. Dillon, 'Indigenous People and Citizenship: A Personal Experience', 50th

Anniversary of Australian Citizenship Conference, University of Melbourne, 21–23 July 1999.

27 B. Attwood, *The Making of the Aborigines*, Allen & Unwin, Sydney, 1989.

28 L. Behrendt, *Achieving Social Justice*, Federation Press, Sydney, 2003, pp. 61–2.

29 P.H. Russell, *Recognizing Aboriginal Title: The Mabo Case and Indigenous Resistance to English-Settler Colonialism*, University of Toronto Press, Toronto, 2005, p. 18.

30 The case in which Indigenous interests and the Commonwealth lined up to defend the NTA was *Western Australia v Commonwealth* (1995) 183 CLR 373; 128 ALR 1. The media debate associated with the period is summarised in G.D. Meyers and S.C. Muller, *Mabo—Through the Eyes of the Media (Part III): The Constitutional Challenge to the Native Title Act*, Murdoch University Law School, Perth, 1997.

31 Chairperson's Report, ATSIC, *Annual Report 1994–1995*.

32 N. Pearson, 'From Remnant Title to Social Justice' in M. Goot and T. Rowse, *Make a Better Offer: The Politics of Mabo*, Pluto Press, Leichhardt (NSW), 1994, p. 179.

33 Quoted in S. Jackson, *When History Meets the New Native Title Era at the Negotiating Table: A Case Study in Reconciling Land Use in Broome, Western Australia*, North Australia Research Unit, Australian National University, Canberra, 1996, p. 42.

34 Chairperson's Report, ATSIC, *Annual Report 1994–1995*.

35 See C. Johnson, 'The 2001 Election Campaign: The Ideological Context' in J. Warhurst and M. Simms (eds), *2001: The Centenary Election*, University of Queensland Press, St Lucia (Qld), 2002.

36 'Karma Waters Agreement Welcomed', ATSIC News Room Media Releases, 28/9/1998, http://pandora.nla.gov.au/pan/41033/20060106/ATSIC/news_room/media_releases/archive/1998/Sep/212.html.

37 G. Djerrkura, 'A Victory for commonsense and fairness', 23/12/1996, ATSIC News Room Media Releases, http://pandora.nla.gov.au/pan/41033/20060106/ATSIC/news_room/media_releases/archive/1996/Dec/82.html.

38 'Native title shapes reconciliation and economic development', 24/10/1997, ATSIC News Room Media Releases, http://pandora.nla.gov.au/pan/41033/20060106/ATSIC/news_room/media_releases/archive/1997/Oct/115.html. Although later, a fine example is: 'Native Title ruling a win for all Australians', 30/5/2001, ATSIC News Room Media Releases, http://pandora.nla.gov.au/pan/41033/20060106/ATSIC/news_room/media_releases/archive/2001/May/636.html.

39 'Native Title and Indigenous Development', NIWG Fact Sheet 5, National Indigenous Working Group—Fact Sheets—accessed from NIWG website http://www.faira.org.au/niwg. See also: 'New report finds native title agreements lead the way', 11/6/1998, ATSIC News Room Media Releases, http://pandora.nla.gov.au/pan/41033/20060106/ATSIC/news_room/media_releases/archive/1998/Jun/169.html. Indeed, Djerrkura claimed in 1997 that the evidence was already positive and that 'native title processes' had 'already begun to deliver' the cherished result of 'moving away' Indigenous people's 'reliance upon charity or welfare'. 'Native title shapes reconciliation and economic development', 24/10/1997, ATSIC News Room Media Releases, http://pandora.nla.gov.au/pan/41033/20060106/ATSIC/news_room/media_releases/archive/1997/Oct/115.html.

40 'Development Agreements on Native Title Lands—"Win-win" Solutions', NIWG Fact Sheet 6, National Indigenous Working Group—Fact Sheets—accessed from NIWG website http://www.faira.org.au/niwg.

41 See S. Maddison, *Black Politics: Inside the complexity of Aboriginal political culture*, Allen & Unwin, Sydney, 2009, Chapter 4.

42 'Introductory Remarks by the Chairman Mr Gatjil Djerrkura' in 'Summary statements from ATSIC's submission to the Parliamentary Joint Committee on Native Title Amendment Bill 1997', 24/9/1997, ATSIC News Room Media Releases, http://pandora.nla.gov.au/pan/41033/20060106/ATSIC/news_room/media_releases/archive/1997/Sep/112.html.

43 ATSIC, *Annual Report 1996–1997*. The political situation had become more vexed with the handing down of *Wik* in December 1996 and the Native Title Branch of ATSIC itself responded by establishing a small unit called the 'Wik Team' to work with NIWG in advancing the national Indigenous position. The Wik Team remained in operation until the passage of the Amendments to the NTA in 1998.

44 ATSIC, *Annual Report 2001–2002*, p. 28.

45 Quoted in N. Watson, 'Referendum '67: Reflections on the 1967 Referendum', 'Opinion', *National Indigenous Times*, Issue 130, 31 May 2007, accessed online at http://www.nit.com.au/opinion/story.aspx?id=11395.

46 *Western Australia v Ward* (2000) 99 FCR 316; 170 ALR 159.

47 'Mabo Day celebrations open to South East Queenslanders on June 3', 2/6/2003, ATSIC News Room Media Releases, http://pandora.nla.gov.au/pan/41033/20060106/ATSIC/news_room/speeches_transcripts/archive/2003/Jun/2747.html. For Geoff Clark's views, see S2. G. Clark,

'Native Title: Finding the Way Forward Address by Geoff Clark, Chair, ATSIC, Native Title 2002 Conference, Geraldton', 3/9/2002, ATSIC News Room, Speech Transcripts, http://pandora.nla.gov.au/pan/41033/20060106/ATSIC/news_room/speeches_transcripts/archive/2002/Sep/2404.html.

48 'Support for Yorta Yorta Nation from across NSW', 23/5/2002, ATSIC News Room Media Releases, http://pandora.nla.gov.au/pan/41033/20060106/ATSIC/news_room/media_releases/archive/2002/May/2224.html.

49 'Native title system means legal dispossession of Indigenous people', 12/12/2002, ATSIC News Room Media Releases, http://pandora.nla.gov.au/pan/41033/20060106/ATSIC/news_room/media_releases/archive/2002/Dec/2562.html. Clark's view was not, of course, universally expressed. In response to winning the Rubibi claim near Broome, ATSIC announced that the case demonstrated that native title was 'not just for those Aboriginal people living traditional lifestyles in remote places' but 'for all . . . who continue to practise their laws and customs': 'Native Title ruling a win for all Australians', 30/5/2001, ATSIC News Room Media Releases, http://pandora.nla.gov.au/pan/41033/20060106/ATSIC/news_room/media_releases/archive/2001/May/636.html. Indeed, Clark himself was inconsistent: in his landmark address to the *Corroboree 2000* event, in which he first called for a treaty, Clark said that 'distinct rights' arose from the 'status as first peoples, . . . relationships with our territories and waters, and our own systems of law and governance': G. Clark, 'Address to Corroboree 2000', 27 May 2000, http://www.austlii.edu.au/au/other/IndigLRes/car/2000/14/speeches/Geoff_Clark.htm. However, Clark was not the only Indigenous leader to believe that descent should have been determinative. ATSIC Commissioner Marion Hansen lamented that many Indigenous people who had 'inherited' land 'from their ancestors' would be denied recognition because 'the ability of Aboriginal groups to prove their native title in the courts is extremely difficult and perhaps impossible in highly developed areas'. 'Ten years on, it's time to deliver justice on native title': Hansen, 1/5/2002, ATSIC News Room Media Releases, http://pandora.nla.gov.au/pan/41033/20060106/ATSIC/news_room/media_releases/archive/2002/May/2238.html.

50 'Treaty more urgent than ever after Federal Court's dismissal of Yorta Yorta appeal': 8/2/2001, ATSIC News Room Media Releases, http://pandora.nla.gov.au/pan/41033/20060106/ATSIC/news_room/media_releases/archive/2001/Feb/574.html.

51 ATSIC, *Annual Report 1998–1999*, pp. 32–3. Indeed it is arguable that Indigenous recourse to international forums and sources of authority had

the unwitting effect of contributing to growing polarisation within Aboriginal affairs in Australia.

52 See, for example, N. Collings, 'Australian Government Exposes Itself before the UN', *Indigenous Law Bulletin*, 5(4), Nov–Dec. 2000, 11–15; D. Dick, '"Second to None?": Australia and Indigenous Human Rights', *Alternative Law Journal*, 26(1), Feb. 2001, 22–6, 40; A. Kent. 'The Unpredictability of Liberal States: Australia and International Human Rights', *The International Journal of Human Rights*, 6(3), Autumn 2002, 55–84; G. Marks, 'Sovereign States vs Peoples: Indigenous Rights and the Origins of International Law', *Australian Indigenous Law Reporter*, 5(2), 2000, 1–9; D. Otto, 'From "Reluctance" to "Exceptionalism": The Australian Approach to Domestic Implementation of Human Rights', *Alternative Law Journal*, 26(5), October 2001, 215–18; L. Behrendt, *Achieving Social Justice: Indigenous Rights & Australia's Future*, Federation Press, Leichhardt (NSW), 2003; R. Pitty, 'Indigenous Peoples, Self-Determination and International Law', *The International Journal of Human Rights*, 5(4), Winter 2001, pp. 44–71 and S. Pritchard (ed.), *Indigenous peoples, the United Nations and Human Rights*, Federation Press, Leichhardt (NSW), 1998. Commonwealth responses are reported in D. Dick, 'Second to None?', *Alternative Law Journal*, 26(1), Feb. 2001, 22 and D. Otto, 'From "Reluctance" to "Exceptionalism": The Australian Approach to Domestic Implementation of Human Rights', *Alternative Law Journal*, 26(5), 219. The gulf between international principle and domestic reality perhaps reached its zenith when a leading UN figure announced her support for 'the principle that peoples and nations have permanent ownership of and control over their natural wealth and resources is a principle that should be applied to the world's indigenous peoples', to which the then Chairperson of ATSIC responded by calling for an 'immediate halt to all mining activities in Australia'. 'All mining should cease until proper payment is made to Indigenous owners of Australia's resources wealth', 22/5/2003, ATSIC News Room Media Releases, http://pandora.nla.gov.au/pan/41033/20060106/ATSIC/news_room/media_releases/archive/2003/May/2717.html.

53 G. Clark, 'Ten Years On', Eddie Mabo Memorial Lecture, Melbourne, 3/6/2002, ATSIC, News Room Speeches Transcripts, http://pandora.nla.gov.au/pan/41033/20060106/ATSIC/news_room/media_releases/archive/2002/Jun/2369.html. See also G. Clark, 'Native Title: Finding the Way Forward Address by Geoff Clark, Chair, ATSIC, Native Title 2002 Conference, Geraldton', 3/9/2002, ATSIC News Room, Speech

Transcripts, http://pandora.nla.gov.au/pan/41033/20060106/ATSIC/news_room/speeches_transcripts/archive/2002/Sep/2404.html.

54 P. Dodson, 'Reaching Agreement', delivered at a conference: 'Moving Forward: Best Practice for Indigenous Relations in Western Australia', 19–20 April 2001, Sheraton Perth Hotel.

55 G. Clark, 'Ten Years On', Eddie Mabo Memorial Lecture, Melbourne, 3/6/2002, ATSIC, News Room Speeches Transcripts, http://pandora.nla.gov.au/pan/41033/20060106/ATSIC/news_room/media_releases/archive/2002/Jun/2369.html.

56 'Critics of the system now include High Court judges and Liberal Senators', ATSIC, *Annual Report 2001–2002*, p. 28.

57 ATSIC, *Annual Report 2001–2002*, p. 29.

58 'Native title system means legal dispossession of Indigenous people', 12/12/2002, ATSIC News Room Media Releases, http://pandora.nla.gov.au/pan/41033/20060106/ATSIC/news_room/media_releases/archive/2002/Dec/2562.html.

59 According to Clark the period was marked by a 'campaign of attrition', waged in the courts, the states and territories and then the Commonwealth Parliament, as the new regimes were either allowed or disallowed in the Senate: G. Clark, Chairperson's Report, *ATSIC Annual Report 2000–2001*, p. 38.

60 The so-called 'Cairns Group' met for the first time in September 2003, consisting of a group of lawyers and Indigenous leaders selected by ATSIC's Native Title Branch. After two meetings, the initiative fizzled out without any discernible product.

61 G. Clark, 'Ten Years On', Eddie Mabo Memorial Lecture, Melbourne, 3/6/2002, ATSIC, News Room Speeches Transcripts, http://pandora.nla.gov.au/pan/41033/20060106/ATSIC/news_room/media_releases/archive/2002/Jun/2369.html.

62 The Native Title Branch was relocated from Canberra to Darwin, back to Canberra, up to Brisbane and back to Canberra within the space of four years.

63 See, for example, M. Moscaritolo and M. Madigan, 'Leader to Fight Sex Attack Case', *Herald Sun*, 7 May 2002, p. 7; S. Rintoul and I. Gerard, 'ATSIC Crisis "Hurting Reconciliation"', *The Australian*, 10 May 2003; M. Schubert and S. Rintoul, 'Sugar Ray Calls It Quits', *The Australian*, 26 June 2003, p. 6; M. McKinnon, S. Rintoul and M. Schubert, 'ATSIC Chief's Wife Runs Up $25,000 Travel Bill', *The Australian*, 14 April 2003, p. 5; and S. Rintoul and M. Schubert, 'Federal Police Raid Sugar Ray's Office', *The Australian*, 2 April 2003, p. 14.

64 See M. Ivanitz, 'The Demise of ATSIC? Accountability and the Coalition Government', *Australian Journal of Public Administration*, vol. 59, no. 1, March 2000, p. 312; KPMG, *Report of the Special Auditor*, Department of the Prime Minister and Cabinet, Canberra, 1996; T. Rowse, 'ATSIC's Regions: The Equity Issue' in T. Rowse, *Indigenous Futures, Choice and Development for Aboriginal and Islander Australia*, UNSW Press, Sydney, 2002, p. 185 and A. Pratt, 'Make or Break? A Background to the ATSIC Changes and the ATSIC Review', *Current Issues Brief*, 29, Department of the Parliamentary Library, Canberra, 2002–03, 1996.

65 *Aboriginal And Torres Strait Islander Commission Act 1989*, s. 3. Rowse's view is that ATSIC was 'white anted from [the] first day. It has been undermined': T. Rowse, 'ATSIC's Regions: The Equity Issue' in T. Rowse, *Indigenous Futures, Choice and Development for Aboriginal and Islander Australia*, UNSW Press, Sydney, 2002, p. 185.

66 P. Ruddock, Minister for Immigration and Multicultural and Indigenous Affairs and Minister Assisting the Prime Minister for Reconciliation, *ATSIC Review Panel Announced*, Media Release, 12 November 2002. Aboriginal and Torres Strait Islander Services (ATSIS) was announced in April 2003 by then Minister for Indigenous Affairs, Phillip Ruddock. The Final Report recommended strengthening the role of the regional councils: John Hannaford, Jackie Huggins and Bob Collins, *In the Hands of the Regions—A New ATSIC: Report of the Review of the Aboriginal and Torres Strait Islander Commission*, November 2003.

67 Transcript of the Prime Minister the Hon. John Howard MP, Joint Press Conference with Senator Amanda Vanstone, Parliament House, Canberra, 15 April 2004.

68 30 March 2004 http://www.abc.net.au/pm/content/2004/s1077404.htm.

69 In May 2004 the Aboriginal and Torres Strait Islander Commission Amendment Bill 2004 was introduced by Senator Vanstone. The *Aboriginal and Torres Strait Islander Commission Amendment Act 2005* (Cwlth) was later passed and received Royal Assent on 22 March 2005.

70 In 2002 Gordon had been appointed to lead an inquiry into family violence and child abuse in Indigenous communities by the WA Labor government.

71 Influenced by the theorising of Hernando de Soto: H. de Soto, *The Mystery of Capital*, Basic Books, New York, 2000.

72 'Selling Native Title', Michael Duffy interview of Warren Mundine on ABC Radio's *Counterpoint*, 24 January 2005, http://www.abc.net.au/rn/counterpoint/stories/2005/1288345.htm.

73 National Native Title Tribunal, *Talking Native Title*, 15 June 2005, p. 4.

74 Its objects are, among others, to 'provide a national voice for Native Title Representative Bodies and Native Title Service Providers on matters of national significance affecting the native title rights of Aboriginal and Torres Strait Islander people.' National Native Title Council, 'Submission to the Senate Legal and Constitutional Affairs Committee on the Native Title Amendment Bill 2006' 25/1/2007.

75 National Native Title Tribunal, *Talking Native Title*, Issue 15, June 2005, p. 4.

76 For example, through repetition of the conflation of tradition and economic participation: 'The NNTC wants the native title process overhauled to give Aboriginal people a better chance of having connection to their traditional lands recognized, thereby achieving stronger protection of their law and customs and quicker attainment of economic independence': Goldfields Land and Sea Council, 'Four-point plan for making native title system work better': Goldfields Land Council, Media Statements, 16 July 2008, availability: http://www.glc.com.au/me_xx/20080716.htm.

77 For example: 'The current process just needs to change and what we'd be looking for from an incoming government is to make sure there's some commitment that this will be settled very quickly so people can participate and enjoy the economic boom times that are around as well': ABC News, 'Native title should be Govt priority: council', 31 October 2007: http://www.abc.net.au/news/stories/2007/10/31/2077521.htm.

78 Although it is true that ATSIC in particular always retained commitment to rights rhetoric, in 2000–01 'the Board endorsed an ATSIC Rights Framework, advocating the inherent rights of Aboriginal and Torres Strait Islander peoples', ATSIC, *Annual Report 2000–2001*, p. 71.

Chapter 3 Like unacknowledged bastards

1 D. Smith, 'Representative Politics and the new wave of native title organisations' in J. Finlayson and D. Smith (eds), *Native Title: Emerging Issues for Research, Policy and Practice*, Research Monograph No. 10, Centre for Aboriginal Economic Policy Research, the Australian National University, Canberra, 1995, p. 61. The relevant legislation is *Aboriginal Land Rights Act (Northern Territory) 1976* (Cwlth). The functioning of the legislation remains politically controversial: See, for example, J. Reeves, *Building on Land Rights for the Next Generation: The Review of the Aboriginal Land Rights (Northern Territory) Act 1976*, Commonwealth of Australia, Canberra, 1998 and J.C. Altman et al., *Land Rights at Risk?*

Evaluations of the Reeves Report, Research Monograph No. 14, Centre for Aboriginal Economic Policy Research, Canberra, 1999.

2 G. Parker et al., *Review of Native Title Representative Bodies*, Aboriginal & Torres Strait Islander Commission, Canberra, 1995, p. viii.

3 D. Smith, 'Representative Politics and the New Wave of Native Title Organisations' in J. Finlayson and D. Smith (eds), *Native Title: Emerging Issues for Research, Policy and Practice*, Research Monograph No. 10, Centre for Aboriginal Economic Policy Research, Australian National University, Canberra, 1995, pp. 60–1.

4 M. Dodson, 'The Role of Representative Bodies in Making Native Title Claims' in AIATSIS, *Proof and Management of Native Title: Summary of Proceedings of a Workshop*, AIATSIS, Canberra, 1994, p. 5.

5 See NTA 1993, s. 202(4). J. Altman and D. Smith, 'The Report of the ATSIC Review of Representative Bodies' in P. Burke (ed.), *The Skills of Native Title Practice: Proceedings of a Workshop*, AIATIS, Canberra, 1995, p. 150.

6 The Aboriginal legal service movement emerged in Australia in the 1970s, as part of the non-governmental sector, providing specialist legal advice services to Indigenous people in a culturally appropriate way.

7 The Kimberley Land Council, for example, although it had no statutory foundation had been operating since 1978.

8 The Yamatji Land and Sea Council, for example, was established in response to *Mabo* for the purpose of becoming an NTRB.

9 J. Altman and D. Smith, 'Funding Aboriginal and Torres Strait Islander Representative Bodies under the *Native Title Act 1993*', *Land, Rights, Laws: Issues of Native Title*, April 1995, Issue Paper No. 8, p. 3.

10 A partial list of the initial functions is provided at: D. Smith, 'Representative Politics and the New Wave of Native Title Organisations' in J. Finlayson and D. Smith (eds), *Native Title: Emerging Issues for Research, Policy and Practice*, Research Monograph No. 10, Centre for Aboriginal Economic Policy Research, the Australian National University, Canberra, 1995, p. 62. Further functions were added in the 1998 Amendments: see Part 11 of the Amended NTA. At the outset there were jurisdictional tensions with the NNTT which also had an 'assistance to applicants' function, but these were soon resolved: National Native Title Tribunal, *Annual Report 1995–96*, p. iv.

11 See G. Parker et al., *Review of Native Title Representative Bodies*, Aboriginal & Torres Strait Islander Commission, Canberra, 1995, p. iii–vii; J. Altman and D. Smith, 'Funding Aboriginal and Torres Strait Islander Representative Bodies under the *Native Title Act 1993*', *Land,*

Rights, Laws: Issues of Native Title, April 1995, Issue Paper No. 8; D. Smith, 'Representative Politics and the New Wave of Native Title Organisations' in J. Finlayson and D. Smith (eds), *Native Title: Emerging Issues for Research, Policy and Practice*, Research Monograph No. 10, Centre for Aboriginal Economic Policy Research, Australian National University, Canberra, 1995, p. 62.

12 Personal communication. Printed with permission.

13 See 'review recommendations' in G. Parker et al., *Review of Native Title Representative Bodies*, Aboriginal & Torres Strait Islander Commission, Canberra, 1995, pp xi–xx.

14 J. Altman and D. Smith, 'The Report of the ATSIC Review of Representative Bodies' in P. Burke (ed.), *The Skills of Native Title Practice: Proceedings of a Workshop*, AIATIS, Canberra, 1995, p. 151.

15 T. Summerfield, 'Native Title Representative Bodies under the Native Title Act Amendments: A Chance to Excel?', *E Law—Murdoch University Electronic Journal of Law*, 7(2), June 2000, para. [2].

16 For a discussion of the greater complexity of the second set of Amendments, see T. Summerfield, 'Native Title Representative Bodies under the Native Title Act Amendments: A Chance to Excel?', *E Law—Murdoch University Electronic Journal of Law*, 7(2), June 2000, para. [6].

17 See G. McIntyre, D. Ritter and P. Sheiner, 'Administrative Avalanche: The Application of the Registration test under the NTA 1993 (Cth)', *Indigenous Law Bulletin*, 4(20), April/May 1999, 8.

18 See *Australian Mining and Petroleum Law Journal*, 17(3) (Special Edition), Oct. 1998.

19 S. Phillips, '"Like Something out of Kafka": The Relationship between the Roles of the National Native Title Tribunal and the Federal Court in the Development of Native Title Practice', *Land, Rights, Laws: Issues of Native Title*, 2(14), April 2002.

20 The process is described in *Pilbara Aboriginal Land Council v Minister for Aboriginal and Torres Strait Islander Affairs* (2000) 175 ALR 706.

21 The re-recognition criteria were set out in the NTA, but given fuller expression in Aboriginal and Torres Strait Islander Commission, *Procedures Relating to Applications for Recognition as a Native Title Representative Body*, Canberra, 1999.

22 See Aboriginal and Torres Strait Islander Commission, *Procedures Relating to Applications for Recognition as a Native Title Representative Body*, Canberra, 1999 and F.N.A. Flanagan, 'ATSIC Native Title

Representative Bodies Recognition Update', *Native Title News*, 4(10), 2000, 181–3.

23 Cape York Land Council, *Annual Report 1998–1999*, p. 5.

24 T. Summerfield, 'Native Title Representative Bodies under the Native Title Act Amendments: A Chance to Excel?', *E Law—Murdoch University Electronic Journal of Law*, 7(2), June 2000.

25 J. Altman and D. Smith, 'The Report of the ATSIC Review of Representative Bodies' in P. Burke (ed.), *The Skills of Native Title Practice: Proceedings of a Workshop*, AIATIS, Canberra, 1995, p. 152.

26 See, for example, 'Mark Love' in K. Calley and N. Pearson (eds), *The Wik Summit Papers*, Cape York Land Council, Cairns, 1997 and M. Love, 'Without Prejudice: The *Wik* Negotiation' in B. Keon-Cohn (ed.), *Native Title in the New Millennium*, AIATSIS, Canberra, 2001.

27 Senator Brennan Rashid and Corrs Chambers Westgarth, *Review of Native Title Representative Bodies*, Canberra, 1999, p. 43.

28 ATSIC Native Title and Legislation Centre, *Capacity Building Program*, Draft Discussion Paper, 2001, p. 1.

29 See, for example,: T. North, 'From the Internet to the Outback—A World Class Court' in B. Keon-Cohn (ed.), *Native Title in the New Millennium*, AIATSIS, Canberra, 2001; J. Sosso, 'The Role of the Tribunal and the Federal Court', paper delivered at *Negotiating Country*, a forum held by the National Native Title Tribunal at Customs House, Brisbane, 3 August 2001; and W. Jonas, *Native Title Report 2001*, Human Rights and Equal Opportunities Commission, Sydney, January 2002, Chapter 2 and sources cited therein.

30 Senator Brennan Rashid and Corrs Chambers Westgarth, *Review of Native Title Representative Bodies*, Canberra, 1999.

31 The problem of under-funding is considered judicially in, for example: *Sampi v Western Australia* [2000] FCA 1018; *Bolton v Western Australia* [2001] FCA 1074; *Wadi Wadi People v Victoria* [2001] FCA 1780; *Gale v Minister for Land and Water Conservation (NSW)* [2001] FCA 1652; *Colbung v Western Australia* [2001] FCA 1342; *Wilkes v Western Australia* [2002] FCA 222; and *Harrington-Smith on behalf of the Wongatha People v Western Australia (No 6)* [2003] FCA 663.

32 R. Potok, *A Report into the Professional Needs of Native Title Representative Body Lawyers: Final Report*, Monash University, 7 April 2005, pp. 2, 4 and passim and D.F. Martin, *Capacity of Anthropologists in Native Title Practice*, National Native Title Tribunal, April 2004, p. 26.

33 See Kimberley Land Council, *Annual Report 2000–2001*, pp. 1, 8, 16.

34 J. Altman and D. Smith, 'The Report of the ATSIC Review of Representative Bodies' in P. Burke (ed.), *The Skills of Native Title Practice: Proceedings of a Workshop*, AIATIS, Canberra, 1995, p. 152.

35 The Howard government's antipathy to collectivism is evidenced by, for example, the unprecedented attack on the principle of collective bargaining in the workplace and on student unionism: see D. Peetz, *Brave New Workplace*, Allen & Unwin, Sydney, 2005 and in relation to so-called 'voluntary student unionism' see F. Rochford, 'Sausage Rolls and Sports Fields: The Debate over Voluntary Student Unionism in Australia', *Education and the Law*, 18(2/3), 2006, 161–76. More generally, see C. Hamilton and S. Maddison, *Silencing Dissent: How the Australian Government is Controlling Public Opinion and Stifling Debate*, Allen & Unwin, Sydney, 2007; D. Marr, *His Master's Voice: The Corruption of Public Debate Under Howard: Quarterly Essay 26*, Black Inc., Melbourne, 2007; and G. Boucher and M. Sharpe, *The Times Will Suit Them: Postmodern Conservatism in Australia*, Allen & Unwin, Sydney, 2008.

36 *Australian Government, Response to Joint Statutory Committee on Native Title and the Aboriginal and Torres Strait Islander Land Account on the Operation of Native Title Representative Bodies March 2006*, http://www.aph.gov.au/senate/committee/ntlf_ctte/rep_bodies/gov_response.pdf.

37 See T. Summerfield, 'Native Title Representative Bodies under the Native Title Act Amendments: A Chance to Excel?', *E Law—Murdoch University Electronic Journal of Law*, 7(2), June 2000, para. [41].

38 In 1995, it was noted that 'at this stage in the development of processes under the NTA, it is not possible to apply generalised performance indicators': J. Altman and D. Smith, 'The Report of the ATSIC Review of Representative Bodies' in P. Burke (ed.), *The Skills of Native Title Practice: Proceedings of a Workshop*, AIATIS, Canberra, 1995, p. 158. It never really became possible.

39 Among the Aboriginal Legal Service's victories were: *Western Australia v Commonwealth* (1995) 183 CLR 373; 128 ALR 1; *Ward v Western Australia* (1998) 159 ALR 483; and *Walley v Western Australia* (1996) 67 FCR 366; 137 ALR 561.

40 See, for example, South West Aboriginal Land and Sea Council, *Annual Report 2004*, pp. 21–2 and Ngaanyatjarra Council, *Annual Report 2001–2002*, p. 5.

41 Personal communication to the author.

42 D. Smith, 'Representative Politics and the new wave of native title organisations' in J. Finlayson and D. Smith (eds), *Native Title: Emerging Issues for Research, Policy and Practice*, Research Monograph No. 10,

Centre for Aboriginal Economic Policy Research, Australian National University, Canberra, 1995, p. 68.

43 Ss. 202(3)(a).

44 Ss. 202 (4).

45 Ss. 203AD(1).

46 Both statutory formulations recognised the difference between traditional connection that may give rise to a determination of native title and historical and contemporary interests which do not have that potential and created only a limited obligation on the part of NTRBs to the latter. Often Indigenous people (and therefore potential native title holders) do not live on the country to which they assert a traditional affiliation and so NTRBs were not infrequently faced with situations where some native title claimants did not live anywhere within the mandate of the representative body, in contrast to other Aboriginal people who were resident within the jurisdiction but were not traditional owners. See D. Martin, 'The Incorporation of "traditional" and "historical" interests in Native Title Representative Bodies' in D. Smith and J. Finlayson, *Fighting over Country: Anthropological Perspectives*, CAEPR, ANU Research Monograph 12, 1997.

47 See, for example, P. Mulder, 'Role of Representative Bodies and Native Title Units in Resolving Some Disputes: Some Dilemmas and Directions' and P. Agius, 'Dispute Resolution Prior to Application: Role of Native Title Representative Bodies' in P. Burke (ed.), *The Skills of Native Title Practice: Proceedings of a Workshop*, AIATIS, Canberra, 1995 and for a rather idealised account F. Tanner, 'Representing Native Title Groups' in L. Strelein (ed.), *Working with the Native Title Act: Alternatives to the Adversarial Method*, AIATSIS, Canberra, 1998.

48 Goldfields Land Council, *Annual Report 2002*, p. 6.

49 See, for example, R.S. French, 'The National Native Title Tribunal and the Native Title Act, Agendas for Change' in G.D. Meyers (ed.), *Implementing the Native Title Act: The Next Step: Facilitating Negotiated Agreements*, National Native Title Tribunal, Perth, 1997, p. 29.

50 North Queensland Land Council, *Annual Report 2000–2001*, p. 1.

51 J. Finalyson, 'Aboriginal Tradition and Native Title Representative Bodies' in D. Smith and J. Finlayson, *Fighting over Country: Anthropological Perspectives*, CAEPR, Research Monograph 12, 1997, p. 147.

52 Subject, of course, to principles of administrative law: but enforcing such rights also requires resources.

53 Kimberley Land Council, *Annual Report 2000–2001*, p. 2.

54 For example, prior to the 1998 Amendments it was considered 'best practice' to simply lodge 'polygon claims' in response to mining tenure applications, so-named because the borders simply mirrored the boundaries of the tenements in question. Later, after the Amendments had been passed, the rush to retain the right to negotiate involved (again as 'best practice') the mass combination of claims, sometimes with fairly arbitrary boundaries and memberships.

55 NTA, ss. 61 and 62A.

56 D. Ivison, *Postcolonial Liberalism*, Cambridge University Press, Cambridge, 2002, p. 150.

57 D. Smith, 'Representative Politics and the New Wave of Native Title Organisations' in J. Finlayson and D. Smith (eds), *Native Title: Emerging Issues for Research, Policy and Practice*, Research Monograph No. 10, Centre for Aboriginal Economic Policy Research, Australian National University, Canberra, 1995, p. 65.

58 Central Queensland Land Council Aboriginal Corporation, *Annual Report 1999–2000*, p. 11.

59 North Queensland Land Council, *Annual Report 2000–2001*, p. 11.

60 For a sample of similar dynamics see: Goldfields Land Council, *Annual Report 1998–1999*, p. 16; South West Aboriginal Land and Sea Council, *Annual Report 2002*, p. 12; and Ngaanyatjarra Council, *Annual Report 2001–2002*. See T. Summerfield, 'Native Title Representative Bodies under the Native Title Act Amendments: A Chance to Excel?', *E Law—Murdoch University Electronic Journal of Law*, 7(2), June 2000, para. [2].

61 The lack of clarity intrinsic in the initial formulation of the NTA was not addressed by the 1998 Amendments: T. Summerfield, 'Native Title Representative Bodies Under The Native Title Act Amendments: A Chance To Excel?', *E Law—Murdoch University Electronic Journal of Law*, 7(2), June 2000, para. [23].

62 See also D. Smith, 'Representative Politics and the New Wave of Native Title Organisations' in J. Finlayson and D. Smith (eds), *Native Title: Emerging Issues for Research, Policy and Practice*, Research Monograph No. 10, Centre for Aboriginal Economic Policy Research, the Australian National University, Canberra, 1995, p. 68.

63 See D. Smith, 'Representative Politics and the New Wave of Native Title Organisations' in J. Finlayson and D. Smith (eds), *Native Title: Emerging Issues for Research, Policy and Practice*, Research Monograph No. 10, Centre for Aboriginal Economic Policy Research, the Australian National University, Canberra, 1995, p. 65.

64 For a clear example of this dynamic at work see S. Woehne-Green, 'Some Ethical Issues for Representative Bodies and Anthropologists Working Together on Native Title Issues' in J. Fingleton and J. Finlayson (eds), *Anthropology in the Native Title Era: The Proceedings of a Workshop*, AIATSIS, Canberra, 1995. See also J. Morris, 'Increasing Aboriginal Claimants' Control of the Native Title Claim Process' in P. Burke (ed.), *The Skills of Native Title Practice: Proceedings of a Workshop*, AIATIS, Canberra, 1995 and the discussion which followed.

65 N. Pearson, 'Honouring Mabo's Legacy—and asking what is left of it', *ATSIC News*, Winter 2003, 20–1.

66 The tendency for a 'racial' division between professional and non-professional employees of NTRBs, because of the small number of Indigenous lawyers and anthropologists, made for an unhelpful perception that the information provided by lawyers and anthropologists was 'whitefellas' talking, rather than individuals doing their best according to disciplinary precepts. It also ignored the reality that for an Indigenous lawyer or anthropologist to be effective, they must be good at their professional duties rather than having a particular ethnicity. In R. Potok, *A Report into the Professional Needs of Native Title Representative Body Lawyers: Final Report*, Monash University, 7 April 2005, p. 61, reports of calls for more Indigenous lawyers were mixed with complaints about conflict of interest. Perhaps, too, any assertion that increasing the number of Indigenous staff necessarily increases 'representativeness' is in any event fundamentally suspect on the basis that it presumes that political authority is predicated on identity rather than process. One might argue, for example, that the process by which a Chief Executive Officer is hired and directed says more about his or her 'representativeness' in a functional sense, than whether or not the person in question is Aboriginal. The politics, of course, remains understandably vexed.

67 Carpentaria Land Council Aboriginal Corporation, *Annual Report 2001–2002*, pp. 2, 7.

68 Central Queensland Land Council Aboriginal Corporation, *Annual Report 1999–2000*, pp. 10–11.

69 J. Morris, 'Increasing Aboriginal Claimants' Control of the Native Title Claim Process' in P. Burke (ed.), *The Skills of Native Title Practice: Proceedings of a Workshop*, AIATIS, Canberra, 1995, pp. 1–2.

70 Which is not to diminish the significance of these matters.

71 Goldfields Land Council, *Annual Report 2002*, p. 14.

72 South West Aboriginal Land and Sea Council, *Annual Report 2002*, p. 4.

73 Carpentaria Land Council Aboriginal Corporation, *Annual Report 2001–2002*, p. 7.
74 Queensland South Representative Body Aboriginal Corporation, *Annual Report 2000–2001*, p. 16.
75 Most obviously, NTRBs were not established to auspice economic development either in terms of their statutory functions or the funding they received from government.
76 Hon. Mal Brough MP, Minister for Families, Community Services and Indigenous Affairs and the Minister Assisting the Prime Minister for Indigenous Affairs, 'Reforms to Native Title Representative Bodies to Benefit Indigenous Australians', Archived Media Releases, 7 June 2007, http://www.facs.gov.au/internet/minister3.nsf/content/ntrb_7jun07.htm.
77 H. Wootten, 'A Cheer for the Mabo Nudgers', *Aboriginal Law Bulletin*, 3(62), 1993, 2.
78 Cape York Land Council, *Annual Report 2000–2001*, p. 15.
79 P. Sullivan, 'Problems of Mediation in the National Native Title Tribunal' in J. Fingleton and J. Finlayson, *Anthropology in the Native Title Era: Proceedings of a Workshop*, AIATSIS, Canberra, 1995, p. 97. Sullivan provides an excruciating account of the potential pitfalls of the mediation process.
80 Kimberley Land Council, *Annual Report 2004*, p. 5.
81 For a definition of this concept see D.B. Rose, 'Land Rights and Deep Colonising', *Indigenous Law Bulletin*, 1996, 28.

Chapter 4 State expectations

1 For standard works see G.F. Sawer, *Modern Federalism*, 2nd edn, Pitman Australia, Carlton (Vic.), 1976 and J. Moon and C. Sharman, *Australian Politics and Government: The Commonwealth, the States and the Territories*, Cambridge University Press, Port Melbourne, 2003.
2 After the *Work Choices Case*, it seems that there are few areas that are necessarily beyond potential Commonwealth control under the corporations head of power: see *New South Wales v Commonwealth* [2006] HCA 52; 81 ALJR 34; 231 ALR 1.
3 *Western Australia v Commonwealth* (1995) 183 CLR 373; 128 ALR 1. See R. French, 'The Race Power: A Constitutional Chimera' in G. Winterton (ed.), *Australian Constitutional Landmarks*, Cambridge University Press, Cambridge; Port Melbourne, 2003. The Australian Capital and Northern Territories, with even less constitutional autonomy than the states, could

be the subject of direct Commonwealth override on any matter: *Constitution*, s. 122.

4 After 1998 the state systems were permitted to be weaker than the NTA in terms of the procedural rights guaranteed to native title claimants, though subject to the final ability of the Commonwealth Senate to disallow alternative state native title regimes: NTA, ss. 43A(9) and 214.

5 R. Court, 'Returning Power to the States: Risky or Responsible?', *Samuel Griffith Society: Conference Proceedings*, 1997, 9, 6–14, p. 6.

6 R.S. French and P.M. Lane, 'Response to Commonwealth Government Discussion Paper Outlining Proposed Amendments to the Native Title Act 1993' in G.D. Meyers (ed.), *Implementing the Native Title Act: The Next Step: Facilitating Negotiated Agreements*, National Native Title Tribunal, Perth, 1996, p. 92.

7 For example, state solicitor's advice could apparently be determinative of government decisions about whether or not to appeal cases, despite the fact that lawyers are there to follow instructions, not give them. See Hon. Eric Ripper MLA, Deputy Premier, Treasurer, Minister for State Development, 'Keynote Address to the AIATSIS Native Title Conference 2008', Perth Convention Exhibition Centre, 5 June 2008, http://www.nativetitle.wa.gov.au/uploadedFiles/Media_and_Publications/Speeches/AIATSIS_DEPUTY_PREMIER.pdf, retrieved 15/12/08.

8 P. Shergold, 'Beyond the silo: connecting government', *Public Sector Informant, Canberra Times*, May, 2004; P. Shergold, 'Connecting Government: Whole-of-Government Responses to Australia's Priority Challenges', a speech to launch *Connecting Government: Whole-of-Government Responses to Australia's Priority Challenges*, 20 April 2004: http://www.pmc.gov.au/speeches/shergold/connecting_government_2004-04-20.cfm and P. Shergold, 'Sharing Responsibility: A New Approach to Delivering Services to Indigenous Australians', National Reconciliation Planning Workshop, Canberra, 31 May 2005: http://www.pmc.gov.au/speeches/shergold/sharing_responsibility_2005-05-31.cfm.

9 Tenements covered by, for example, s. 237 of the NTA.

10 See D. Ritter, 'Many Bottles for Many Flies: Managing Conflict over Indigenous Peoples' Cultural Heritage in Western Australia', *Public History Review*, 13, 2006.

11 Most commonly the 'creation of a right to mine', the subject of a notice under s. 29 of the NTA.

12 This process is discussed at length in D. Ritter, *The Native Title Market*, UWA Press, Perth, 2009.

13 See D. Martin, 'Deal of the Century? A Case Study from the Pasminco Century Project', *Indigenous Law Bulletin*, 34; 4(11), 1998.
14 See, for example, 'Burrup Peninsula' in Human Rights and Equal Opportunity Commission, *Native Title Report 2003*, Sydney, 2004, 84–7.
15 See, for example, Hon. Eric Ripper MLA, Deputy Premier, Treasurer, Minister for State Development, 'Keynote Address to the AIATSIS Native Title Conference 2008', Perth Convention Exhibition Centre, 5 June 2008, http://www.nativetitle.wa.gov.au/uploadedFiles/Media_and_Publications/Speeches/AIATSIS_DEPUTY_PREMIER.pdf, retrieved 15/12/08.
16 Compare *Hayes v Northern Territory* [1999] FCA 1248 (9 September 1999), para. [26] with W. Treasure, 'Whatever Happened to the Long-standing Principle that the Crown Sets an Example to Others by Behaving as a Model Litigant', *Native Title News*, 7(11), 2006, 205–7.
17 R.S. French, 'Personal Reflections on the National Native Title Tribunal', *Melbourne University Law Review*, 2003, 27, 488–522, p. 502.
18 M. Dillon, 'Native Title: A View from the Commonwealth' in F. McKeown (ed.), *Opportunities for Understanding*, National Native Title Tribunal, Perth, 1994, p. 207.
19 R.S. French, 'Pathways to Agreement' in G.D. Meyers, *The Way Forward: Collaboration and Cooperation in Country*, National Native Title Tribunal, Perth, 1996, p. 24.
20 R.S. French and P.M. Lane, 'Response to Commonwealth Government Discussion Paper Outlining Proposed Amendments to the Native Title Act 1993' in G.D. Meyers (ed.), *Implementing the Native Title Act: The Next Step: Facilitating Negotiated Agreements*, National Native Title Tribunal, Perth, 1996, p. 91.
21 J. Finlayson, 'Anthropology and Connection Reports in Native Title Claim Applications' presented at the *Native Title Forum*, Customs House, Brisbane, August 2001, p. 2.
22 J. Finlayson, 'Anthropology and Connection Reports in Native Title Claim Applications', presented at the *Native Title Forum*, Customs House, Brisbane, August 2001, p. 4.
23 Government of Western Australia, *General Guidelines Native Title Determinations and Agreements*, March 2000, p. 2.
24 Western Australian Office of Native Title, *Guidelines for the Provision of Information in Support of Applications for a Determination of Native Title*, October 2004, p. 4. The guidelines that offered perhaps the greatest promise of flexibility were those of the Bracks Labor government in Victoria, released in October 2001, but even then the state was clear that the 'proof required for a consent determination of native title' required

the rights claimed to be 'substantiated' and meant a connection report would have to contain evidence that was 'of a high standard': Native Title Unit of the Department of Justice, *Guidelines for Native Title Proof in Victoria*, October 2001, p. 6.

25 At least two connection reports were subsequently published as freestanding ethnographies: see S. Cane, *Pila Nguru: The Spinifex People*, Fremantle Arts Centre Press, Fremantle, 2002 and G. Bagshaw, *The Karajarri Claim: A Case-Study in Native Title Anthropology*, Oceania Publications, Sydney, 2003.

26 Transcript of videoconference directions before North J., *Hayes v Western Australia* WAD 6113 of 1998, 12.35 pm, Thursday, 24 March 2005, p. 2.

27 See C. Wilson-Clark, 'Working Group Report Damns Labor', *The West Australian*, 9 April 2003.

28 From Hon. Eric Ripper MLA, Deputy Premier, Treasurer, Minister for State Development, 'Keynote Address to the AIATSIS Native Title Conference 2008', Perth Convention Exhibition Centre, 5 June 2008, http://www.nativetitle.wa.gov.au/uploadedFiles/Media_and_Publications/Speeches/AIATSIS_DEPUTY_PREMIER.pdf, retrieved 15/12/08, p. 4.

29 See Hon. Eric Ripper MLA, Deputy Premier, Treasurer, Minister for State Development, 'Keynote Address to the AIATSIS Native Title Conference 2008', Perth Convention Exhibition Centre, 5 June 2008, http://www.nativetitle.wa.gov.au/uploadedFiles/Media_and_Publications/Speeches/AIATSIS_DEPUTY_PREMIER.pdf, retrieved 15/12/08.

30 The full list of consent determinations of native title can be found on the Tribunal's register at http://www.nntt.gov.au/Applications-And-Determinations/Search-Determinations/Pages/Search.aspx.

31 See J. Clarke, 'Key Aspects of the Western Australian Government's Policy on Native Title and Commercial Ventures with Aboriginal Communities', paper given at *Joint Ventures and Commercial Alliances with Aboriginal Communities Conference*, 29–30 July 1996, Mercure Hotel, Perth; J. Clarke, 'Western Australia's Approach to Native Title' in *Native Title: A One Day Conference Concerning Implications for Investment & Growth in the Resources and Infrastructure of Western Australia following the Last Federal Government Response*, 24 April 1997; and S. Wood, 'State Government—The New Role: Western Australian Government', paper given at *Living with Wik: The New Native Title Laws*, 16–17 November 1998, Sydney.

32 'From 23 December 1996 to 5 September 2000 no section 29 notices were issued in the Northern Territory. It is understood that during this time few or no exploration or prospecting titles were granted in the

Northern Territory. At 21 March 2000 there existed a backlog of over 1000 mining title applications and 12 petroleum permit applications. During this period, there was considerable agitation by mining interests and various State and Territory governments for amendments to the NTA to achieve "certainty" over native title issues': Aboriginal and Torres Strait Islander Social Justice Commissioner, *Native Title Report 2001*, Human Rights and Equal Opportunity Commission, 2001, http://www.hreoc.gov.au/social_justice/ntreport_01/chap1.html#nor, 1 June 2007. See also C. Athanasiou and G. Borchers, 'The Northern Territory's Alternative' in B. Keon-Cohn, (ed.), *Native Title in the New Millennium*, AIATSIS, Canberra, 2001.

33 *Anderson v Western Australia* [2000] FCA 1717 (28 November 2000); *Clarrie Smith and others v State of Western Australia and others* [2000] FCA 149 (29 August 2000) and 'Yamatji Co-operation Agreement', *Native Title News*, 4(12), December 2000.

34 In the middle of 2000, the State of Western Australia began a policy of granting mining tenements without going through the future act processes of the NTA on the basis of the Full Court decision in *State of Western Australia v Ward* [2000] FCA 191. Essentially, under what became known as 'the Ward Policy', the state granted tenements where it deemed that native title had been extinguished because of 'improvements to or enclosures on' pastoral leases. On appeal the High Court decided that improvements and enclosures were irrelevant to the question of extinguishment, rendering all tenements granted under the Ward Policy to be of questionable validity.

35 Press release from the Premier, Peter Beattie, 'Premier Sets Three-Month Timetable for Native Title Agreement', Friday, 17 July 1998.

36 See J. Fitzgerald, 'Queensland Alternative Provisions' in B. Keon-Cohn, (ed.), *Native Title in the New Millennium*, AIATSIS, Canberra, 2001.

37 From 8 September 2000 to 31 March 2003 the Queensland Government had implemented its alternative state regime through the *Mineral Resources Act 1989 (Qld)*. In 2003 the Queensland Government amended the *Mineral Resources Act 1989 (Qld) (Natural Resources and other Legislation Amendment Act 2003 (Qld))* with the effect that the right to negotiate procedures established under the NTA applied to applications made under the *Mineral Resources Act 1989 (Qld)*.

38 *Buck v New South Wales* (Fed C of A, Lockhart J, NG 6002 of 1996, 7 April 1997, unreported). See, for example, 'The Crescent Head Agreement', *Australian Indigenous Law Reporter*, (2)1, 1997, 100–5; S. Blackshield, 'Crest Head Native Title Agreement', *Aboriginal Law Bulletin*,

3(88), 1997, 9–10; and rather more evocatively T. Condie, 'At Last! Tears of Joy Flow after Historic Native Title Breakthrough by Dunghutti People', *Koori Mail*, (137), 23 October 1996, 1–3.

39 *Wilson v Anderson* (2002) 213 CLR 401.

40 *Lovett v Victoria* [2007] FCA 474 and *Clarke v Victoria* [2005] FCA 1795.

41 Yorta Yorta Co-operative Management Agreement 2004. See Jesse Hogan and Fergus Shiel, 'Historic Yorta Yorta deal signed,' *The Age*, 11 June 2004, http://www.theage.com.au/articles/2004/06/10/1086749839804.html?from=storylhs.

42 Agreement between the Territory and ACT Native Title Claim Groups (2001).

43 Eric Ripper, Deputy Premier, keynote address to *Moving Forward: Best Practice for Indigenous Relations in Western Australia*, Conference, Sheraton Hotel Perth, 19 April 2001.

44 See C. Athanasiou, 'Land Rights or Native Title: What's Going on in the Northern Territory?', *Indigenous Law Bulletin*, 14(12), 1998, 14–17 and D. Carment, 'The Northern Territory Government and the Debate on Aboriginal Native Title 1992–1995', *Journal of Northern Territory History*, 9, 1998, 81–90.

45 *Hayes v Northern Territory* [1999] FCA 1248 (9 September 1999), para. 26.

46 See A. Andrejewski, CEO, SA Mines and Energy Department at *Native Title: Commercial Realities of the Coalition's Change Agenda*, 27 August 1996, p. 1 and T. Wooley, 'The Alternative Scheme in South Australia' in B. Keon-Cohen (ed.), *Native Title in the New Millennium*, AIATSIS, Canberra, 2001.

47 The South Australian Aboriginal Legal Rights Movement ('ALRM'), which became the only native title representative body for the state after the rationalisation of NTRBs which occurred following the 1998 Amendments. The state also continued to fund litigation against native title: P. Agius et al., 'Negotiating Comprehensive Settlement of Native Title Issues: Building a New Scale of Justice in South Australia', *Land Rights Laws: Issues of Native Title*, 2(20), 2002, 5–6.

48 P. Agius et al., 'Negotiating Comprehensive Settlement of Native Title Issues: Building a New Scale of Justice in South Australia', *Land Rights Laws: Issues of Native Title*, 2 (20), 2002. The technical detail of the South Australian approach received judicial consideration in *Jones v South Australia* [2003] FCA 538.

49 South Australian Government, South Australian Native Title Resolution homepage, http://www.iluasa.com.

50 South Australian Government, 'News and Recent Developments' South Australian Native Title Resolution homepage, http://www.sanativetitleresolution.com.au/developments/index.asp.
51 Premier of South Australia, 'Historic native title settlement' News Media Release, 28 August 2006, http://www.ministers.sa.gov.au/news.php?id=536.
52 For an earlier digest of state approaches see J. Finlayson, 'Anthropology and Connection Reports in Native Title Claim Applications', presented at the Native Title Forum, Customs House, Brisbane, August, 2001, p. 4.
53 To choose one example of many see: Premier of South Australia, 'Historic native title settlement', News Media Release 28 August 2006, http://www.ministers.sa.gov.au/news.php?id=536.
54 H. Wootten, 'Native Title in a Long Perspective: A View from the Eighties' at 'Outcomes and Possibilities', 3–5 September 2002, Geraldton (WA), p. 4.
55 Western Australian Aboriginal Native Title Working Group, *Reaching Agreement: A Better Approach to Native Title in Western Australia*, Perth, 1999, p. 5.
56 The term is inexact: S. Bradfield, 'Agreeing to Terms: What is a "Comprehensive" Agreement?', *Land, Rights, Laws: Issues of Native Title*, March 2(26), 2004, p. 7.
57 http://www.dia.wa.gov.au/Policies-in-Focus/State-Strategy/Statement-of-Commitment/
58 See, for example, C. Wilson-Clark, 'Working Group report damns Labor', *The West Australian*, 9 April 2003.
59 H. Wootten, 'Native Title in a Long Perspective: A View from the Eighties' at 'Outcomes and Possibilities', 3–5 September 2002, Geraldton (WA), p. 4.
60 For two examples of state interests being set out plainly, see T.K. Griffin, Attorney General and Minister for Consumer Affairs, 'South Australia's Approach to Native Title—A Different Approach', Joint Ventures and Commercial Alliances with Aboriginal Communities conference, 29–30 July 1996, Mercure Hotel Perth and P. Beattie, 'Premier sets three-month timetable for native title agreement', Ministerial Media Statement, 17 July 1998.
61 For example: S. Wood, 'Western Australian Government' at Living with Wik: The New Native Title Laws, Sydney Sheraton Airport Hotel, 16–17 November 1998, p. 5.
62 P. Beattie, 'Wik: Transcript of answers given to a media conference by Peter Beattie Today', 2 July 1998. The issue has so far remained purely

hypothetical throughout the period under study, because no compensation payment has yet been ordered by a court.

63 See, for example, P. Ruddock, 'The Government's Approach to Native Title', Native Title Representative Bodies Conference, Adelaide, 4 June 2004.

64 J. Kennett, 'News Release from the Office of the Premier', 28 October 1998.

65 E. Ripper, Deputy Premier, address to Moving Forward: Best Practice for Indigenous Relations in Western Australia, conference, Sheraton Hotel Perth, 19 April 2001, p. 2.

66 Which is not to say that all litigated cases will produce definite results: see *Harrington-Smith on behalf of the Wongatha People v State of Western Australia (No 9)* [2007] FCA 31.

67 See, for example, R. Borbidge, 'Cabinet Reaffirms Support for Aboriginal Land at Hopevale', Ministerial Media Statement, 11 November 1997.

68 J. Altman, 'Native Title Act 1993—Issues and Considerations for Resource Developers', presented at AIC Worldwide's Doing Business with Aboriginal Communities, conference, Sheraton Wentworth, 14–15 June 1995, p. 3.

69 C. Scholtz, 'Land Claims: A Negotiated Option' in *Limits & Possibilities of a Treaty Process in Australia*, 27 August 2001, Canberra, p. 4. See further C. Scholtz, *Negotiating Claims: The Emergence of Indigenous Land Claim Negotiation Policies in Australia, Canada, New Zealand, and the United States*, Routledge, New York, 2006.

70 Transcript of videoconference directions before North J, *Hayes v Western Australia* WAD 6113 of 1998, 12.35 pm, Thursday, 24 March 2005, p. 2.

71 See C. Scholtz, *Negotiating Claims: The Emergence of Indigenous Land Claim Negotiation Policies in Australia, Canada, New Zealand and the United States*, Routledge, New York, 2006, p. 151.

72 E. Ripper, Deputy Premier, address to Moving Forward: Best Practice for Indigenous Relations in Western Australia, conference, Sheraton Hotel Perth, 19 April 2001.

73 For an important judicial exploration of this theme see *Lovett v Victoria* [2007] FCA 474.

74 From Hon. Eric Ripper MLA, Deputy Premier, Treasurer, Minister for State Development, 'Keynote Address to the AIATSIS Native Title Conference 2008', Perth Convention Exhibition Centre, 5 June 2008, accessed via Office of Native Title website, p. 7, http://www.nativetitle.wa.gov.au/uploadedFiles/Media_and_Publications/Speeches/AIATSIS_DEPUTY_PREMIER.pdf, retrieved 15/12/08, p. 4.

75 S. Bradfield, 'Agreeing to Terms: What is a "Comprehensive" Agreement?', *Land, Rights, Laws: Issues of Native Title*, 2(26), March 2004, p. 7.

Chapter 5 Mining rules and the sheep's back

1 NTA, ss. 68 and 84(2); after the Amendments: ss. 66(3)(a) and 84. See *Byron Environment Centre Inc v Arakwal People* (1997) 78 FCR 1; 148 ALR 46 and *Woodridge v Minister for Land and Water Conservation (NSW)* (2001) 108 FCR 527.

2 In *Yorta Yorta*, for instance, approximately 500 parties were involved: P. Seidel, 'The Yorta Yorta Native Title Determination Application' in L. Strelein (ed.), *Working with the Native Title Act: Alternatives to the Adversarial Method*, AIATSIS, Canberra, 1998, p. 130.

3 Generally, interests seeking party status were not contested and, when they were, usually without success. The extent to which parties actually actively participated in the process varied greatly.

4 The purpose of peak industry groups was never to advocate in relation to specific matters or to participate in particular sets of negotiations, and indeed successive Federal Court decisions rendered it impossible for such bodies to actually become party to specific native title claims. See J.K. Ellis, 'Indigenous Land Use Agreements: A Minerals Industry Perspective' in G. Meyers (ed.), *The Way Forward: Collaboration and Cooperation 'in Country'*, National Native Title Tribunal, Perth, 1996, p. 169 and *Harrington-Smith on behalf of the Wongatha People v Western Australia* [2002] FCA 184.

5 R.S. French, 'Personal Reflections on the National Native Title Tribunal', *Melbourne University Law Review*, 2003, 27, 488–522, p. 502.

6 G. Leyland, 'Native Title and the Fishing Industry' in F. McKeown (ed.), *Native Title: An Opportunity for Understanding*, National Native Title Tribunal, Perth, 1994, p. 176.

7 *Yarmirr v Northern Territory* (1998) 82 FCR 533; *Commonwealth v Yarmirr* (1999) 101 FCR 171; *Commonwealth v Yarmirr* (2001) 208 CLR 1.

8 J. Ellis, 'Transcript of Presentation', *Meeting of Key Stakeholders on Native Title Convened by the Council of Aboriginal Reconciliation*, Canberra International Hotel, 2 June 1996, p. 1.

9 See generally in relation to the function of heritage assessment surveys: D. Ritter, 'Many Bottles for Many Flies: Managing Conflict over Indigenous Peoples' Cultural Heritage in Western Australia', *Public History Review*, 13, 2006.

10 As described in 'Secret White Men's Business', 20 March 2000, *Four Corners*, http://www.abc.net.au/4corners/stories/s111958.htm.

11 A. Solomon, 'Mediation and Negotiation: "Yes, But I have a Life Too"' in L. Strelein (ed.), *Working with the Native Title Act: Alternatives to the Adversarial Method*, AIATSIS, Canberra, 1998, p. 59.

12 For example, the WA Chamber of Minerals and Energy worked closely with the Australian Mining Industry Council and other industry associations including the Association of Mining and Exploration Companies, Australian Tourism Industry Association, Australian Petroleum Exploration Association, Chamber of Commerce and Industry, Forest Industries Federation, Pastoralists and Graziers Association of WA, WA Farmers' Federation, and WA Fishing Industry Council: 'Report of the Aboriginal Affairs Committee' in The Chamber of Minerals and Energy of Western Australia, *Annual Report 1994*, pp. 7–8.

13 F. Brennan, *The Wik Debate: Its Impact on Aborigines, Pastoralists and Miners*, UNSW Press, Sydney, 1998, p. 28.

14 See generally M.W. Hunt, *Mining Law in Western Australia*, Federation Press, Leichhardt (NSW), 2001.

15 See, for example, S. Hawke and M. Gallagher, *Noonkanbah: Whose Land, Whose Law*, Fremantle Arts Centre Press, Fremantle, 1989; R.A. Dixon and M.C. Dillon (eds), *Aborigines and Diamond Mining*, University of Western Australia Press, Perth, 1990; G. Stokes, 'Special Interests or Equality?: The Mining Industry's Campaign against Aboriginal Land Rights in Australia', *Australian Canadian Studies*, 5(1), 1987, 61–78; G. Stokes, 'Mining Corporations and Aboriginal Land Rights in Australia: A Critique and Proposal', *Australian Quarterly*, 59(2), Winter 1987, 182–98; T. Duncan, 'How Land Rights Choke off New Mining Hopes: Business and Investment', *The Bulletin*, 31 Jan. 1984, 90–2; and T. Rowse, 'Land Rights, Mining and Settler Democracy', *Meanjin*, 45(1), Mar. 1986, 58–67.

16 The hard strategy was partially successful in ensuring that the legislative regime provided weaker procedural rights to claimants than the land rights regime in the Northern Territory, but unsuccessful in that the NTA was passed and included the right to negotiate. See, for example, P. Ellery, 'Report of the Chief Executive Officer', The Chamber of Minerals and Energy of Western Australia, *Annual Report*, 1994, p. 4.

17 'Appendix 4: The Impact of the Commonwealth Native Title Act 1993 on Exploration in Australia' in Australian Mining Industry Council, *Minerals Industry Survey '94*, Canberra, 1994, p. 32.

18 Minerals Council of Australia, *Native Title and the Australian Minerals Industry*, February 1998. See also, for example, 'Appendix 4: The Impact of the Commonwealth Native Title Act 1993 on Exploration in Australia' in Australian Mining Industry Council, *Minerals Industry Survey '94*, Canberra, 1994, p. 32; S. Williamson, 'Native Title and the Mining Industry: A View from the WA Chamber of Mines' in F. McKeown (ed.), *Native Title: An Opportunity for Understanding*, National Native Title Tribunal, Perth, 1994; P. Ellery, 'Report of the Chief Executive Officer', The Chamber of Minerals and Energy of Western Australia, *Annual Report*, 1994; 'Report of the Aboriginal Affairs Committee', The Chamber of Minerals and Energy of Western Australia, *Annual Report*, 1994.

19 See C. Senior, 'The Yandicoogina Process: A Model for Negotiating Land Use Agreements', *Land, Rights, Laws: Issues of Native Title*, February 1998, Regional Agreements paper no. 6.

20 See, for example, I. Manning, *Native Title, Mining and Mineral Exploration*, ATSIC, Canberra, 1997 and I. Manning, *Native Title, Mining and Mineral Exploration: A Postscript*, ATSIC, Canberra, 1998 and the references cited therein.

21 M. Macpherson, 'President's Address', presented at the *Minerals Outlook Seminar*, 11 May 1994, p. 3.

22 See A. Lavelle, 'Native Title and Recent Australian Mineral Exploration Trends', *Journal of Australian Political Economy*, 47, June 2001, pp. 27–46.

23 See, for example, A. de Soyza, 'Engineering Unworkability', *Land, Rights, Laws: Issues of Native Title*, 1(26), October 1998.

24 See, for example, *Technical Taskforce on Mineral Tenements and Land Title Applications: Final Report*, State Government of Western Australia, November 2001, s. 5.1.

25 The basic philosophy of the *WA Mining Act (1978)* is that tenements must be worked, that is, have exploration money spent on them, or surrendered. Tenement parking refers to the practice of resource interests applying for tenements in order to secure priority over the ground in question, but in the knowledge that the native title backlog would prevent the application from being processed quickly. The advantage for savvy companies was in obtaining precedence over prospective ground but without having to expend money on exploration.

26 At least as early as 1994, resources industry peak bodies were talking up the performance of resource interests in relation to Indigenous employment and engagement and expressing the industry's reconciliation credentials. 'Report of the Aboriginal Affairs Committee', Chamber of Minerals and Energy of Western Australia, *Annual Report*, 1994, p. 8.

27 G. Savell, 'Minerals Development is a Very Public Affair', presented at AIC Worldwide Public Affairs in Minerals & Energy Conference, 18–19 March 1996, Hyatt Hotel, Sydney, pp. 7, 15.

28 M. Gordon, 'A Lesson in the Art of Lobbying', *The Australian*, 27 July 1996, 27.

29 D. Buckingham, head of Minerals Council of Australia, quoted in M. Gordon, 'A Lesson in the Art of Lobbying', *The Australian*, 27 July 1996, p. 27.

30 See 'Appendix 4: The Impact of the Commonwealth Native Title Act 1993 on Exploration in Australia' in Australian Mining Industry Council, *Minerals Industry Survey '94*, Canberra, 1994; Australian Mining Industry Council, *Minerals Industry Survey '95*, Canberra, 1995, p. 4; and Australian Mining Industry Council, *Minerals Industry Survey '96*, Canberra, 1996, p. 4.

31 Australian Mining Industry Council, *Minerals Industry Survey '97*, Canberra, 1997, p. 6. The same section is repeated a year later in Australian Mining Industry Council, *Minerals Industry Survey '98*, Canberra, 1998, p. 7.

32 'Dick Wells' in K. Calley and N. Pearson (eds), *The Wik Summit Papers*, Cape York Land Council, Cairns, 1997, p. 83.

33 See, for example, S. Williamson, 'Native Title and the Mining Industry: A View from the WA Chamber of Mines' in F. McKeown (ed.), *Native Title: An Opportunity for Understanding*, National Native Title Tribunal, Perth, 1994, pp. 170–1 and J. Ellis, 'Transcript of Presentation', *Meeting of Key Stakeholders on Native Title Convened by the Council of Aboriginal Reconciliation*, Canberra International Hotel, 2 June 1996, p. 1.

34 See, for example, Chamber of Minerals and Energy of Western Australia Inc., *Let's Make Native Title Work*, Issue Paper No. 1, March 1998, p. 1 and Chamber of Minerals and Energy of Western Australia Inc., *We Need a System to Sort Out the Current Native Title Mess*, Issue Paper No. 3, March 98, p. 1.

35 Minerals Council of Australia, *Annual Report 1998*, p. 15.

36 In the original, the question is capitalised. Chamber of Minerals and Energy of Western Australia Inc., *Let's Make Native Title Work*, Issue Paper No. 1, March 1998, p. 1.

37 The principal win for the mining industry was the creation of the potential for the winding back of the right to negotiate by state governments, but in practice this did not occur for the reasons outlined in Chapter 4. The kinds of tenure made subject to the right to negotiate were reduced and the process was tightened, with a swathe of lesser

procedural rights introduced in replacement. Stringent new registration testing procedures precipitated the elimination of most overlapping claims and the prevention of any recurrence of the proliferation. Finally, the Amendments also created provision for Indigenous Land Use Agreements.

38 Minerals Council of Australia, *Annual Report 1998*, p. 16.

39 Minerals Council of Australia, *Annual Report 1999*, p. 16.

40 See, for example, G. Savell, 'Land Rights, Native Title and the Mining Industry', paper presented to *An Indigenous Future? Challenges and Opportunities*, Bennelong Society Conference, 2003. See Minerals Council of Australia, *Annual Report 1999*, pp. 16–17 and Minerals Council of Australia, *Annual Report 2000*, pp. 18–19.

41 See T. Corbett and C. O'Faircheallaigh, 'Unmasking the Politics of Native Title: The National Native Title Tribunal's Application of the NTA's Arbitration Provisions', *The University of Western Australia Law Review*, 33(1), December 2006, 153–76.

42 Discussed in detail in D. Ritter, *The Native Title Market*, UWA Press, Perth, 2009.

43 For example: 'Many Aboriginal people welcome mineral development, provided it does not endanger or compromise cultural beliefs and customs': Chamber of Minerals and Energy of Western Australia Inc., *Let's Make Native Title Work*, Issue Paper No. 1, March 1998, p. 4.

44 National Native Title Tribunal, *Talking Native Title*, 17 December 2005, p. 6.

45 Speaking in 1996, Hal Wootten noted a high degree of distrust of those representing Aboriginal communities; H. Wootten, 'Mediating between Aboriginal Communities and Industry' in G.D. Meyers (ed.), *Implementing the Native Title Act: The Next Step: Facilitating Negotiated Agreements*, National Native Title Tribunal, Perth, 1996, p. 181. J. Ellis, 'Transcript of Presentation', *Meeting of Key Stakeholders on Native Title Convened by the Council of Aboriginal Reconciliation*, Canberra International Hotel, 2 June 1996, p. 4. In 1996, for example, the Minerals Council of Australia described proposals to give greater authority to NTRBs as 'essentially an issue for the Government and indigenous people', but indicated that it would 'be concerned if statutory powers disenfranchise legitimate indigenous interests'. The coded language was characteristic, but provided a clear indication that the MCA was strongly opposed to what it perceived as NTRBs gaining a stranglehold on representation.

46 D. Smith, 'Representative Politics and the new wave of native title organisations' in J. Finlayson and D. Smith (eds), *Native Title: Emerging*

Issues for Research, Policy and Practice, Research Monograph No. 10, Centre for Aboriginal Economic Policy Research, the Australian National University, Canberra, 1995, p. 64.

47 Minerals Council of Australia, Submission to the Parliamentary Joint Committee on Native Title and the Aboriginal and Torres Strait Islander Land Fund Inquiry into Native Title Representative Bodies, 16/07/04, Parliamentary Joint Committee on Native Title and the Aboriginal and Torres Strait Islander Land Account, Completed Inquiries, Native Title Representative Bodies, http://www.aph.gov.au/Senate/committee/ntlf_ctte/rep_bodies/index.htm.

48 See, for example, P. Ruddock, 'The Government's Approach to Native Title', Native Title Representative Bodies Conference, Adelaide, 4 June 2004, p. 13.

49 Minerals Council of Australia, Submission to the Parliamentary Joint Committee on Native Title and the Aboriginal and Torres Strait Islander Land Fund Inquiry into Native Title Representative Bodies, 16/07/04, Parliamentary Joint Committee on Native Title and the Aboriginal and Torres Strait Islander Land Account, Completed Inquiries, Native Title Representative Bodies, http://www.aph.gov.au/Senate/committee/ntlf_ctte/rep_bodies/index.htm, p. 2.

50 See Minerals Council of Australia, Australian Petroleum Production & Exploration Association Limited, Submission to the Senate Legal and Constitutional Affairs Committee on the Native Title Amendment Bill 2006, 19/1/2007, Senate Legal and Constitutional Affairs Committee, Completed Reports, Inquiry into the Native Title Amendment Bill 2006, at http://www.aph.gov.au/Senate/committee/legcon_ctte/completed_inquiries/2004–07/native_title/submissions/sublist.htm.

51 See Association of Mining and Exploration Companies, Submission to the Senate Legal and Constitutional Affairs Committee on the Native Title Amendment Bill 2006, http://www.aph.gov.au/senate/committee/ntlf_ctte/rep_bodies/submissions/sub06.pdf, p. 2.

52 G. Savell, 'Land Rights, Native Title and the Mining Industry', paper presented to *An Indigenous Future? Challenges and Opportunities*, Bennelong Society Conference 2003.

53 See R. Bartlett, *Native Title in Australia*, Butterworths, Sydney, 2004 pp. 346–9.

54 'John Mackenzie' in K. Calley and N. Pearson (eds), *The Wik Summit Papers*, Cape York Land Council, Cairns, 1997, p. 74. See also 'Mark Love' in K. Calley and N. Pearson (eds), *The Wik Summit Papers*, Cape York Land Council, Cairns, 1997.

55 See, for example, 'John Mackenzie' in K. Calley and N. Pearson (eds), *The Wik Summit Papers*, Cape York Land Council, Cairns, 1997, p. 74; J. MacKenzie quoted in 'Outcome on Agreements', *Meeting of Native Title Stakeholders*, Canberra, 14–16 June 1996, convened by the Council of Aboriginal Reconciliation: '[o]ur view, based on legal advice, is that . . . a valid pastoral lease grants exclusive possession and extinguishes Native Title completely. This has been recognized in the preamble to the Native Title Act' and R. Boswell, 'We All Believed Title had been Extinguished', *The Australian*, 15 April 1997, p. 14.

56 See R. Farley, 'The Mabo Spiral: A Farm Sector Perspective' in M. Goot and T. Rowse, *Make a Better Offer: The Politics of Mabo*, Pluto Press, Leichhardt (NSW), 1994.

57 J. Mackenzie (Treasurer, NFF), 'National Farmers' Federation—Native Title and Voluntary Agreements' in G. Meyers (ed.), *The Way Forward: Collaboration and Cooperation 'in Country'*, National Native Title Tribunal, Perth, 1996, p. 176. Ironically, while the pastoralists would long remain adamant that native title had been extinguished by their tenure, peak mining adopted what one industry spokesperson described as the 'very conservative position that pastoral leases do not extinguish native title'. S. Williamson, 'Native Title and the Mining Industry: A View from the WA Chamber of Mines' in F. McKeown (ed.), *Native Title: An Opportunity for Understanding*, National Native Title Tribunal, Perth, 1994, p. 170. The key difference was that while pastoralists risked nothing by assuming that native title had been extinguished on their leases, the validity of new tenure obtained by miners and explorers could be placed in jeopardy if granted over land where a claim was subsequently made out. Tenements granted without complying with the NTA 1993 were potentially invalid. When *Wik* was handed down the Minerals Council of Australia denounced the decision as having 'changed one of the fundamental understandings reached when the NTA was passed': Minerals Council of Australia, *Annual Report 1997*, p. 13 and Minerals Council of Australia, *Annual Report 1998*, p. 15.

58 Though it was never really clear why this was the case. Given that any native title determination will more or less precisely record what rights are possessed by the traditional owners and where they continue to exist, it is not clear why there is any need for a more precise codification of the rules of interaction. In Western Australia, Queensland, the Northern Territory and South Australia, Aboriginal people held and enjoyed certain statutory rights of access to pastoral properties without there ever being any need for any regulation of the right in the manner envisaged

under access protocols. The *Land Act 1910* (Qld) includes a right of access to remove indigenous produce, rock, soil (s. 199). The *Land Act 1898* (WA) includes a right of Aboriginal access and use: s. 107 and 24th Sch, as well as a right of access to remove indigenous produce, rock, soil: s. 107, 24th Sch. The *Land Act 1980* (Qld) includes a right of Aboriginal access and use: Lease form, reg. 39, see R. Bartlett, *Native Title in Australia*, Butterworths, Sydney, 2004, pp. 346–7.

59 R.S. French, 'The National Native Title Tribunal and the Native Title Act, Agendas for Change' in G.D. Meyers (ed.), *Implementing the Native Title Act: The Next Step: Facilitating Negotiated Agreements*, National Native Title Tribunal, Perth, 1997, pp. 30 and 34.

60 *Re Waanyi People's Native Title Application (No 2)* (1995) 129 ALR 118; *North Ganalanja Aboriginal Corporation v Queensland* (1995) 61 FCR 1; 132 ALR 565 and *Wik Peoples v Queensland* QG104/1993 (unreported), 29 January 1996.

61 *Wik Peoples v Queensland* (1996) 187 CLR 1; 141 ALR 129. The case was, of course, much commented upon. See, for example, G. Hiley (ed.), *The Wik Case: Issues and Implications*, Butterworths, Sydney, 1997. In 1997 the NFF, with the support of the PGA, launched an advertising campaign lobbying for legislation to extinguish native title on pastoral leases: G. Armstrong, A. Burns and J. MacDonald, 'Anger as NFF Launches Wik Campaign', *The West Australian*, 21 March 1997, p. 27.

62 The fears and expectations proved in the most part correct with the unexpected exception proving to be New South Wales, where native title was held by the High Court to have been extinguished by the local form of pastoral tenure: *Wilson v Anderson* (2002) 213 CLR 401.

63 As an example of the PGA's antagonistic contributions to the native title process, in 1997 the PGA explicitly advised pastoralists 'not to co-operate in native title mediation': D. Jopson, 'Mother Country', *Sydney Morning Herald*, 20 December 1997, p. 20 and stated that its policy was to refuse to negotiate formal access agreements with Aborigines through the National Native Title Tribunal: Z. Kovacs, 'PGA "No Deals" Policy', *The West Australian*, 29 April 1997, p. 6.

64 See K. Calley and N. Pearson (eds), *The Wik Summit Papers*, Cape York Land Council, Cairns, 1997 and R.S. French, 'Model codes for pastoral access could offer way forward', National Native Title Tribunal Media Release, 22 January 1997.

65 NTA, Pt 2, Div. 3, Subdiv. G, NTA: ss. 24GA–24GE. See also R. Bartlett, *Native Title in Australia*, Butterworths, Sydney, 2004, p. 419.

66 J. Howard, 'Address to Participants at the Longreach Community Meeting to Discuss the *Wik* Ten Point Plan, Longreach, Queensland', 17 May 1997, reproduced as an appendix to Native Title and Aboriginal and Torres Strait Islander Land Fund Senate Committee, *Sixteenth Report: Consistency of the Native Title Amendment Act 1998 with Australia's International Obligations under the Convention on the Elimination of all Forms of Racial Discrimination (CERD)*, 28 June 2000, p. 277.

67 For example, the Aboriginal and Torres Strait Islander Social Justice Commissioner drawing attention to one instance where a Seafood Industry Association obtained funding to participate in claims over land even though the organisation held no interest beyond the high-water mark. *Submission of Aboriginal and Torres Strait Islander Social Justice Commissioner to the Inquiry into the Capacity of Native Title Representative Bodies*, Joint Statutory Committee on Native Title and the Aboriginal and Torres Strait Islander Land Account, Inquiry into the Operation of Native Title Representative Bodies, pp. 6, 10–11.

68 N. Pearson, 'Where We've Come From and Where We're At with the Opportunity that is Koiki Mabo's Legacy to Australia', Mabo Lecture, Native Title Representative Bodies Conference, Alice Springs, p. 6.

69 *Smith v Western Australia* [2000] FCA 1249 (29 August 2001).

70 Clauses 13 and 20, *Smith Pastoral Access Protocols: Smith v Western Australia* [2000] FCA 1249 (26 August 2001).

71 Clause 15 *Smith Pastoral Access Protocols: Smith v Western Australia* [2000] FCA 1249 (26 August 2001).

72 See clauses 21–7 of the *Smith Pastoral Access Protocols: Smith v Western Australia* [2000] FCA 1249 (26 August 2001). It was not clear how the NWN community were expected to access funding for this purpose.

73 H. Esbenshade, 'The Pastoralists' Perspective on Mediating Native Title Claims', *Native Title News*, 5(4), 2001, p. 63.

74 See, for example, M. Riley, 'Winning Native Title: The Experience of the Nharnuwangga, Wajarri and Ngarla People', *Land, Rights Laws: Issues of Native Title*, 2(19), 2002.

75 P. Jarvis, 'Decision Eases Doubts', *The West Australian*, 15 August 2002.

76 The case for pastoral access protocols is put at its best in M. Love, 'Without Prejudice: The Wik Negotiation' in B. Keon-Cohen (ed.), *Native Title in the New Millenium*, AIATSIS, Canberra, 2001 and 'Mark Love' in K. Calley and N. Pearson (eds), *The Wik Summit Papers*, Cape York Land Council, Cairns, 1997.

77 See, for example, G. Neate, 'Native Title and Related Outcomes', *Queensland Native Title Forum*, Brisbane, 17 December 2003, p. 22.

78 National Native Title Tribunal, *Talking Native Title*, 26 March 2008, p. 1.

79 National Farmer's Federation, 'Practical Moves to Make Native Title Claims Workable', Media Release, 24 August 2006, http://www.nff.org.au/read/2428457165.html?hilite=native, retrieved 24/12/08.

80 R.B. Reich, *Supercapitalism: The Transformation of Business, Democracy and Everyday Life*, Knopf, New York, 2007, Chapter 5.

81 R.T. De George, 'The Myth of Corporate Social Responsibility: Ethics and International Business' in J.W. Houck and O.F. Williams (eds), *Is the Good Corporation Dead?*, Rowman & Littlefield, Lanham (Maryland), 1996, p. 18.

82 L. Davis, 'The Corporate Sector and Social and Community Commitment', *Journal of Indigenous Policy*, 2, 2002, 37–41, p. 37. On Rio Tinto more generally see R. Howitt, 'Recognition, Respect and Reconciliation: Steps Towards Decolonisation?', *Australian Aboriginal Studies*, 1, 1998, 28–34 and B. Harvey, 'Rio Tinto's Agreement Making in Australia in a Context of Globalisation' in M. Langton, M. Tehan, L. Palmer and K. Shain (eds), *Honour Among Nations? Treaties and Agreements with Indigenous People*, Melbourne University Press, Melbourne, 2004.

83 See R.B. Reich, *Supercapitalism: The Transformation of Business, Democracy and Everyday Life*, Knopf, New York, 2007.

84 See, for example, M. Macpherson, 'President's Address', presented at the *Minerals Outlook Seminar*, 11 May 1994, pp. 2–3 and Chamber of Minerals and Energy of Western Australia Inc., *Let's Make Native Title Work*, Issue Paper No. 1, March 1998, p. 4.

85 R.J. Carter, 'Report of the President, The Chamber of Minerals and Energy of Western Australia, *Annual Report*, 1996, p. 8–9.

86 B. Cusack, 'Report of the President', The Chamber of Minerals and Energy of Western Australia, *Annual Report*, 1997, pp 8–9.

87 Chamber of Minerals and Energy of Western Australia Inc., *Let's Make Native Title Work*, Issue Paper No. 1, March 1998, p. 4. Long after the battle over the Amendments to the NTA was over, AMEC was still rather disingenuously trying to claim that although 'there is a legal difference between a "right to consult" and a "right to negotiate", the end result in terms of compensation is exactly the same'. AMEC, *Submission to the House of Representatives Standing Committee on Industry & Resources Inquiry into Resources Exploration Impediments from Association of Mining and Exploration Companies Inc*, July 2002, p. 31.

88 By 2001 and 2002, for example, the MCA's Annual Report mentioned native title briefly and benignly. Minerals Council of Australia, *Annual*

Report 2001, p. 17 and Minerals Council of Australia, *Annual Report 2002*, p. 21. Even when the Howard administration unexpectedly gained control of the Senate at the 2004 federal election, there was little interest from industry in legislatively revisiting the NTA.

89 G. Savell, 'Land Rights, Native Title and the Mining Industry', paper presented to *An Indigenous Future? Challenges and Opportunities*, Bennelong Society Conference, 2003.

Chapter 6 Poets and slaves

1 R.S. French, 'The Role of the National Native Title Tribunal', *Native Title News*, 1(2), 1994, 70.

2 The Act also referred to conciliation, and in the first month of his tenure French said that '[t]he role of the Tribunal is somewhere in the grey area between mediation and conciliation': P. Van Hattem and R.S. French, 'New President of National Native Title Tribunal', *Brief*, June 1994, 12–21, p. 17. In practice, as will be seen in the remainder of this chapter, the NNTT regarded its work as mediation, not conciliation.

3 R.S. French, 'The Role of the National Native Title Tribunal', *Native Title News*, 1(2), 1994, 70. See also R. Farley, 'Native Title: Two Laws, Many Cultures' in G.D. Meyers (ed.), *Implementing the Native Title Act: The Next Step: Facilitating Negotiated Agreements*, National Native Title Tribunal, Perth, 1996, p. 117. In his efforts to make the Act work, French—a science fiction aficionado—was fond of invoking this favoured saying from Captain Jean Luc Picard from *Star Trek: The Next Generation.*

4 The initial acting President was Justice Jane Matthews of the Federal Court, who later served as a part-time member of the NNTT from July 1994 to January 1999. French once stood for the Liberal Party as a candidate for the safe federal Labor seat of Fremantle. French agreed to extend his term twice, initially until December 1997, 'to enable a reasonable degree of continuity in the leadership of the Tribunal through what is, for all concerned, a difficult time': *National Native Title Tribunal Annual Report, 1996–1997*, p. 8. His term was then extended further to allow the new President to begin operation once the Amendments had been enacted. He finally finished as President in December 1998.

5 French was required to make key rulings on interpretation while as a consequence of changes in the law, Neate never found himself in a position of having to rule on contentious matters of statutory interpretation. As it turned out, French had misinterpreted the NTA to the detriment of Indigenous interests, purporting to exercise more power

than the appeal courts held that the statute permitted. See R.S. French, 'A Moment of Change—Personal Reflections on the National Native Title Tribunal 1994–1998', *Melbourne University Law Review*, 27, 2003, 488–522, pp. 508–11.

6 French's willingness sometimes led to controversy, most notably the 'cargo-cult' affair of late 1995: see R.S. French, 'A Moment of Change—Personal Reflections on the National Native Title Tribunal 1994–1998', *Melbourne University Law Review*, 27, 2003, 488–522, p. 507.

7 P. Lane, 'Have We got a Deal for You?', in L. Strelein and K. Muir, *Native Title in Perspective: Selected Papers from the Native Title Research Unit 1998–2000*, Aboriginal Studies Press, Canberra, 2000, p. 36.

8 P. Hayes, 'National Native Title Tribunal: Effective Mediator or Bureaucratic Albatross? A User's Perspective', *Indigenous Law Bulletin*, 5(18), 2002, 4–7, p. 4.

9 See NTA, s. 110.

10 Notwithstanding their pro-Indigenous credentials, the appointment of Viner and Chaney, both former federal Liberal Ministers from Western Australia, by the Keating government meant that the new Tribunal could be less easily caricatured as a creature of the Australian Labor Party.

11 Writing in 2002, one experienced native title lawyer observed of the then fourteen members of the NNTT: '[t]he great majority are non-Indigenous. The great majority are male. The great majority are lawyers by training. The great majority are from the *big end of town*. The early days of the NNTT, which had a number of imaginative appointments, seem to have passed us by': P. Hayes, 'National Native Title Tribunal: Effective Mediator or Bureaucratic Albatross? A User's Perspective', *Indigenous Law Bulletin*, 5(18), 2002, 4–7, p. 6. See also T. Corbett and C. O'Faircheallaigh, 'Unmasking the Politics of Native Title: The National Native Title Tribunal's Application of the NTA's Arbitration Provisions', *The University of Western Australia Law Review*, 33(1), December 2006, 153–76, p. 175. The composition of the Tribunal's membership was also altered by some premature retirements. One member, Seán Flood, who had already made a series of very passionate speeches while a member, resigned in 1997 after directly attacking the Commonwealth Government in an address. French noted in the Presidential Overview to National Native Title Tribunal, *Annual Report 1997–1998*, that 'Mr Sean Flood resigned from the Tribunal on 13 October 1997. His resignation followed his public commitment to a position of opposition to the proposed amendments to the Native Title Act and strong criticism of the government in relation to them': p. 8.

12 National Native Title Tribunal, Submission to the Senate Legal and Constitutional Affairs Committee on the Native Title Amendment Bill 2006, 9/2/07, Senate Legal and Constitutional Affairs Committee, Completed Reports, Inquiry into the Native Title Amendment Bill 2006, at http://www.aph.gov.au/Senate/committee/legcon_ctte/completed_inquiries/2004-07/native_title/submissions/sublist.htm, p. 5.

13 R.S. French, 'Personal Reflections on the National Native Title Tribunal', *Melbourne University Law Review*, 27, 2003, 488–522, p. 505.

14 P. Van Hattem and R.S. French, 'New President of National Native Title Tribunal', *Brief*, June 1994, 12–21, p. 20. In August 1995, Cabinet approved a substantial increase in the NNTT's budget to $20,041,000 for 1995–96, representing an increase of about $11 million: National Native Title Tribunal, *Annual Report 1995–1996*, p. 1.

15 In February 1995, the High Court handed down a decision which fundamentally altered the capacity of the NTA to operate as Parliament had intended. In *Brandy v Human Rights and Equal Opportunity Commission* (1995) 127 ALR 1; (1995) 69 ALJR 191; (1995) 183 CLR 245, the High Court held that a statutory scheme which allowed an administrative body to make a determination which, upon registration, took effect as an order of the Federal Court was impermissible under the Commonwealth Constitution because under Australian public law judicial functions cannot be invested in a non-judicial body. The NNTT responded by noting that in the event that agreement had been in fact achieved between the parties, then the claim could be referred to the Federal Court to make consent orders in the terms which had been settled, thereby providing a practical solution to the problem, but nevertheless the fact remained that some of the architecture of the Act had been demolished. It was confirmed that *Brandy* applied to the NNTT in *Fourmile v Selpam* (1998) 80 FCR 151. In relation to various other statutory provisions, it was just not entirely clear how the NTA was meant to operate. R.S. French, 'A Moment of Change—Personal Reflections on the National Native Title Tribunal 1994–1998', *Melbourne University Law Review*, 27(2), 2003, 488–522, p. 516.

16 See R.S. French, 'A Moment of Change—Personal Reflections on the National Native Title Tribunal 1994–1998', *Melbourne University Law Review*, 27, 2003, 488–522, pp. 508–11.

17 In its *Annual Report 1994–1995*, the Tribunal noted that by 30 June 2005 it had received approximately 500 notices issued by the State of Western Australia pursuant to s. 29 of the Act and had established a Future Act section, dedicating a member (the Hon. Chris Sumner) to its

management: p. v. In relation to other ambiguities associated with the early operation of the NNTT see R.S. French and P.M. Lane, 'Response to Commonwealth Government Discussion Paper Outlining Proposed Amendments to the Native Title Act 1993' in G.D. Meyers (ed.), *Implementing the Native Title Act: The Next Step: Facilitating Negotiated Agreements*, National Native Title Tribunal, Perth, 1996; National Native Title Tribunal, *Annual Report 1995–1996*, p. 171; and R. Farley, 'Native Title: Two Laws, Many Cultures' in G.D. Meyers (ed.), *Implementing the Native Title Act: The Next Step: Facilitating Negotiated Agreements*, National Native Tribunal, Perth, 1996, p. 117. The combination of alternative dispute resolution and adjudicative functions within the same administrative body created obvious stress because, as the President and Registrar of the NNTT recognised as early as 1995, the Tribunal having a decision-making function in relation to future acts inevitably meant that disgruntled parties would be critical of the results of proceedings, potentially creating 'tension between the roles of the Tribunal as a decision-maker and as mediator'. R.S. French, 'Issues to Date' in G.D. Meyers, *Implementing the Native Title Act: First Steps, Small Steps*, National Native Title Tribunal, Perth, 1996, p. 74 and see R.S. French and P.M. Lane, 'Response to Commonwealth Government Discussion Paper Outlining Proposed Amendments to the Native Title Act 1993' in G.D. Meyers (ed.), *Implementing the Native Title Act: The Next Step: Facilitating Negotiated Agreements*, National Native Title Tribunal, Perth, 1996, p. 99.

18 See P. Lane, 'Western Australia's Response to the High Court Decision' in G.D. Meyers, *Implementing the Native Title Act: First Steps, Small Steps*, National Native Title Tribunal, Perth, 1996.

19 *Dann v Western Australia* (1997) 74 FCR 391; 144 ALR 1.

20 *Re Koara People* (1996) 132 FLR 73; see also *Western Australia v Thomas* (1996) 133 FLR 124.

21 This was a consequence of the statutory scheme that required tenements to be continually reduced and upgraded to encourage ground to be turned over, which resulted in many mining leases being applied for, effectively in order for the company in question to simply continue exploration.

22 *Evans v Western Australia* (1997) 77 FCR 193.

23 The Tribunal's role in the future act system had also been to some extent displaced by new procedures including by the quaintly named 'Independent Person', a state-appointed officer with arbitral authority in relation to a right to consult that now applied to some future acts: NTA, s. 24MD(6B)(f).

24 Among the changes, the conditions for an act attracting the expedited procedure provisions were tightened, making it much harder for native title claimants to successfully object: *Smith on behalf of the Gnaala Karla Booja People v Western Australia* [2001] FCA 19 (19 January 2001); *Little v Western Australia* [2001] FCA 1706; and *Little v Oriole Resources Pty Ltd* 146 FCR 576, 225 ALR 202.

25 See, for example, T. Corbett, 'The National Native Title Tribunal's Façade of Indigenous Advocacy', *Social Alternatives*, 25(2), 2006, 37–42; R. Bartlett, 'Dispossession by the National Native Title Tribunal', *Western Australian Law Review*, (26), July 1996, 108; D. Ritter, 'A Sick Institution? Diagnosing the Future Act Unit of the National Native Title Tribunal', *Australian Indigenous Law Reporter*, 7(2), 2002, 1–13; T. Corbett and C. O'Faircheallaigh, 'Unmasking the Politics of Native Title: The National Native Title Tribunal's Application of the NTA's Arbitration Provisions', *The University of Western Australia Law Review*, 33(1), December 2006, 153–76; S. Choo, 'How High Can You Jump? Raising the Bar for Expedited Procedure Matters', Paper presented to the Native Title Conference, Geralton. 2002; C. O'Faircheallaigh, 'Aborigines, Mining Companies and the State in Contemporary Australia: A New Political Economy or "Business as Usual"?', *Australian Journal of Political Science*, 41(1), 2006, 1–22; and T. Burton and C. Davies, 'Major Disturbance or Miner Disturbance?: *Little and Ors v Oriole Resources Pty Ltd* (2005) 146 FCR 576', *Indigenous Law Bulletin*, 6(19), 2006, 10–12.

26 See R. Blowes and D. Trigger, 'Negotiating the Century Mine Agreements: Issues of Law, Culture and Politics' in M. Edmunds (ed.), *Regional Agreements in Australia: Vol. 2: Case Studies*, AIATSIS, Canberra, 1999, p. 96.

27 In 1999–2000, the Tribunal reformulated a new two-year strategic plan to replace its Business Plan which had as its goals: to assist people to develop agreements that resolve native title issues; to have a fair and efficient process for making arbitral and registration test decisions; to provide accurate and comprehensive information about native title matters to clients, governments and communities; to have a highly skilled, flexible, diverse and valued workforce: *Strategic Plan 2000–2002, National Native Title Tribunal Annual Report, Appendix 1.*

28 See D.L. Ritter, 'A Sick Institution? Diagnosing the Future Act Unit of the National Native Title Tribunal', *Australian Indigenous Law Reporter*, 7(2), 2002, 1–13.

29 For some examples: the National Native Title Tribunal Submission to the House of Representatives Standing Committee on Industry and

Resources Inquiry into Resources Exploration Impediments, 26 July 2002 included statistics on native title and tenements 'cleared for grant.' The Tribunal stated in its submission to the *Parliamentary Joint Committee on Native Title and the Indigenous Land Fund Inquiry into the Effectiveness of the National Native Title Tribunal* (November 2002, Submission 22) that 'Tribunal practices also take into consideration commercial deadlines and pressures': [378]. The Tribunal also commented that '[t]he general effectiveness of the Tribunal in processing applications was noted approvingly recently by the Northern Territory Minister for Mines.'

30 D. Ritter, 'A Sick Institution? Diagnosing the Future Act Unit of the National Native Title Tribunal', *Australian Indigenous Law Reporter*, 7(2), 2002, 1–13.

31 T. Corbett and C. O'Faircheallaigh, 'Unmasking the Politics of Native Title: The National Native Title Tribunal's Application of the NTA's Arbitration Provisions', *The University of Western Australia Law Review*, 33(1), December 2006, 153–76, p. 175.

32 See C. O'Faircheallaigh, 'Aborigines, Mining Companies and the State in Contemporary Australia: A New Political Economy or "Business as Usual"?', *Australian Journal of Political Science*, 41(1), 2006, 1–22.

33 See G. Clark, 'Mediation under the Native Title Act 1993: Some Structural Considerations', *James Cook University Law Review*, Special Issue, 9, 2002/3, pp. 103–6.

34 Curiously, the preamble did not refer to 'mediation' at all.

35 R. Fisher, *Getting to Yes: Negotiating an Agreement Without Giving In*, Random House, London, 1999. A concise background is set out in G. Clark, 'Mediation under the Native Title Act 1993: Some Structural Considerations', *James Cook University Law Review*, Special Issue, 9, 2002/3, pp. 90–1. First enshrined by the Tribunal at para. 11.3, pp. 52–3 of National Native Title Tribunal, *Annual Report 1993–1994* and para. 11.3, p. 152 in National Native Title Tribunal, *Annual Report 1994–1995*.

36 H. Wootten, 'Some Thoughts on Native Title and Doing Business' in G.D. Meyers, *Implementing the Native Title Act: First Steps, Small Steps: Selected Discussion Papers of the National Native Title Tribunal (1994–95)*, National Native Title Tribunal, Perth, 1996, p. 49.

37 R.S. French, 'Opening Address' in F. McKeown (ed.), *Native Title: An Opportunity for Understanding*, National Native Title Tribunal, Perth, 1995, p. 5.

38 R.S. French, 'Pathways to Agreement' in G.D. Meyers (ed.), *The Way Forward: Collaboration and Cooperation 'in Country'*, National Native Title Tribunal, Perth, 1996, p. 22. See also p. 17, where French refers to

'recognition of the legal and moral rights of indigenous Australians and building upon that foundation'.

39 See P. Sheiner, 'The Beginning of Certainty: Consent Determinations of Native Title', *Land, Rights, Laws: Issues of Native Title*, 2(12), Nov. 2001, p. 4.

40 R.S. French, 'Pathways to Agreement' in G.D. Meyers, *The Way Forward: Collaboration and Cooperation 'in Country'*, National Native Title Tribunal, Perth, 1996, p. 22.

41 R.S. French, 'Opening Address' in *Native Title: An Opportunity for Understanding*, National Native Title Tribunal, Perth, 1995, p. 5.

42 The Tribunal's 'Cooperation and Collaboration in Country' conference held in September 2005 was an explicit effort to guide Australia down the path of regional agreements.

43 R.S. French, 'Opening Address' in Native Title: An Opportunity for Understanding, National Native Title Tribunal, Perth, 1995, p. 5. This is acknowledged in R.S. French, 'Personal Reflections on the National Native Title Tribunal', *Melbourne University Law Review*, 2003, 27, 488–522, see also the sources cited at n. 82 therein.

44 The expression is used in R.S. French, 'Personal Reflections on the National Native Title Tribunal', *Melbourne University Law Review*, 27, 2003, 488–522, p. 503.

45 Tellingly, the proceedings of the NNTT's first major public conference of stakeholders were published as *Native Title: An Opportunity for Understanding*. The inaugural collection of conference papers invoked the metaphor of a child learning in the subtitle 'First Steps, Small Steps': G.D. Meyers, *Implementing the Native Title Act*, National Native Title Tribunal, Perth, 1996.

46 Some splendid examples of public inaccuracies are set out in National Native Title Tribunal, *Native Title: A Five Year Retrospective 1994–1998: Report on the Operations of the Native Title Act 1993 and the Effectiveness of the National Native Title Tribunal*, Perth, 1999.

47 R.S. French, 'Personal Reflections on the National Native Title Tribunal', *Melbourne University Law Review*, 27, 2003, 488–522, p. 503. The extent to which the Tribunal regarded remedying the perceived information deficit as a top strategic priority is illustrated by budgetary and staffing figures from the organisation's first full year of operation: almost 20 per cent of the full-time staff were employed to perform 'community liaison', and almost half of the total outsourcing budget went to a media consultancy: National Native Title Tribunal, *Annual Report 1994–1995*, p. 78. See also p. 27.

48 The other two objectives of the policy were to 'Inform Aboriginal and Torres Strait Islander people and the wider public about the claims process' and 'Assist applicants and potential applicants to manage their applications and publicize the process in a way that minimizes the incidence of community responses based on fear, uncertainty, ignorance or prejudice'. National Native Title Tribunal, *Annual Report 1994–1995*, p. 134.

49 National Native Title Tribunal, *Annual Report 1994–1995*, p. 139.

50 So, in mid-1997, for example, when the NTA had been in operation for more than three years, French foregrounded an 'emphasis on information programs' leading to 'reasonable understanding of the basic concepts and processes' as an 'express corporate goal' of the Tribunal which was 'essential to effective participation in native title mediation: R.S. French, 'Introduction—President's Report' in National Native Title Tribunal, *Annual Report 1996–1997*, p. 5. See, for example, 'The Typical Scenario' in G. Clark, 'Mediation under the Native Title Act 1993: Some Structural Considerations', *James Cook University Law Review*, Special Issue, 9, 2002/3, p. 108.

51 See generally M. Grattan (ed.), *Essays on Australian Reconciliation*, Black Inc., Melbourne, 2000.

52 S. Flood, '"The Spirit of Mabo"—The Land Needs the Laughter of Children: Native Title and the Achievements of Aboriginal People' in G.D. Meyers (ed.), *Implementing the Native Title Act: The Next Step: Facilitating Negotiated Agreements*, National Native Title Tribunal, Perth, 1996, p. 105.

53 R.S. French, 'A Moment of Change—Personal Reflections on the National Native Title Tribunal 1994–1998', *Melbourne University Law Review*, 27(2), 2003, 488–522, p. 489.

54 S. Flood, '"The Spirit of Mabo"—The Land Needs the Laughter of Children: Native Title and the Achievements of Aboriginal People' in G.D. Meyers (ed.), *Implementing the Native Title Act: The Next Step: Facilitating Negotiated Agreements*, National Native Title Tribunal, Perth, 1996, p. 109.

55 R.S. French, 'The National Native Title Tribunal and the Native Title Act, Agendas for Change' in G.D. Meyers (ed.), *Implementing the Native Title Act: The Next Step: Facilitating Negotiated Agreements*, National Native Title Tribunal, Perth, 1996, p. 43.

56 R.S. French, 'Opening Address' in F. McKeown (ed.), *Native Title: An Opportunity for Understanding*, National Native Title Tribunal, Perth, 1995, p. 4.

57 See, for example, G. Clark, 'Mediation under the Native Title Act 1993: Some Structural Considerations', *James Cook University Law Review*, Special Issue, 9, 2002/3, p. 105.
58 'Fred Chaney' in K. Calley and N. Pearson (eds), *The Wik Summit Papers*, Cape York Land Council, Cairns, 1997, p. 47.
59 'Justice French' in K. Calley and N. Pearson (eds), *The Wik Summit Papers*, Cape York Land Council, Cairns, 1997, p. 63.
60 Curiously, although the rationale for pastoral access protocols is actually both legalistic and rooted in social mistrust, the need for them is often expressed in populist terms, as a solution worked out 'by the people who are actually on the ground': 'Mark Love' in K. Calley and N. Pearson (eds), *The Wik Summit Papers*, Cape York Land Council, Cairns, 1997, p. 113. In reality, far from being sorted through and negotiated by individual pastoralists and Aboriginal people in a spirit of folksy bonhomie, pastoral access protocols have largely been generated by bureaucrats, peak bodies and lawyers.
61 NTA, s. 225(b).
62 H. Wootten, 'Mediating between Aboriginal Communities and Industry' in G.D. Meyers (ed.), *Implementing the Native Title Act: The Next Step: Facilitating Negotiated Agreements*, National Native Title Tribunal, Perth, 1996, p. 169.
63 R.S. French, 'Pathways to Agreement' in G.D. Meyers (ed.), *The Way Forward: Collaboration and Cooperation 'in Country'*, National Native Title Tribunal, Perth, 1996, p. 22.
64 R.S. French, 'Opening Address' in F. McKeown (ed.), *Native Title: An Opportunity for Understanding*, National Native Title Tribunal, Perth, 1995, p. 4. See also P. Van Hattem and R.S. French, 'New President of National Native Title Tribunal', *Brief*, June 1994, 12–21, p. 17 and R.S. French, 'Issues to Date' in G.D. Meyers (ed.), *Implementing the Native Title Act: First Steps, Small Steps: Selected Discussion Papers of the National Native Title Tribunal (1994–95)*, National Native Title Tribunal, Perth, 1996.
65 Some memorable attacks are repeated in *Native Title: A Five Year Retrospective 1994–1998: Report on the Operations of the Native Title Act 1993 and the Effectiveness of the National Native Title Tribunal*, Perth, 1999.
66 P. Van Hattem and R.S. French, 'New President of National Native Title Tribunal', *Brief*, June 1994, 12–21, p. 14. See also R.S. French, 'Introductory Notes for Mediation Conference (First Mediation Conference—Wiradjuri Wellington Town Common Committee and

Parties)' in G.D. Meyers, *Implementing the Native Title Act: First Steps, Small Steps: Selected Discussion Papers of the National Native Title Tribunal (1994–1995)*, National Native Title Tribunal, Perth, 1996 and French's recollections of the Wellington Common mediation in R.S. French, 'A Moment of Change—Personal Reflections on the National Native Title Tribunal 1994–1998', *Melbourne University Law Review*, 27(2), 2003, 488–522.

67 R.S. French, 'Pathways to Agreement' in G.D. Meyers (ed.), *The Way Forward: Collaboration and Cooperation 'in Country'*, National Native Title Tribunal, Perth, 1996, p. 22.

68 As French would later acknowledge: R.S. French, 'Personal Reflections on the National Native Title Tribunal', *Melbourne University Law Review*, 27, 2003, 488–522, p. 502.

69 *National Native Title Tribunal Annual Report 1996–1997*, 'President's Overview', p. 5: 'Intra-indigenous issues were a dominant feature of the Tribunal's work in 1996/97 requiring its involvement in the attempted resolution of overlapping claims and the formation of working groups so that divergent interests of conflicting claimants might be managed by them in a way that enabled them to engage more effectively with governments and others': p. 5. *National Native Title Tribunal Annual Report 1997–1998*, 'President's Overview', p. 7: 'Intra-indigenous conflict still dominates the native title process throughout the country, manifesting in multiple and overlapping claims'.

70 Patricia Lane, the then Registrar of the NNTT, noted in 1996 that whether 'simply counting the number of agreements reached will represent a true picture of the Tribunal's performance' was arguable but, she conceded, '[a] lmost inevitably one measure of "success" of a mediator will be the number of agreements reached however superficial that measure might be'. P. Lane, 'Have We Got a Deal for You?' in L. Strelein and K. Muir, *Native Title in Perspective: Selected Papers from the Native Title Research Unit 1998–2000*, Aboriginal Studies Press, Canberra, 2000, p. 36.

71 'Presidential Overview', *National Native Title Tribunal Annual Report 1997–1998*, p. 6. In June 1998 the Tribunal conducted 'the first national audit of agreements since the introduction of the Native Title Act', which 'revealed that, despite the controversy over the Native Title Act, 1100 agreements had been struck between different Indigenous groups, miners, industry bodies and governments showing that many groups and individuals have been focusing on the practical business of making agreements': *Annual Report 1997–1998*, p. 41. The audit documented future act agreements and 'native title settlement, partial and progress

agreements' including agreements to amend or withdraw applications, reconciliation agreements, site protection agreements, framework agreements and draft determinations of native title: p. 41. It identified 227 native title determination related agreements (in which it included 'non-native title outcomes') and 873 future act related agreements: p. 42.

72 National Native Title Tribunal, *Annual Report 1997–1998*, pp. 7, 30.

73 National Native Title Tribunal, Submission to *Parliamentary Joint Committee on Native Title and the Indigenous Land Fund Inquiry into the Effectiveness of the National Native Title Tribunal* (November 2002, Submission 22), p. 12.

74 The Parliamentary Joint Committee on Native Title and the Aboriginal and Torres Strait Islander Land Fund has since changed its name following amendments to the Act by *Financial Framework Legislation Amendment Act 2005*, Number 8 of 2005, date of assent: 22 Feb. 2005, s. 4, Schedule 1 (items 208–10). It is now the Parliamentary Joint Committee on Native Title and the Aboriginal and Torres Strait Islander Land Account, previously the Land Fund. The Native Title Committee's Terms of Reference are set out in NTA, Pt 12, s. 206.

75 There are a mixture of views in evidence. The issue on which there was the most agreement was the disparity in resources between NTRBs and the NNTT.

76 Cape York Land Council, Submission to *Parliamentary Joint Committee on Native Title and the Indigenous Land Fund Inquiry into the Effectiveness of the National Native Title Tribunal* (November 2002, Submission 32), p. 2.

77 Cape York Land Council, Submission to *Parliamentary Joint Committee on Native Title and the Indigenous Land Fund Inquiry into the Effectiveness of the National Native Title Tribunal* (November 2002, Submission 32), p. 10.

78 G. Clark, 'Views through different lenses—the role of the National Native Title Tribunal in the mediation of claims; *Frazer v Western Australia*', *Native Title News*, 6(5), 2003, 71–5. p. 75.

79 Queensland Government, Submission to *Parliamentary Joint Committee on Native Title and the Indigenous Land Fund Inquiry into the Effectiveness of the National Native Title Tribunal* (November 2002, Submission 24), p. 3.

80 *Frazer and Others v State of Western Australia* [2003] FCA 351 at [12].

81 P. Hayes, 'National Native Title Tribunal: Effective Mediator or Bureaucratic Albatross? A User's Perspective', *Indigenous Law Bulletin*, 5(18), 2002, 4–7, p. 4.

82 P. Hayes, 'National Native Title Tribunal: Effective Mediator or Bureaucratic Albatross? A User's Perspective', *Indigenous Law Bulletin*, 5(18), 2002, 4–7, p. 6.

83 National Farmers' Federation Native Title Taskforce, Submission to the Senate Legal and Constitutional Affairs Committee on the Native Title Amendment Bill, 2006 15/1/2007, pp. 1–2, Senate Legal and Constitutional Affairs Committee, Completed Reports, Inquiry into the Native Title Amendment Bill 2006, at http://www.aph.gov.au/Senate/committee/legcon_ctte/completed_inquiries/2004-07/native_title/submissions/sub05.pdf.

84 Minerals Council of Australia, Australian Petroleum Production & Exploration Association Limited, Submission to the Senate Legal and Constitutional Affairs Committee on the Native Title Amendment Bill 2006, 19/1/2007, Senate Legal and Constitutional Affairs Committee, Completed Reports, Inquiry into the Native Title Amendment Bill 2006, at http://www.aph.gov.au/Senate/committee/legcon_ctte/completed_inquiries/2004-07/native_title/submissions/sublist.htm.

85 As O'Fairchaellaigh has explained: 'NTRB funding has declined slightly in real terms (by 2.4% in 1997 dollars, from $44,277,000 in 97–98 to $43,199,000 in 2002–03: ATSIC Annual Reports 1997/98–2002/02). In contrast, the Federal Government has substantially increased real funding for the Commonwealth NNTT (by 43% between 1998–99 and 2003–04)': C. O'Faircheallaigh, 'Aborigines, Mining Companies and the State in Contemporary Australia: A New Political Economy or "Business as usual"?', *Australian Journal of Political Science*, 41(1), 1–22, p. 11.

86 This is repeated in the later Annual Reports and in various speeches by Neate and others.

87 Section 86A.

88 G. Clark, 'Mediation under the Native Title Act 1993', *James Cook University Law Review*, 9, 2002/3, pp. 90, 108. See also G. Neate, C. Jones and G. Clark, 'Against All Odds: The Mediation of Native Title Agreements in Australia', paper presented to the Second Asis Pacific Mediation Forum, Singapore, 19–22 November 2003, p. 27.

89 G. Clark, 'Mediation under the Native Title Act 1993: Some Structural Considerations', *James Cook University Law Review*, Special Issue, 9, 2002/3, p. 108.

90 See G. Clark, 'Mediation under the Native Title Act 1993: Some Structural Considerations', *James Cook University Law Review*, Special Issue, 9, 2002/3, pp. 96–7.

91 Including detailing staff to attend and take notes, even though the hearings were transcribed by the Commonwealth: *Official Committee Hansard, Joint Committee on Native Title and the Aboriginal and Torres Strait Islander Land Fund: Reference Effectiveness of the National Native Title Tribunal*, Perth, Western Australia, 12 June 2003, p. 375.

92 National Native Title Tribunal, *Annual Report 2002–2003*, Table 17 and G. Neate, C. Jones and G. Clark, 'Against All Odds: The Mediation of Native Title Agreements in Australia', paper presented to the Second Asia Pacific Mediation Forum, Singapore, 19–22 November 2003.

93 National Native Title Tribunal, Submission to the Senate Legal and Constitutional Affairs Committee on the Native Title Amendment Bill 2006, 9/2/07, Senate Legal and Constitutional Affairs Committee, Completed Reports, Inquiry into the Native Title Amendment Bill 2006, at http://www.aph.gov.au/Senate/committee/legcon_ctte/completed_inquiries/2004–07/native_title/submissions/sublist.htm, p. 11.

94 See T. Burton, 'Deconstructing Native Title Stories: Rights, Recognition, Relationships', *Onyx*, 13(3), October 2004.

95 G. Neate, 'Exploring the Role of the NNTT in Reaching Agreements over Native Title', paper presented to *Assessing the Impact of Native Title and Cultural Heritage in 2002: Negotiating Balanced Outcomes for All Parties*, Brisbane, 16 April 2002, p. 43.

96 Similarly, when the examples relied upon by the Tribunal to assert that the process was functional were by their very nature anomalous, none of the parties involved were inclined to disavow an 'outcome' being heralded as a success, allowing diverse interests to participate in consensus-building. For useful relevant insights, see D. Mosse, 'Good Policy is Unimplementable? Reflections on the Ethnography of Aid Policy and Practice', paper presented at the EIDOS Workshop on 'Order and Disjuncture: The Organisation of Aid and Development', SOAS, London, 26–28 September 2003, p. 19.

97 The full quote is, unusually, in a 'Postscript' to the judgment: *Re Waanyi People* [1995] NNTTA 4 (14 February 1995); (1995) 129 ALR 118; (1995) 124 FLR 1.

98 See D. Mosse, 'Good Policy is Unimplementable? Reflections on the Ethnography of Aid Policy and Practice', paper presented at the EIDOS Workshop on 'Order and Disjuncture: The Organisation of Aid and Development', SOAS, London 26–28 September 2003.

99 Cape York Land Council, submission to *Parliamentary Joint Committee on Native Title and the Indigenous Land Fund Inquiry into the*

Effectiveness of the National Native Title Tribunal (November 2002, Submission 32), p. 1.

100 T. Lee, 'The Natives are Restless: A Personal Reflection on Ten Years of Native Title' in C. Choo and S. Hollbach (eds), *Studies in Western Australian History: History and Native Title*, 23, 2003, 29–39, p. 33. Lee's term as a Member was not renewed by the Commonwealth Government when it expired in June 2003.

101 F. Chaney, 'The Rules for Engagement' in S. Toussaint (ed.), *Crossing Boundaries—Cultural, Legal, Historical and Practice Issues in Native Title*, Melbourne University Press, Melboure, 2004, p. 101. When he resigned from the NNTT, Fred Chaney conceded that 'the results are still way below what we would have hoped': talking to Kerry O'Brien on 19 Feb. 2007 on the ABC *7.30 Report*.

Chapter 7 You can take the judge out of the court . . .

1 C. Scholtz, 'Land Claims: A Negotiated Option' in *Limits & Possibilities of a Treaty Process in Australia*, Canberra, 27 August 2001, p. 4. See further C. Scholtz, *Negotiating Claims: The Emergence of Indigenous Land Claim Negotiation Policies in Australia, Canada, New Zealand, and the United States*, Routledge, New York, 2006.

2 See *Federal Court of Australia Act* (1976), Part II, Div. I, s. 5 'creation of the court' and Part III 'jurisdiction of the court'. The Federal Court was created pursuant to s. 71 of the Australian Constitution.

3 See R. French, 'Federal Courts Created by Parliament' in B. Opeskin and F. Wheeler, *Australian Federal Judicial System*, Melbourne University Press, Carlton (Vic.), 2000.

4 See R. French, 'Federal Courts Created by Parliament' in B. Opeskin and F. Wheeler, *Australian Federal Judicial System*, Melbourne University Press, Carlton (Vic.), 2000, p. 123.

5 *De Rose v South Australia* [2002] FCA 1342; BC200206460 at [271].

6 *Ward v Western Australia* (1998) 159 ALR 483; BC9806200 and *Yorta Yorta Aboriginal Community v Victoria* (FCA, Olney J, No. 6001/95, 18 December 1998, BC9806799, unreported); NTS [60,425].

7 R.S. French, 'Discussion Paper on Proposed Changes to the Native Title Act 1993' in G.D. Meyers, *Implementing the Native Title Act, First Steps: Small Steps. Selected Discussion Papers of the National Native Title Tribunal (1994–1995)*, National Native Title Tribunal, Perth, 1996, p. 79.

8 L. Anderson, 'Managing Native Title in the Federal Court', paper given at 'Negotiating Country', National Native Title Forum, Brisbane, 3 August 2001, p. 3.
9 J. Finlayson, 'Managing Competing Agendas: Strategic Partnerships Across the Native Title Operational Environment', *Indigenous Law Bulletin*, 5(9), July 2001, 4–6, p. 6.
10 The Chief Justice is responsible for managing the administrative affairs of the Federal Court, a function which is performed with the assistance of the Registrar and may be delegated to other judges: Pt IIA, ss. 18A–18Y, *Federal Court of Australia Act.*
11 Federal Court of Australia, Chapter 2 'The Work of the Court', Section 2.2, *Annual Report 1998–1999.* See also G. Hiley, 'Report on Recent Federal Court User Group Meetings', *Native Title News*, 6(3), 35.
12 Federal Court of Australia, Chapter 3 'The Work of the Court', Section 3.2, *Annual Report 2000–2001.*
13 Australian Law Reform Commission, Discussion Paper 62, *Review of the Federal Civil Justice System*, 1999, 10.31, pp. 275–6.
14 Federal Court of Australia, Chapter 2 'The Work of the Court', Section 2.4, *Annual Report 1998–1999.*
15 Commonwealth Attorney General, *Access to Justice—An Action Plan*, Commonwealth of Australia, Canberra, 1995, p. 393.
16 Federal Court of Australia, Chapter 2 'The Work of the Court', Section 2.3, *Annual Report 1998–1999* and Australian Law Reform Commission, Discussion Paper 62, *Review of the Federal Civil Justice System* at [10.50–51].
17 Federal Court of Australia, Chapter 2 'The Work of the Court', Section 2.3, *Annual Report 1998–1999.*
18 Federal Court of Australia, Chapter 2 'The Year in Review', Section 2.2, *Annual Report 1999–2000.*
19 Federal Court of Australia, Chapter 3 'The Work of the Court', Section 3.2, 'Time span of active caseload', *Annual Report 1999–2000.*
20 Federal Court of Australia, Chapter 3 'The Work of the Court', Section 3.2, 'Time span of active caseload', *Annual Report 1999–2000.* The three-year time goal was set in October 1999: Federal Court of Australia, Chapter 3 'The Work of the Court', Section 3.2, *Annual Report 2000–2001.*
21 G. Neate, 'Native Title Ten Years On: Getting on with the job or sitting on the fence?', paper delivered to Native Title Update Forum National Farmers' Federation Carnarvon, Western Australia, 21 May 2002, p. 49.
22 Courts in Australia are not party-politicised in a narrow sense, though as one former High Court judge has suggested, whether 'consciously or

unconsciously', perhaps judges 'cannot escape the currents of their times'. M. McHugh, 'The Constitutional Jurisprudence of the High Court: 1989–2004', Inaugural Sir Anthony Mason Lecture in Constitutional Law, 26 November 2004, Sydney, p. 6.

23 See, for example, G. Clark, 'Ten Years On', Eddie Mabo Memorial Lecture, Melbourne, 3 June 2002, p. 3 and ATSIC, *Annual Report 2003–2004*, p. 54.

24 S. Phillips, '"Like Something out of Kafka": The Relationship between the Roles of the National Native Title Tribunal and the Federal Court in the Development of Native Title Practice', *Land, Rights, Laws: Issues of Native Title*, 2(14), April 2002, p. 5.

25 Compare *Harrington-Smith on behalf of the Wongatha People v Western Australia (No 6)* [2003] FCA 663, para. [38].

26 Federal Court of Australia, Chapter 3 'The Work of the Court', Section 3.2, 'Court initiatives', *Annual Report 1999–2000.*

27 S. Phillips, '"Like Something out of Kafka" The Relationship between the Roles of the National Native Title Tribunal and the Federal Court in the Development of Native Title Practice', *Land, Rights, Laws: Issues of Native Title*, 2(14) April 2002, 1–12. See also L. Anderson, 'Managing Native Title in the Federal Court', paper given at 'Negotiating Country', National Native Title Forum, Brisbane, 3 August 2001, pp. 5–6.

28 Federal Court of Australia, Chapter 3 'The Work of the Court', Section 3.2, 'Native title workload', *Annual Report 1999–2000.*

29 Federal Court of Australia, Chapter 3 'The Work of the Court', Section 3.2, *Annual Report 2001–2002.*

30 Federal Court of Australia, Appendix 5 'Performance Information 1999–2000', Table 5.1 'Performance Information and Level of Achievement 1999–2000', *Annual Report 1999–2000.*

31 Federal Court of Australia, Appendix 6 'Performance Information 2001–2002', Table 6.1 'Performance Information and Level of Achievement 2001–2002', *Annual Report 2001–2002*; Federal Court of Australia, Appendix 6 'Performance Information 2000–2001', Table 6.1 'Performance Information and Level of Achievement 2000–2001', *Annual Report 2000–2001*; and Federal Court of Australia, Appendix 5 'Performance Information 1999–2000', Table 5.1 'Performance Information and Level of Achievement 1999–2000', *Annual Report 1999–2000.*

32 Federal Court of Australia, Chapter 3 'The Work of the Court', Section 3.2, *Annual Report 2000–2001.*

33 The Court noted that in 2000–01, 106 native title applications had been completed, with an average time from filing to disposition of two years and one month, but these figures were inflated through the inclusion of the withdrawal or discontinuance of applications: Federal Court of Australia, Chapter 3 'The work of the Court', Section 3.2, *Annual Report 2000–2001.*

34 Federal Court of Australia, '3.2 Management of Cases and Deciding Disputes by the Court—Disposition of Native Title Matters', *Annual Report 2000–2001.*

35 L. Anderson, 'Managing Native Title in the Federal Court', paper given at 'Negotiating Country', National Native Title Forum, Brisbane, 3 August 2001, pp. 7–8.

36 Federal Court of Australia, Chapter 3 'The Work of the Court', Section 3.2, *Annual Report 2001–2002.*

37 The Committee also endorsed the 'adoption of local timeframe targets'. Federal Court of Australia, Chapter 3 'The Work of the Court', Section 3.2, *Annual Report 2001–02.*

38 L. Anderson, 'Managing Native Title in the Federal Court', paper given at 'Negotiating Country', National Native Title Forum, Brisbane, 3 August 2001, pp. 7–8.

39 Quoted in Western Australian Native Title Working Group press release, 31 May 2001.

40 A.M. North, 'From the Internet to the Outback—A World Class Court' in B Keon-Cohen (ed.), *Native Title in the New Millennium*, AIATSIS, Canberra, 2001, pp. 28–9.

41 Indeed, ATSIC claimed that it was its approach that 'resulted' in the Court 'adopting a more flexible disposition timeframe in February 2003': ATSIC, *Annual Report 2003–2004*, p. 93.

42 J. Thurtell, *Review of Practice and Procedure in the Conduct of on Country Hearings in Native Title Cases for the Federal Court of Australia*, March 2004, p. 112.

43 *Colbung v Western Australia* [2001] FCA 1342.

44 See, for example, *Sampi v Western Australia* [2000] FCA 1018 and *Bolton v Western Australia* [2001] FCA 1074.

45 Federal Court of Australia, Chapter 3 'The Work of the Court in 2002–2003', Section 3.2, *Annual Report 2002–2003.*

46 W. Soden, 'The Federal Court and Native Title Outcomes. Not only limits but opportunities', June 2003, p. 5.

47 Federal Court of Australia, Chapter 3 'The Work of the Court', Section 3.2, *Annual Report 2004–2005.*

48 Federal Court of Australia, Chapter 3 'The Work of the Court', Section 3.2, *Annual Report 2004–2005.*

49 See, for example, Federal Court of Australia, Chapter 3 'The Work of the Court', Section 3.2, 'Matters completed' and 'Matters on hand', *Annual Report 1999–2000* in conjunction with Federal Court of Australia, Appendix 6 'Workload Statistics', Table 6.1 'Summary of Workload Statistics', *Annual Report 1999–2000* plus the graphs in Appendix 6. The same pattern continues in the later annual reports from 2001 to 2005.

50 NTA, s. 82(1) and (2).

51 NTA, s. 82(3).

52 *Federal Court of Australia Act 1975* (Cwlth) s. 59.

53 *Federal Court Rules, Order 78—Native Title Proceedings.*

54 NTA, s. 82(1).

55 NTA, s. 82(2).

56 In general, see M. Black, 'Developments in Practice and Procedure in Native Title Cases', *Public Law Review*, (13), March 2002. See also the discussion in *Jango v Northern Territory (No 2)* [2004] FCA 1004; BC200404855 at [16]–[18].

57 M. Black, 'Developments in Practice and Procedure in Native Title Cases', *Public Law Review*, (13), March 2002, 16, p. 18.

58 *Federal Court Rules*, O. 78, r. 34 and M. Black, 'Developments in Practice and Procedure in Native Title Cases', *Public Law Review*, (13), 16 March 2002, p. 22.

59 For example *Wilkes v Western Australia* [2003] FCA 156.

60 For example *Yarmirr v Northern Territory* (1997) 74 FCR 99; 143 ALR 687. See also M. Black, 'Developments in Practice and Procedure in Native Title Cases', *Public Law Review*, (13), 16 March 2002.

61 See *Western Australia v Ward* (1997) 76 FCR 492; 145 ALR 512; *Yarmirr v Northern Territory* (1997) 74 FCR 99; 143 ALR 687; and *Smith v Western Australia* [2000] FCA 526.

62 *De Rose v South Australia* [2002] FCA 1342, para. [249]. His Honour then outlined many examples of potential miscommunication that had occurred in the trial, paras [254]–[259].

63 Commonwealth Attorney General, *Access to Justice—An Action Plan*, Commonwealth of Australia, Canberra, 1995, p. 48.

64 See http://www.aija.org.au/pastprog.htm.

65 Justice Olney QC, for example, was a lively contributor at a conference session on native title at the annual conference of the Australian Anthropological Society held at the University of Sydney in September 1994. M. Edmonds (ed.), *Claims To Knowledge, Claims To Country: Native*

Title, Native Title Claims and the Role of the Anthropologist, Native Title Research Unit, Australian Institute of Aboriginal and Torres Strait Islander Studies, Canberra, 1994. For criticism of Justice Olney's participation in this event see J.R.S. Forbes, 'Judicial Tidy-up or Takeover? Centralism's Next Stage', *Upholding the Australian Constitution: Proceedings of the Eleventh Conference of the Samuel Griffith Society* vol. 11, ch. 7, 1999.

66 Federal Court, 'A Quiet Revolution: Achieving major change in the Federal Court of Australia', Federal Court of Australia Public Information Unit, Melbourne, Australia, 2004.

67 M. Black, 'Developments in Practice and Procedure in Native Title Cases', *Public Law Review*, (13), 16, March 2002, pp. 19–20.

68 Federal Court of Australia, Chapter 3 'The Work of the Court', Section 3.6, *Annual Report 2000–1001.*

69 It was at a 'time when the court was enlarging its experience with television, radio and still photography in the courtroom': M. Black, 'Foreword' to D. Stepniak, *Electronic Coverage of Courts—A Report Prepared for the Federal Court of Australia by Daniel Stepniak*, Commonwealth of Australia, Canberra, vols 1 and 2, 1998. See also Federal Court of Australia, Chapter 3 'The Work of the Court', Section 3.3, *Annual Report 2004–2005*; Federal Court of Australia, Chapter 3 'The Work of the Court in 2002–2003', Section 3.3, *Annual Report 2002–2003*; and Federal Court of Australia, Chapter 3 'The Administration of the Court', Section 3.10 'Video Conferencing', *Annual Report 1998–1999.*

70 M. Black, 'Developments in Practice and Procedure in Native Title Cases', *Public Law Review*, (13), 16, March 2002, pp. 16–18.

71 A.M. North, 'From the Internet to the Outback—A World Class Court', *Native Title Representative Bodies Legal Conferences*, The Chifley on Flemington, Melbourne, 16–20 April 2000, p. 11.

72 *Mabo v Queensland (2)* 107 ALR 1, p. 79.

73 *Mabo v Queensland (2)* 107 ALR 1, p. 28.

74 See, for example, S. Donaghue, 'The Clamour of Silent Constitutional Principles', *Federal Law Review*, 24, 1996, 133; J. Goldsworthy, 'Implications in Law, Language and the Constitution' in G. Lindell (ed.), *Future Directions in Australian Constitutional Law*, Federation Press, Leichardt (NSW), 1994 and B. Kercher, *An Unruly Child: A History of Law in Australia*, Allen & Unwin, Sydney, 1995.

75 *Minister for Immigration v Teoh* (1995) 183 CLR 273.

76 *Yorta Yorta Aboriginal Community v Victoria* (FCA, Olney J, No. 6001/95, 18 December 1998, BC9806799, unreported), paras [126] and [129].

77 *Yorta Yorta Aboriginal Community v Victoria* (FCA, Olney J, No. 6001/95, 18 December 1998, BC9806799, unreported), paras [17] and [21].

78 J. Torpey, 'Making the Whole What has been Smashed: Reflections on Reparations', *The Journal of Modern History*, Chicago, 73(2), June 2001, 333–58.

79 See for some examples of many: W. Atkinson, '"Not One Iota" of Land Justice: Reflections on the Yorta Yorta Native Title Claim 1994–2001', *Indigenous Law Bulletin*, 5(6), Feb.–March 2001; B. Golder, 'Law, History, Colonialism: An Orientalist Reading of Australian Native Title Law', *Deakin Law Review*, 9(1), 2004, 41–60; V. Kerruish and C. Perrin, 'Awash in Colonialism', *Alternative Law Journal*, 24(1), Feb. 1999, 3; G. MacDonald, 'Does "Culture" have "History"'? Thinking about Continuity and Change in Central New South Wales', *Aboriginal History*, 25(2001) 176; R. Pitty, 'A Poverty of Evidence: Abusing Law and History in Yorta *Yorta v Victoria* (1998)', *Australian Journal of Legal History*, 2000 (6), 41; A. Reilly, 'The Ghost of Truganini: Use of Historical Evidence as Proof of Native Title', *Federal Law Review*, (28), 2000, 453; D. Ritter, 'The Judgment of the World: The Yorta Yorta Case and the "Tide of History"', *Australian Historical Studies*, 35(123), April 2004, 106–21; J.F. Weiner, 'Diaspora, Materialism, Tradition: Anthropological Issues in the Recent High Court Appeal of the Yorta Yorta', *Land, Rights, Laws: Issues of Native Title*, 2002(2), 18; and S. Young, *The Trouble with Tradition: Native Title and Cultural Change*, Federation Press, Annandale (NSW), 2008.

80 M. Morgan: http://www.hreoc.gov.au/racial_discrimination/beyond_tolerance/speeches/morgan.html. See also M. Morgan, 'The Yorta Yorta Experience', conference paper delivered at the Annual Native Title Representative Bodies Conference, *Outcomes and Possibilities*, Geraldton, Western Australia, September 3–5, http://www.aiatsis.gov.au/rsrch/ntru/research/yorta_yorta/mmorgan.pdf. Clark said *Yorta Yorta* marked the 'sorriest day in this country's history . . . the genocide of Aboriginal people in this country . . . this is the terrorism that has continued for 200 years': B. Haslem, S. Rintoul, M. Schubert, 'Clark Claims Genocide on Ruling', *The Australian*, 13 December 2002, p. 4.

81 H. Wootten, 'Conflicting Imperatives: Pursuing Truth in the Courts' in I. McCalman and A. McGrath, *Proof & Truth: The Humanist as Expert*, Australian Academy of the Humanities, Canberra, 2003, p. 36.

82 H. Wootten, 'Conflicting Imperatives: Pursuing Truth in the Courts' in I. McCalman and A. McGrath, *Proof & Truth: The Humanist as Expert*, Australian Academy of the Humanities, Canberra, 2003, p. 48.

83 N. Pearson, 'Where we've come from and where we're at with the opportunity that is Koiki Mabo's Legacy to Australia', *Native Title Representative Bodies Conference*, Alice Springs, 3 June 2003, p. 17.

84 'The Yorta Yorta Judgement: The Saddest History, the Harshest Verdict', 18/12/1998, ATSIC News Room Media Releases, http://pandora.nla.gov.au/pan/41033/20060106/ATSIC/news_room/media_releases/archive/1998/Dec/226.html.

85 Compare his predecessors: writing in 1995, O'Donoghue accepted that 'most Indigenous Australians' would not 'benefit directly from the *Mabo* judgment since the processes of colonization have deprived them of their native title rights': 'Chairperson's Report' in ATSIC *Annual Report 1994–1995*. Two years later, Djerrkura acknowledged that, '[o]f course in some circumstances native title has been extinguished or become defunct': 'Native title shapes reconciliation and economic development', 24/10/1997, ATSIC News Room Media Releases, http://pandora.nla.gov.au/pan/41033/20060106/ATSIC/news_room/media_releases/archive/1997/Oct/115.html.

86 A. Moreton-Robinson, 'The Possessive Logic of Patriarchal White Sovereignty: the High Court and the *Yorta Yorta* decision', *borderlands e-journal*, 3(2), para. 24. Of course, whether Justice Olney had correctly interpreted the evidence before him was another matter, open to the same kind of scholarly and normative debate as any other judicial decision within a liberal democracy.

87 *Members of the Yorta Yorta Aboriginal Community v Victoria* [2002] HCA 58; 214 CLR 422; 194 ALR 538; 77 ALJR 356 (12 December 2002) at para. [50].

88 *Wik Peoples (McNaught Ngallametta) v Queensland* (FCA, QG6001/98, 17 April 2000).

89 See, for example, *Munn for the Gunggari People v Queensland* (2001) 115 FCR 109; [2001] FCA 1229; *Masig People v Queensland* [2000] FCA 1067; *Poruma People v Queensland* [2000] FCA 1066; *Mabuiag People v Queensland* [2000] FCA 1065; *Dauan People v Queensland* [2000] FCA 1064; *Smith v Western Australia* (2000) 104 FCR 494; [2000] FCA 1249; and *Wik Peoples v Queensland* [2000] FCA 1443.

90 *Lovett v Victoria* [2007] FCA 474, paras [37]–[38]. Authorities cited are omitted from the passages.

91 *Yorta Yorta Aboriginal Community v Victoria* (FCA, Olney J, No. 6001/95, 18 December 1998, BC9806799, unreported), paras [17] and [21].

92 *Nangkiriny v State of Western Australia* [2002] FCA 660, para. [27].

93 *Clarrie Smith v State of Western Australia* [2000] FCA 1249, para. [31].

94 *Kaurareg People v State of Queensland* [2001] FCA 657, para. [13].
95 *Clarke v Victoria* [2005] FCA 1795, paras [2].
96 *Lovett v Victoria* [2007] FCA 474, para. [55].
97 Federal Court of Australia, *25 Years of the Federal Court of Australia*, video presentation, 2002.
98 A.M. North, 'From the Internet to the Outback—A World Class Court' in B Keon-Cohen (ed.), *Native Title in the New Millennium*, AIATSIS, Canberra, 2001.
99 Australian Government, Attorney General's Department, 'Claims Resolution Review', http://www.ag.gov.au/www/agd/agd.nsf/Page/Indigenouslawandnativetitle_Nativetitle_Claimsresolutionreview.
100 Office of the Registrar, Federal Court of Australia, Submission to the Senate Legal and Constitutional Affairs Committee on the Native Title Amendment Bill 2006, 25/1/2007, Senate Legal and Constitutional Affairs Committee, Completed Reports, Inquiry into the Native Title Amendment Bill 2006, at http://www.aph.gov.au/Senate/committee/legcon_ctte/completed_inquiries/2004–07/native_title/submissions/sublist.htm.
101 For a general discussion of the Court/Tribunal debate, see A. Chalk, 'Redefining the role of the Federal Court in settling native title matters', paper presented to the 3rd Annual Negotiating Native Title Forum, Melbourne, 19–20 February 2009.
102 National Native Title Tribunal, Submission to the Senate Legal and Constitutional Affairs Committee on the Native Title Amendment Bill 2006, 9/2/07, Senate Legal and Constitutional Affairs Committee, Completed Reports, Inquiry into the Native Title Amendment Bill 2006, at http://www.aph.gov.au/Senate/committee/legcon_ctte/completed_inquiries/2004-07/native_title/submissions/sublist.htm. p. 19.
103 R.S. French, 'Plus ca change, plus c'est la meme chose?—The 2007 amendments to the Native Title Act', *Land, Rights, Laws: Issues in Native Title*, Native Title Research Unit, Volume 3, Issue Paper No. 12, February 2008, p. 6.

Chapter 8 The end of uncertainty

1 J.A. Scutt, 'The Privatisation of Justice: Power Differentials, Inequality, and the Palliative of Counseling and Mediation', *Women's Studies International Forum*, 11(5), 1988, 503–520, p. 513.
2 G. Neate, 'Exploring the Role of the NNTT in Reaching Agreements over Native Title', paper presented to *Assessing the Impact of Native Title and*

Cultural Heritage in 2002: Negotiating Balanced Outcomes for All Parties, Brisbane, Queensland, 16 April 2002, p. 43.

3 National Native Title Tribunal, *Talking Native Title*, Issue 30, March 2009, p. 5.

4 *Jango v Northern Territory* [2006] FCA 318.

5 F. Chaney, *Vincent Liangiari Lecture 2007*, 11 August 2007.

6 C. Lawrence, 'The "Emergency Intervention" in Northern Territory Indigenous Communities', *The New Critic*, 7, May 2008: http://www.ias.uwa.edu.au/new-critic/seven/intervention.

7 R.S. French, 'Rolling a Rock Uphill?—Native Title and the Myth of Sisyphus', Judicial Conference of Australia National Colloquium, 10 October 2008: http://www.hcourt.gov.au/speeches/frenchcj/frenchcj10Oct08.pdf.

INDEX

For Product Safety Concerns and Information please contact our EU representative GPSR@taylorandfrancis.com
Taylor & Francis Verlag GmbH, Kaufingerstraße 24, 80331 München, Germany

www.ingramcontent.com/pod-product-compliance
Lightning Source LLC
LaVergne TN
LVHW011121300926
849160LV00008B/461
9781742370200